the phishing manual

dean budnick

the
phishing
manual

a compendium
to the music
of phish

 HYPERION new york

Library of Congress Cataloging-In-Publication Data

Budnick, Dean.
    The Phishing manual : a compendium to the music of Phish / by
Dean   Budnick.
        p.   cm.

    ISBN 0-7868-8203-4
    1. Phish (Musical group)   2. Rock musicians—United States—
Biography.   I. Title.
ML421.P565B83   1996
782.42166'092'2—dc20
    [B]   96-22947
                                                                        CIP
                                                                        MN

BOOK DESIGN BY KATHY KIKKERT

FIRST EDITION

10   9   8   7   6   5   4   3   2   1

For everyone who's shared the groove with
me over the years, in particular: Manny S., Stacy B.,
Andrew W., Stella L., Jon C., Phoebe D., Rob T., Alec G.,
Tom S., Joe R., Tim S., Joe U., Greg N., New York Joe,
and of course Leanne B. (for encouragement,
assistance, and a generous blind spot).

acknowledgments

The idea for this book arose during a long, dazzling drive from Telluride to Red Rocks with my sister and company. The project solidified in a moment of epiphany while I watched one phan browbeat another for the "sins" of failing to recognize the Rhombus and using a Halloween costume as a waste receptacle. Since then a number of people have provided friendship, technical assistance, and general fervor for this work. Most notably I wish to thank my agent, Daniel Bial; my editor, Jennifer Lang (a welcome voice of insight and good humor); my computer consultants and saviors, Kristin Blais, Brad Leupen, and Andrew Wagner (merely a consultant, not quite a savior); my parents, Janet and Alfred Budnick (burgeoning phans/guppies); my fellow tapers and tape traders who enabled me to amass a collection of nearly 1500 hours of Phish, which became my Rosetta Stone as I worked on this project; Jeff Holdsworth; the Phish.net community, and in particular thse Phish.netters past and present who have provided me with many hours of entertainment, information, and occasional infuriation, in particular I:)@J( )e, Downerman, Shelly, Pandian (remember?), Dirk420, Rosemary and you too ZZYZX; Alec Gowan and Margaret Briggs, who indulged/endured an extensive audio research session at the Briggs family cabin in Maine; my wife, Leanne Barrett (I owe you a trip to Denmark), and the many others whose names appear throughout this book. No flies on any of you.

This all began with the music of course, on a fateful day ten years ago when I stumbled onto the magic and majesty of Phish.

contents

the phishing manual

1 vermont's phinest

Phish's story begins neither in Nectar's nor in the Sculpture Room of Goddard College but rather in the student lounges of the University of Vermont's Redstone campus. It was here that a freshman named Ernest Anastasio III (Trey for short) met a sophomore electrical engineering student named Jeff Holdsworth. Both hailed from a similar region of the country that stretches from southwest New Jersey to eastern Pennsylvania. They discovered that they shared a similar taste in music that included such acts as the Allman Brothers Band, Led Zeppelin, and Pat Metheny. More important, they both loved to play their guitars.

Trey and Jeff began to play those guitars together in the dorm lounges. Although he had practiced on drums for many years, Trey had started playing the guitar only in eleventh grade. Jeff had a bit more experience under the formal guidance of an instructor. Ultimately, after a number of lounge sessions, Trey and Jeff concluded that they had complementary musical styles and tastes, so they decided to form a band.

Trey had some prior band experience. As a high school sophomore at the Taft School in Watertown, Connecticut, he had joined an eight-member group called Red Tide. The group performed "classic rock" tunes such as "Smoke on the Water" and "Sunshine of Your Love." Initially Trey served only as a vocalist in Red Tide, which ultimately disbanded due to the many clashing personalities in the group. By his senior year, a few remaining members of Red Tide, who were committed to performing less conventional and more challenging music, formed a new band, which they named Space Antelope. This group, which played at school assemblies and at a dance or two, also featured a friend named Steve Pollak, aka the Dude of Life, who would eventually travel with Trey to the University of Vermont. (The Dude's self-penned hit single was "Fire at the Taft School," and he also encouraged audience members to run like space antelopes, out of control.) Perhaps Space Antelope's most notable performance was a complete rendition of Pink Floyd's "Dogs," before a captive school assembly audience ("Dogs" is a seventeen-minute composition from Floyd's *Animals* album). The epic was not well received, and the band dissolved soon afterward.

Trey's high school band experiences made him realize that he and Jeff would need committed players who would be willing to practice intensely and extensively in order to master the complicated music and the improvisational style that they sought to achieve. Their first recruit was a freshman drummer named Jon "Fish" Fishman. Trey's first memory of Fish is seeing him walking by and instantly identifying him as one of the goofiest-looking people he'd ever seen. Fish first remembers Trey bursting into his room while he practiced in order to encourage him to play in the fledgling group.

Fish agreed, although initially he continued to perform with another band as well. Fish had grown up in DeWitt, New York, which is just outside Syracuse. There he had locked the door to his bedroom and taught himself to play the drums. Fish would throw various records onto his turntable in an effort to copy their sound. His early favorites included Black Sabbath and Led Zeppelin. By the time he'd entered college, however, his enthusiasm for drumming had moved away from traditional rock and toward both jazz and hardcore.

The trio now needed a bass player. Not finding any immediate success by word of mouth, they resorted to flyers. Trey posted a number of them on dormitory bulletin boards, soliciting bass players who wanted to form a band. The flyers said that the other members' musical interests included the Allman Brothers Band and Led Zeppelin. Soon after, Mike Gordon read the posting and decided that this sounded like fun. Fish, Jeff, and Trey welcomed him aboard.

Mike was from Sudbury, Massachusetts, and he had been performing on the bass for a couple years. He also had played in the Tombstone Blues Band with some of his friends while attending high school. Unlike Fish, Mike was not self-taught. He had received formal training under the tutelage of a bass instructor. Like Fish, Mike had a penchant for locking himself in his room. He did this in order to enter a large black box that hung from the ceiling and that would enable him to concentrate on music, without any visual stimulation to interfere with his experience.

As the four students began their first informal practice sessions, Trey and Jeff learned of an impending ROTC formal Halloween dance. The pair approached the dance's organizers and convinced them to hire the quartet as the evening's musical entertainment. It was the band's first gig. Unfortunately, since they had just started playing together, they weren't sure if they could muster enough material to provide music for the entire dance. So the fledgling group practiced like crazy, preparing an odd collection of 1960s and '70s rock and soul hits.

The first gig took place at the ROTC formal on Sunday, October 30, 1983. The band showed up prepared to give it their best. They did not, however, show up in appropriate dress. The ROTC students' formal wear contrasted sharply with the band members' flannel wear. Additionally, the music the group had prepared was out of fashion. The ROTC students were not interested in "I Heard It through the Grapevine" or "Long Cool Woman in a Black Dress"; they wanted to hear current music. This was the time when Michael Jackson's *Thriller* and the soundtrack to *Footloose* topped the charts. So most of those in attendance did their best to ignore the ragtag collection of minstrels performing in the corner and eventually drowned out the live music with a tape player.

At this inauspicious debut the career of Phish began. The band selected its name as a play on Jon's nickname, with a nod to the shoddy spelling of the Beatles as well. Trey soon designed a logo for the band, the image that persists to this day. Over the ensuing months the band continued to hone their skills, juggling school responsibilities with band practice. They also continued to perform in various common rooms and basements throughout the Redstone campus.

After a year or so of performing on campus, Phish felt they were ready to perform in Burlington. The group had a number of original tunes to complement their selection of covers. After some initial gigs as happy-hour entertainment at a small lounge called Dillon's, they approached Nectar Rorris, the proprietor of a popular downtown restaurant and bar, who presented music free-of-charge for his patrons every night of the week. Nectar decided to give the band a chance, although this first Nectar's gig did not take place at the more prestigious bar downstairs but rather in the smaller upstairs room (which has long since been remodeled and now serves as the home of the Metropolis music club). So on Friday, December 1, 1984, Phish performed its first of many gigs on Main Street in Burlington.

The band's lineup had swollen in time for the Nectar's show with the addition of percussionist Marc Daubert. Trey knew Marc because he belonged to what some phans refer to as the Princeton mafia. In the time before Trey's enrollment at Taft, he attended the Princeton Day School in Princeton, New Jersey. Here he met a number of people who shared his creative tendencies and his love of music. During Trey's formal Princeton schooling and in subsequent years, these friends met at various places both to hear and play music. They often made day trips and nighttime visits to a metal rhombus tucked into the woods less than a forty-five-minute drive away. Trey later celebrated these gatherings and the geography that inspired them with his music.

To many phans the kingpin of the Princeton mafia (or at least

the tallest member, nearly six-and-a-half-feet tall in stockinged feet) is Tom Marshall. Tom's correspondence with Trey while Trey lived in Burlington became the source and inspiration for some of Trey's music. In turn, Tom became Trey's writing partner, a relationship that continues to this day. Some of Phish's earlier songs also feature the contributions of Marc Daubert, Dave Abrahams, Bob Szuter, and Aaron Woolfe. Indeed, the Princeton Day School contributed so deeply to the band that Phish formally presented a plaque to the school to thank the music department after the band's *A Live One* release achieved gold record status.

Phish's initial gig at Nectar's proved to be a successful showcase for the band. Some of their music during this period also is reflected on a few demo tapes that have circulated over the years. One of them features a number of songs that Trey and Mike worked on while they were living in the UVM dorms. A second one collects some music that Trey recorded at home over winter break in 1985. These two tapes offer stripped-down versions of songs that Phish played during this era ("Slave to the Traffic Light," "Letter to Jimmy Page") as well as a few that as yet have never made it to the stage in their original form ("Minkin," "And So to Bed," "Hamburger").

Marc left the area soon after the Nectar's gig, and Phish again returned to its initial four-piece lineup. But this was not destined to last. Following the band's performance at the 1985 Goddard College Springfest, keyboardist Page McConnell introduced himself to the members of Phish and expressed a desire to join the group. Soon he was brought aboard.

Page came from Basking Ridge, New Jersey. He had initially attended Southern Methodist University in Dallas for two years. Ultimately, however, he decided to return north and pursue a career in music. He felt that Goddard College would provide him with such an opportunity so he transferred to the school (a move that would shortly become a trend).

Page had another influence on the band. Trey and Steve Pollak (the Dude) had found themselves in hot water at UVM due to a prank that had gotten out of hand (so to speak). Page saw Trey's situation and suggested that his new bandmate transfer to Goddard. During this period Goddard's enrollment had dropped dramatically. In an effort to stimulate enrollment, the college encouraged its students to recruit new undergraduates. Indeed, Goddard offered a small stipend to any student whose recruiting efforts proved successful. Page was doubly blessed when both Trey and Fish decided to enroll, earning the keyboard player $100.

Goddard College was founded in 1938 on 250 acres of former farmland to promote the founders' idea of a progressive education. Through the Goddard Work Program, every student is required to devote eight hours a week to the administrative and physical maintenance of the school. Students also help to design their own academic program through the assistance of faculty advisers who meet with their advisees for an hour every week. This collaborative yet individualized approach results in graduation exercises that feature no single valedictorian but rather commencement commentaries from each of the graduates.

Another integral part of the Goddard College curriculum is the

Senior Study. This is an exhaustive independent study that is completed during a student's final semester in school. These studies often result in elaborate essays or reports that relate the senior's experiences during this semester of work. For many students it is the culmination of their collegiate career at Goddard.

Page, Trey, and Fish all completed Senior Studies, and each of these works is intimately connected to the band members' roles in Phish. Page's Senior Study, which he completed in 1987 under the tutelage of his adviser, Karl Boyle, is entitled "The Art of Improvisation." (Boyle is an early guest musician with Phish.) Page's study lists his musical influences: Bill Evans, Duke Ellington, and Art Tatum. It also draws extensively on the book *Zen and the Art of Archery* to articulate Page's ultimate performance goal of becoming egoless.

Trey's study, which he submitted a year later, is called "The Man Who Stepped into Yesterday." This project is a thematically linked song cycle. It consists of a tape of recorded music along with an accompanying essay that explores the origins and approaches of these various songs. "The Man Who Stepped into Yesterday" presents the initial Gamehendge saga that Phish would later perform.

Finally, Fish's study, which he submitted in time to graduate in 1990, is entitled "A Self-Teaching Guide to Drumming Written in Retrospect." It is an account of how Fish taught himself to become an effective player and performer. It recounts his personal musical development, placing particular emphasis on listening to others while also stressing the important personal unifying elements of heart, mind, and body.

At Goddard College the band members met a number of like-minded creative people who would continue to work with them over the years. One of these people was Jim Pollock, an artist whose cartoons were often featured in the *Goddard Review*. Pollock has come to design much of the band's promotional materials and merchandise (most recently he contributed the artwork to Phish's mail-order tickets). Another Goddard friend was Nancy Taube, who graciously permitted the band to perform two of his songs ("I Didn't Know" and "Halley's Comet"). A third is J. Willis Pratt, who aided Phish as a roadie–spiritual adviser, particularly in the group's early days.

Willis is also an experimental guitarist who has recorded a few tapes' worth of material with Fish backing him on drums. (The band sold one of these at its merchandise table during the 1993 spring tour.) Finally, Tim Rogers came to operate the Phish light board for a few years and occasionally played a bit of harmonica with the band.

Trey's experience with the music department at UVM had been quite limiting. He wanted to compose music, but he soon learned that he would not be allowed to compose until his senior year. Eventually this led him to Ernie Stires, who would become Trey's mentor and friend. Ernie was a jazz pianist who had come to the Green Mountain State at the request of Vermont Symphony Orchestra founder Alan Carter. Stires's particular interest in the big bands of the 1930s and '40s later served as a model for Trey's own musical work with Phish. While working with Stires, Trey came to understand that many big bands produced music that could be enjoyed on a number of levels—it could be danced to, but someone could also appreciate the musical complexity of the arrangements. Trey took this to heart as his work with Stires led him to integrate complex elements and themes along with particular formal structures such as fugues into his music. The impact of Stires's teachings can be heard in such Phish songs as "Flat Fee," "Asse Festival," "Divided Sky," "David Bowie," "Foam," and "Split Open and Melt."

Trey's love of composition continues to this day. While on tour, he views set-list construction as one way to satisfy this creative urge. As a result, before each night's show Trey sits back and considers the band members' particular attitudes and moods, the songs that Phish has played on the previous few nights, and the songs that the band played on its previous visit to that venue (or geographic region). In turn, he composes a minisuite of music that takes all these factors into account. Of course, in most instances this does not represent the final list. For instance, Page will look it over and make some amendments. Additionally, the band often will deviate from the list while onstage, based on spontaneous impressions and musical inspiration. On some occasions they've gone so far as to perform no songs from the proposed list.

Of course, in the band's early years none of this was required, as

Phish barely had enough songs to complete two sets of music. Still, with continued rehearsals and ongoing songwriting efforts, the group's playlist began to grow along with the band's bookings. Phish moved from the upstairs room at Nectar's down to the bar proper. They also started to gig at some of Burlington's other venues, such as Hunt's, where they occasionally appeared on double bills with other local bands such as Lamb's Bread and The Jones.

Meanwhile, Phish continued to perform at its members' respective colleges as well. One notable show took place in the Goddard College cafeteria in November 1985. This performance served as a crucial turning point for Mike. While playing, he experienced a moment of transcendence, a period of absolute inner peace and love that led him to realize that he had found his life's calling. The other band members took notice as a grinning Mike began to jump up and down. To this day Mike strives to re-create that moment through his efforts at lucid dreaming, blurring the distinction between waking and sleeping consciousness. He also strives to help his phans achieve similar experiences through the music that he creates.

Mike functioned as the band's de facto manager during these early years, dealing with finances and booking because no one else assumed much of this responsibility. Additionally, as the band's phan base continued to grow over the years, Mike took the time to answer personally all of Phish's mail. To this day Mike continues to answer much of the phan mail himself. He is also the band member most often seen outside a venue before a show, speaking casually with phans or grabbing a bit of preshow exercise on his bike.

Phish's five-piece lineup continued until the spring of 1986 when Jeff left the group. He was scheduled to graduate with his engineering degree in May. While he enjoyed playing in Phish, he didn't envision life as a professional musician, and he didn't intend to remain in Burlington after graduation. Jeff's religious convictions also had some role, as he acquired a distaste for Phish's electric music. (Jeff's subsequent history has been the matter of much speculation in certain circles. Let me offer a few clarifications. After graduation Jeff did not join Jimmy Swaggart's traveling musical road show nor did he enter the pit band for the Moral Majority. Rather, he settled into the life of an engineer and businessman. He no longer wields an electric guitar, but he does continue to play his acoustic and enjoys fingerpicking for family and friends alike.)

Jeff's departure had some immediate impact on the sound of the band. The loss of that second guitar opened some musical space for the other members of the band to fill, most notably Page. (If you listen to tapes from this period, the change is discernible.) Also, the band began to explore that space a bit further. In many ways Jeff had kept them grounded (in the best possible sense). He saw the group for what it was: a rock band that performed both covers and originals. With his departure the remaining members started to anticipate what the band could be—an amalgam of many tones, styles, and influences that could strive to create something more challenging than prototypical roots rock music. It took a while for Phish's execution to approach this vision, but the band's ultimate success is a product of it.

Initially, the band sought to improve itself through elaborate rehearsal exercises and sessions. One ongoing goal has been to enhance the band members' onstage communication. In effect, Phish has sought to practice improvisation. While this might sound like an oxymoron, it really reflects the band's work ethic and their devotion to their craft. As Ernie Stires has said on numerous occasions, just as a stand-up comedian doesn't make up his jokes on the spot, musical improvisation is the product of discipline and practice.

One such exercise that Phish developed is called "including your own hey." This begins with one person presenting a melody. The other three band members then perform a complementary melody of their own. When the three finally have achieved this complementary melody, all four band members say "hey." Then the adjacent person alters his melody a bit, and the three remaining band members are required to modify their own melodies in a corresponding manner. Once this is done, everyone says "hey" and the next band member makes an adjustment. This exercise teaches each of them to become unconscious of his own performance while simultaneously listening to the performance of the three others (becoming egoless, as Page indicated in his Senior Study).

Phish also has developed a number of variations on this exercise that takes these listening and performance skills a step further. For instance, one version called "filling the hey hole" prohibits any of the band members from playing on the downbeats together—an act that requires intense concentration and fluidity on one's instrument. If you want to hear a simple example of some of these exercises put into action, pull out your favorite "You Enjoy Myself" vocal jam and listen closely. When you have that one mastered, listen to one of Phish's epic "Tweezers" (you can find a list in chapter 2) or just throw on the "Tweezer" from *A Live One* (11/2/94 if you have the tape).

Another technique that the band has implemented over the years is learning to perform other genres of music. This has allowed Phish to apply new methods and techniques to its own performances. For instance, the band studied with a barbershop quartet teacher. While this form of music may appear rather simple, it actually requires the participant to produce a number of distinct sounds through particular positions of the facial muscles.

Similarly, for a period in the late '80s Phish transformed itself into a jazz band. The group performed in Burlington as the Johnny B. Fishman Jazz Ensemble. The ensemble solely played jazz standards with horn accompaniment (Russ Remington, who later appeared with the first Giant Country Horns, is an ensemble veteran). These gigs allowed the band members to learn a bit more about this genre, while also absorbing the musical perspective of a horn player.

Most recently, during November 1994, Phish brought Reverend Jeff Mosier on tour with them for a week to educate the band in the art of bluegrass. As with the jazz ensemble, the bulk of Phish's education occurred live onstage. Mosier accompanied Phish on banjo and vocals while working through a number of traditional bluegrass selections. The members of Phish have credited all these efforts with improving the performance of their own music (and these exercises also have added a few new options to set lists).

To return to the earlier period, a significant event took place when Phish hired Paul Languedoc as its sound engineer, a role he continues to play to this day. His relationship with the band began a bit earlier, since he worked in a guitar shop that designed one of Trey's guitars. By 1985, Paul had assumed that duty personally, and he soon began to build Mike's basses. In turn, the band asked Paul to help produce its live sound. He also has come to build much of the equipment both to produce that sound and to lug it about from show to show. The band has acknowledged many of his contributions from the stage over the years—in fact Paul's first show behind the sound board on 10/15/86 includes such an introduction from Trey.

Momentum continued to build. Phish soon settled into a series of gigs at Nectar's, performing once a month on Sunday through Tuesday. They also supplemented these shows with a few other performances at the area's colleges. Meanwhile, the group contin-

Photo credit: Rich Luzzi

ued to practice as extensively as their work and school schedules would permit.

The band's grueling efforts finally began to yield some distinct rewards in 1988. In April of that year Phish took first place at the Battle of the Bands at The Front, a club that had recently opened on Main Street. While Phish certainly was one of Burlington's more popular groups, particularly among the city's college students, up to that time Phish had been denied a measure of critical respect. Other local bands such as Screaming Broccoli and Hollywood Indians, who performed a rougher-edged, louder music, often were praised to the exclusion of Phish. Thus, many phans and the band itself took some pride in the victory (anticipated by a naked Jon Fishman).

Another fortuitous event occurred that spring. Amherst College junior John Paluska, who was skiing in the Burlington area with some friends, decided to take in a Phish performance. One of John's friends from his home region of Woolrich, Maine, was Mike Billington, who had recently emigrated to Burlington with his band, Ninja Custodian. Mike had recommended Phish to John as a group he might enjoy. So one evening after returning from the slopes, John decided to go to Nectar's to see the band in action. He was overwhelmed both with the musical abilities of the band and also with the fervid yet respectful support of their phans. The next day John called Mike and asked him how to get in touch with the band. Ninja Mike gave John the coveted phone number and the rest, as they say, is Phishtory.

John was the social director of a cooperative house at Amherst College. He invited Phish to come and play at Humphries House's next all-campus party, which was held during the full moon. Phish made the trip to The Zoo, as Humphries House also was known, for the full moon party, the band's debut performance outside of Vermont. The gig was an overwhelming success.

A friendship quickly formed between John and Phish that soon solidified into an alliance. John thoroughly enjoyed Phish's music and felt that many others would feel the same way. So he became the band's western Massachusetts contact, pushing various clubs and organizations to invite Phish to perform. He brought Phish back to Amherst, also to Hampshire College, and eventually to a club in Northampton called Pearl Street.

Meanwhile, Phish wanted to find additional areas to play. More gigs meant more money. It also meant the possibility of performing music full-time, which ultimately would result in the production of more music. This is where John's friend Ben Hunter enters the picture. Like John, Ben had looked to Mike Billington as a sort of musical mentor when they were growing up. So Ben, too, made a trip to Nectar's in the spring of that year for a live Phish experience. His reaction was similar to John's. In fact, he may have even been more enthusiastic. His exuberance led him to walk up to Fish after the show to give him a big hug. Ben was a student at Boston University at this time and a voracious consumer of live music. He occasionally rented out a local club to host a band or two.

After John's success in the western part of the state, Fish, Mike, Page, and Trey agreed with the two friends that Ben should try to introduce Phish to a new audience in Boston. Unable to secure a club date for the band, Ben rented out Molly's, a club on Brighton Avenue in the Allston section of Boston frequented by Boston University students. Ben furiously posted handbills and handed out notices of the band's debut Boston gig on November 3, 1988. The show was such a success that Ben rented out the club once again on December 2, filling the place with audience members who had heard of Phish's last performance. A number of prospective phans were turned away at the door.

After two gigs Phish had already outgrown Molly's, so Ben and John struggled to find a new, larger place for the band to play. The one they deemed most appropriate, the Paradise, had a capacity of 650. However, the club had never heard of Phish and refused to book them despite Ben's promises of success. So Ben and John decided to take matters into their own hands. They rented out the Paradise, charging $5 for tickets and inviting anyone over the age of eighteen to attend. Meanwhile, back in Burlington a group of enthusiastic phans encouraged others to make the four-hour ride to Boston to attend the gig, in order to demonstrate that Phish was a legitimate draw. The Burlington contingent sent a caravan of phans south to the Boston area. The show sold out, affirming area support for the band and silencing some of the Paradise employees who had scoffed while watching the band unload its beaten-up amps into the club.

A partnership soon developed among Ben, John, and the band. The two friends formed Dionysian Productions to handle Phish's business affairs, and they brought Phish into new markets. During the course of 1989, Phish played in Syracuse, then Geneva, then New York City at Wetlands Preserve. Phish also solidified its hold on prior regions, as it outgrew Nectar's and moved up the street to the larger Front. The members of the band were finally able to quit their day jobs and concentrate on their music.

Ben's nickname, by the way, is Junta. It was in appreciation of his efforts that the tape that Phish began selling at its performances bears his name. *Junta* was recorded off and on over a one-year period at Euphoria Sound Studios in Revere, Massachusetts. Gordon Hookaloo engineered the sessions, which cost the band about $5,000. This sum had been raised partly by donating all the band's profits from gigs, putting everything back into the music. To this day the band members credit these sessions as being freer and more representative of their sound than any subsequent recordings. The song selection includes many tunes that the band continues to perform before appreciative phans, including "You Enjoy Myself," "David Bowie," "Divided Sky," and "Fluffhead."

The summer of 1988 also featured another milestone in the history of the band—Phish's first visit west. Through the efforts of phriends, the band was invited to perform for a week in Telluride, Colorado. In preparation for their departure, Phish celebrated with a triumphant good-bye party at Nectar's. Then they learned that the deal had fallen apart. They opted to get into the van and travel west anyhow, eventually performing a series of gigs in Telluride at the Roma in exchange for the door receipts. This trip proved important as it cemented many friendships that would flourish over the years.

Meanwhile, the band members finally were able to cast aside their day jobs, and Phish improved the totality of its live performances. Trampolines, vacuums, and Chris Kuroda soon entered the picture. Chris assumed the role of lighting director, which he holds to this day, adding an element of subtlety to the light show while complementing the explosive nature of the band's music. The trampolines and vacuums contributed no subtlety whatsoever. Fish's vacuum solo, which he performed in addition to his trombone solos, placed him at center stage more frequently and ultimately led to the development of Henrietta's Theme, "Hold Your Head Up." This also gave the band additional opportunities to construct nicknames for the drummer. In turn, Phish celebrated the end of 1989 and welcomed the new decade from the stage at the Boston World Trade Center Exhibition Hall on December 31, 1989, the first of many such annual affairs arranged by Dionysian Productions.

Then, just as the band started to hit its stride, along came the *Lawn Boy* debacle. Phish had entered Archer Studios in spurts and stops over the first six months of 1989 to record with engineers Dan Archer and Dean LaBrie. To Phish's initial pleasure, Absolute a Go Go Records agreed to release the product of these sessions as *Lawn Boy*. Absolute a Go Go was an affiliate of Rough Trade, which guaranteed national distribution. Approximately 10,000 copies were pressed on vinyl and shipped to stores. In a matter of days, however, Rough Trade went out of business. The record sold out, but Phish could not arrange for an additional pressing.

Frustrated but undaunted, the band continued to write and perform music. After a three-month break over the summer of 1990, Phish returned to the Wetlands in New York City to debut a collection of new songs. The group then traveled west for the first of two annual Halloween gigs at Colorado College. The year came to a triumphant close with a second New Year's Eve extravaganza at Boston's World Trade Center Exhibition Hall. A spring 1991 tour carried the band south and then west as Phish finally touched down in California in April before traveling back east across the northern states, Phish's first true national tour. Word continued to spread about this group that would enter a city and play two energized, exhausting sets of music, no matter how large the audience (which invariably led to a larger audience the next time around).

During the summer of 1991 Phish bookended studio sessions around a short but celebrated tour. June found Phish in Burlington's White Crow Studios, recording a number of tunes for a follow-up to *Lawn Boy* that the band intended to release in some manner. Phish spent the end of that month and early July polishing up horn charts as they embarked on a long-promised, and finally realized horn tour. Carl Gerhard, Dave Grippo, and Russ Remington joined Phish as the Giant Country Horns for two weeks of shows along the East Coast. Phans enjoyed a number of innovative arrangements of Phish compositions along with some jazz standards and a select new cover or two (most notably Fish's "Touch Me"). Phish then celebrated the completion of this tour and toasted their phans with three sets of music at the horse farm of "phirst phan" Amy Skelton on Saturday, August 3, 1991. From here it was back to the studio to complete the sessions for what would become *Picture of Nectar*.

However, the group still did not have a label on which to release this material. The band left these concerns to John Paluska as it began another cross-country tour in late September, which featured a second Colorado College Halloween performance. Phish also earned the distinction of becoming the first band without a recording contract to sell out two nights at the Great American Music Hall in San Francisco. When the group returned home in November 1991, Fish, Mike, Page, and Trey elected to end such feats by signing a series of two-record contracts with Elektra.

Elektra agreed to release the album that Phish had recorded over the summer of 1991 and also to rerelease *Junta* and *Lawn Boy*. Due to the length of the original *Junta* tape, Elektra opted to produce two CDs, which allowed the band to complete the package with some additional live performances. Elektra's version of *Lawn Boy* appeared without "Fee," which had appeared on the original pressing, because the song already appeared on *Junta*. Also, the new version of the song "Lawn Boy" was remastered a bit slower, gaining fifteen seconds in the process.

Elektra released *Picture of Nectar* with some fanfare on February

15, 1992. "Chalkdust Torture" was sent to radio stations as a single, and a number of phans winced at the possibility of the band's increased renown. The album sold moderately well, but there was no groundswell of national support. This was partially because of the album itself, which tried to demonstrate every facet of the band's music. Bluegrass, jazz, Latin, mellow guitar instrumentals, short rock blasts, composed epics, and extensive improvisational music all appeared next to one another on *Picture of Nectar*, and no one knew quite what to make of it.

This did not deter Phish, who returned to their routine of composing and performing. A two-night stand at New Hampshire's Portsmouth Music Hall in March introduced eleven new songs, which the band took with them on another national tour. Once again, Phish traveled across the country, this time reaching the Warfield Theater in San Francisco before turning the van around and heading home. In June Phish left for a short European tour, most of which was spent opening for the Violent Femmes. When Phish returned to America, they joined many of their musical friends and allies for four dates on the inaugural HORDE tour (Colonel Bruce Hampton and Aquarium Rescue Unit, Widespread Panic, Spin Doctors, and Blues Traveler). Phish headlined two of these shows, the initial one at Cumberland County Civic Center in Portland, Maine, and the band's final one at Jones Beach Theater in Wantagh, New York. Then they embarked on the only national tour they would ever make as a supporting act, opening for Carlos Santana.

The band's experience with Santana affected the group in a number of ways. For starters, it exposed Phish to many new audiences and gave the group its first extended taste of performing in amphitheaters. Perhaps more important, it placed the band members in proximity to one of their heroes. Trey had dedicated the performance of "Landlady" on 9/13/90 "to the spirit of Carlos." During this month and a half on the road, Fish, Mike, Page, and Trey had an opportunity to learn from Carlos Santana through conversation, observation, and performance. Phish joined Santana's band for a few songs on a number of occasions, but on 7/25/92 in Stowe,

Vermont, Santana did Phish the great honor of joining them on-stage during their set. Carlos also provided a metaphor for Phish music that phans still employ today. On one occasion after watching Phish perform, Carlos told the band members that when they were playing he imagined the audience as a sea of flowers, the music as water, and the band as the hose.

Photo credit: Rich Luzzi

The hose has become the persistent metaphor used by phans to describe particularly awe-inspiring jams. The band members also often repeat this quote, as it reflects their own musical philosophy, suggesting that they are only conduits for their music. The members of Phish often express their belief that music exists in a space independent of the group. If the band members are doing their jobs properly and not thinking too hard about it (becoming egoless, as Page might say, or entering a dream state, as Mike might suggest) then true magic occurs because the music flows from that special place and cascades through Phish and into the audience. They often quote Marvin Gaye, who had told Santana that musicians don't actually create music, they can merely train themselves to become better mediums for it. Similarly they quote Colonel Bruce Hampton, who describes this phenomenon in less elevated terms, as vomiting, because the individual musician has lost all personal control.

After returning from the Santana tour, Phish entered the studio to record its first album under the auspices of Elektra. These sessions had great potential because Barry Beckett had agreed to work with the band. Beckett is a legendary figure whose producing credits include Bob Dylan's *Slow Train Coming*, and Dire Straits' *Communiqué*. Beckett had also played with Duane Allman and the Muscle Shoals Rhythm Section. However, right from the start Phish indicated that they intended to exert a great deal of creative control over the work. As a result, the sessions took place in Burlington at White Crow Studios as opposed to a studio more familiar to Beckett. Additionally, Phish elected not to use one of Beckett's engineers but rather Kevin Halpin, who had served in this capacity on *A Picture of Nectar*.

Although the band tied Beckett's hands quite a bit, he did succeed in making *Rift* more cohesive than *Picture of Nectar*. Phish agreed with this goal, as in retrospect they felt that *Picture of Nectar* was too scattered, too much of an effort to showcase the various forms and styles that Phish had assimilated. *Rift* responded to this failing on a few levels. First, the work was thematically linked. The songs, which primarily focus on the issue of romantic difficulties, were tied together through a night's worth of dreams by one individual (which helps to explain the song snippets compressed into the second "Lengthwise" on *Rift*). Also, neither the style of the songs nor their lengths varied as much from one cut to the other.

The band was ready for the departure that *Rift* represents. "Fast Enough for You," for example, demonstrates something that Phish had not yet proven: They had the ability to perform slower songs with more personal messages and themes. Indeed, there is not a multibeast to be found anywhere on *Rift*. Plus, as a hint toward the *Hoist* recording process that was yet to come, Phish held back "Fast Enough for You" from live performances until they had recorded it in the studio. The group hoped to capture the moment when this song finally came together (although the band did use the studio to copy an additional chorus and add it to the mix).

The album successfully achieved the goals that it set out to meet. However, many phans find the vocals a bit weak. Others feel that the whole album sounds a bit sludgy, not quite crisp, without the energy that one expects from the band. At any rate, Elektra released *Rift* on February 2, 1993, and its sales improved from those of *Picture of Nectar*. The label also released "Fast Enough for You" to radio as a single, and it received some airplay, particularly on adult-contemporary formats. However, many felt that this was a curious single to pull and an odd format in which to push it.

Phish's first show of 1993 took place on the day after the release of *Rift,* and the band remained on the road for nearly seven months without a break. The year before had ended on a strong note: In November Phish had sold out two shows at the Capitol Theater in Port Chester, New York, in less than five hours, and on New Year's Eve the band had performed to a sold-out crowd at the Worcester Memorial Auditorium in Worcester, Massachusetts, the largest Phish gig to date. Nineteen ninety-three would exceed the expectations and standards set by the previous year. A spring tour of small theaters and halls led to a summer where Phish headlined at a number of northeast amphitheaters for the first time. From a musical standpoint, the month of August in particular is recognized by many phans as one of Phish's finest periods of consistently exceptional live performances. The band came off the road in September to record *Hoist* but returned for its four-show New Year's run, which culminated with a New Year's Eve show at the Worcester Centrum that sold out the same day that tickets went on sale. Also, Phish hired Chris MacGregor, who had previously worked with eyeball-wearing performance artist—composers the Residents to design a special set for the run. All told, the band performed more than one hundred shows during the year, selling more than three hundred thousand tickets to these performances and earning $5.6 million in gross receipts. More important to most phans, despite the group's move into larger venues, Phish remained amusing, entertaining, innovative, and committed to their music.

When the band prepared to record *Hoist*, they decided to create an album that would take full advantage of the studio and the medium (something they felt that they had failed to do with *Rift*). As they looked for a producer, Trey asked Kelvin Halprin what album he deemed best from a sound engineer's perspective. Halprin named XTC's *Oranges and Lemons*. Phish eventually decided to approach the producer of that work, Paul Fox, whose more recent producing credits included 10,000 Maniacs, *Our Time in Eden*, and the Sugarcubes' *Stick Around For Joy*. However, Fox was somewhat reluctant to work with the band, as he was not particularly impressed with *Rift*. So Phish brought him out to their show at the Waterloo Village Music Center in Stanhope, New Jersey, on July 25, 1993. After watching the band perform live, Paul agreed to produce the album.

This experience was very different from early Phish studio efforts. First, the band agreed to move out to Fox's home territory, as they recorded at the American Recording Company just outside of Los Angeles, California. Also, the band ceded more creative control to Fox, allowing him to use his own engineer, Ed Thacker, who rapidly impressed the band with his skills behind the board. Finally, most of the songs first reached the studio as a four-track demo as Phish decided primarily to record material that they had not performed live. They felt that some of *Rift*'s weaknesses resulted from the fact the band had performed most of that release's songs before a live audience for a long while. Phish's prior performances of those songs had fed off audiences' energy, which the band couldn't tap into in the studio setting, causing the music to fall a bit flat.

Paul also made a number of other suggestions in order to provide *Hoist* with a distinct sound. For instance, he tried to vary the band's instruments from song to song. Trey plays a different guitar on every cut. Mike plays different basses. Fish's kit also varies. Finally, Paul enthusiastically welcomed guest musicians into the mix, particularly the Tower of Power Horns, the Ricky Grundy Chorale, Rose Stone, Bela Fleck, Alison Krauss, and Jonathan Frakes.

Phish accompanied *Hoist* with the band's first video, for "Down with Disease." In the past few years, but especially since they had signed with Elektra, the members of the band had spent many hours on the road debating whether or not to make a music video. Trey presented one end of the spectrum, uncomfortable with the corporate influence of MTV and, more important, unhappy with the creativity that is denied to someone who sees a video and is unable to remove that image from her mind. Mike, on the other hand, thought it could be a satisfying form of artistic expression that could enhance one's enjoyment of a song without imposing a view. Of course, Mike was somewhat biased because he was a filmmaker who had completed a senior film project while at UVM.

Most phans feared that the video would expose many more people to the band and increase Phish's popularity. One story that Mike often relates is that of a woman crying after Phish moved from Nectar's to the Front because she felt that Phish wasn't her band anymore. Ironically, this sentiment now was shared by thousands of phans regarding the music video. They resented sharing their heroes with others. With each successive new album release and tour, similar cries resurfaced, along with allegations that the band had sold out. Indeed, Phish is probably one of the few bands in the history of American music with so many supporters who are obsessed with limiting the size of the group's audience. This is the ultimate in flattery but without question becomes a bit frustrating to the band.

A hit single would have presented another problem, a rapid increase of phans who only came to shows expecting to hear the hits. The members of Phish have often expressed a great admiration for the willingness of their audiences to allow the band to take chances. A successful radio song might have altered this dynamic. The example often used by the band members is the Spin Doctors, who have become chained to their radio hits, unable to produce much musical experimentation without offending people in their audiences.

Ultimately, the band agreed to make a video (if only to end the debate as to whether or not they should make one). Mike directed it with assistance from his UVM adviser Ted Lyman. The video combines footage of the band's plunge into the Phish tank on New Year's Eve along with other shots of the band members, their phriends, and their phamily. The work is framed by the image of Trey's dog, Marley, looking into a phish tank that the band members have entered. The "Down with Disease" video received some moderate rotation on MTV, then disappeared. It later surfaced on an episode of *Beavis and Butthead* (where the pair comment about swimming in one's own toilet).

The "Down with Disease" video was not the band's first experience with MTV. Although they've probably driven this one deep into their collective subconscious, in 1992 Phish appeared as the house band on *Hanging with MTV*. This program broadcast a few moments of the band's selections before the show cut to commercials or videos. These musical snippets included "Buried Alive," "Landlady," and "Big Black Furry Creatures from Mars." Phish also performed a trampoline segment after which they were jokingly asked who was a bigger influence on the band, the Grateful Dead or Mary Lou Retton.

The band performed a number of memorable shows over the course of 1994. The spring tour opened in April with a benefit performance at the Flynn Theater in Burlington featuring a new six-piece Giant Country Horns. The band continued west, eventually performing three-show runs at the Beacon Theater and the Warfield. Other noteworthy events during the year included a steady flow of acoustic performances and Jeff Mosier's touring bluegrass academy.

Perhaps the band's most innovative and entertaining idea was the Halloween costume. Phish did an on-air radio interview in Richmond on June 30 in which they announced that they intended to don a musical Halloween costume and perform any album of music by any band voted upon by the majority of their phans (the DJ voted for the first Flock of Seagulls album). Word of the band's radio announcement soon spread, but many phans remained skeptical until their fall newsletter arrived with voting instructions. The identity of the Halloween album remained a secret until the night of the show, with the band throwing in teases, quotes, and single songs from many albums in the shows leading up to Halloween. Phish performed the winner, the Beatles' White Album, at the Glens Falls, New York, Civic Center in an epic three-set show that ended at three-thirty in the morning.

The band ended the year with its four-show New Year's Eve run. December 30 marked the band's premiere performance at Madison Square Garden, and Trey later admitted that it was the first time that he really thought about the scope of a particular performance space. While growing up in New Jersey, he had viewed Madison Square Garden as the zenith of live sites. On New Year's Eve Phish ushered in the

Photo credit: Jon Richter

final year of the Boston Garden, with all four band members serenading the crowd from a flying hot dog at midnight. (A rabbi had come in before the show to prounounce the dog kosher.)

At this time Phish also made its network television debut. Before appearing at Madison Square Garden on December 30, the group performed "Chalkdust Torture" on the *Late Show with David Letterman*. The song was a special request made by Letterman. Dave seemed to enjoy the selection as well, offering to drive the group back to Vermont after the show. Seven months later he invited them back to his program, and Phish performed "Julius" with Dave Grippo and the CBS Orchestra.

Phish spent the better part of six months off the road in the beginning of 1995. The group briefly returned to debut nine new songs at a Voters for Choice benefit on May 16, before a summer tour began on June 7. This abbreviated tour moved from Idaho to Vermont over the course of a month as the band began performing the songs that it had introduced at the Lowell Memorial Auditorium in Lowell, Massachusetts, along with four new additional ones. The summer also marked the debut of Trey's percussion setup, which he utilized on occasions, affording Fish the opportunity to explore some more complex rhythms. The new song "Free," in particular, benefited from the addition.

On June 27 the group also released a double live CD package entitled *A Live One*. Phans were treated to 140 minutes of music along with a colorful thirty-two-page photo booklet. The songs primarily were drawn from the previous fall's tour, and the band members had spent much of their free time in early 1995 agreeing on particular selections. By most phans' accounts *A Live One* was a welcome addition to their collections of recorded music.

Phish resumed touring in late September and continued to perform all the way through New Year's Eve. The result was an all-time record for Phish ticket sales, which reached $27 million, more than doubling the gross sales of 1994 ($10.3 million). It is hard to imagine that many of the people who attended these concerts left disappointed. As the New Year approached, it became clear to many phans that Phish's commitment to absorbing, liberating live performances had not left. The Halloween performance at Rosemont Horizon in Chicago featured the Who's *Quadrophenia*, performed with the assistance of a horn section. The band also introduced some additional new compositions early in the tour along with the band-phan chess match. The New Year's Eve run, comprised of two shows at the Worcester Centrum and two shows at Madison Square Garden, proved particularly noteworthy, as for the first time in the history of this four-night stand, the band did not repeat a song. Indeed, as Fish motioned to Trey to take it around one more time during the band's rendition of "Johnny B. Goode" that ended the performance year of 1995, it became abundantly clear that an auspicious future awaits, one filled with many more golden hoses and transcendent moments. The group's supporters certainly agree, recognizing that Phish is a band that loves its phans, loves live performance, and above all loves music.

2 welcome to gamehendge

the entries in this chapter relate facts and anecdotes about the many songs that Phish has composed and performed. Since the band permits phans to audio record its shows from a designated taper's section, these entries also recommend versions of songs that appear on tapes and circulate among phans.

"AC/DC Bag"

Just what is an "AC/DC Bag"? Well according to its creator, Mr. Ernest Anastasio III, an AC/DC Bag is a robotized hangman used by Wilson's government to execute enemies of state in Prussia in the land of Gamehendge. The song "AC/DC Bag" describes the execution of Mr. Palmer, former accountant to the evil Wilson, who had been embezzling money from his boss in order to fund the counterrevolutionaries.

"AC/DC Bag" premiered in the beginning of 1986. Early versions of the song move along a bit more slowly than later ones and sound different from the current batch since Trey has a different guitar tone (this is before Paul constructed Trey's present guitar in 1987).

If you want to hear a few of these early versions, find 4/1/86 ("Help"—"Slip"—"AC/DC Bag"!) or 4/15/86.

"AC/DC Bag" has appeared consistently on set lists with the exception of the period from December 1991 through February 1993. "AC/DC Bag" appeared only once during this time, at the Orpheum Theater in Boston on 5/16/92. It returned to the rotation after 2/19/93 at the Roxy in Atlanta, where it appeared as an encore dedicated to a phan who had requested the tune on his birthday. Since then it has become a common (and welcome) song, which the band performed twenty-six times in 1995. If you want to hear some other interesting "Bags," check out 9/24/88 (plenty of quotes and teases), 5/12/91 (horn help), 4/5/94, and 6/30/95.

One final point. Contrary to rumors, the chord progressions in the song do not spell out A-C-D-C-B-A-G, they spell A-C-D-C-F-A-G.

"Acoustic Army"

This one blew them away in Boise. No one knew what to make of it at the University Pavilion show on 6/7/95. Instead of retreating behind his drums after his rendition of "Lonesome Cowboy Bill," Fish remained at the front of the stage, where he was soon joined by Page, Mike, and Trey. The crew brought stools to each of the band members and also handed each an acoustic guitar. What form of Phishy madness was this? Inspired Phish madness to say the least. The band paused and tuned, then began a rollicking instrumental selection that featured each member of the band providing his own particular contribution to the sonic whole. One false ending later and the concert debut of "Acoustic Army" was complete.

Initially no one called it "Acoustic Army." In fact, no one knew what to call it except "sweet." Most set lists from those first few "Acoustic Army" performances (6/9/95 and 6/13/95) tried to capture the essence of the song with appropriate metaphors that suggested streams, creeks, and running water in general. Eventually, the name "Acoustic Army" stuck, and until the band says differently, "Acoustic

Photo credit: Jon Richter

Army" it is (although the word "army" really belies the gentle beauty of this song).

"All Things Reconsidered"

"All Things Reconsidered" is a variation on the theme song of the *All Things Considered* National Public Radio program. As the story goes, this was not Trey's intention when he first composed this short instrumental, but after someone pointed out the similarity to him, he modified his own arrangement a bit. Phish premiered this song at the Colonial Theater in Keene, New Hampshire, on 9/26/91, then immediately dropped it from their rotation. The group started playing it again in the spring, and when Phish returned to the Colonial Theater on 3/11/92, Trey promised the crowd that the group had actually learned to perform this one quite nimbly in the intervening six months. On occasion Trey has added vocals to "All Things Reconsidered" to make it sound like the beginning of the radio show (listen to 2/6/93, for instance).

"Alumni Blues"

"Alumni Blues" was Phish's first signature song. In the early years of the band, Phish performed this one almost every evening to the delight of appreciative phans. "Alumni Blues" combines goofy call-and-response lyrics, a catchy melody, and a pounding jam segment. The words to this song are quintessentially Phishy, as they approach conventions only to defy them. Most notably, the opening lines describe the narrator's "walking blues," which prevent him from walking anywhere because he doesn't have any . . . legs. The obvious rhyme here is "shoes," but Phish avoids the obvious rhyme (except for a few glorious versions such as 5/14/88, when Trey finally succumbs to convention).

Although the music to "Alumni Blues" has remained somewhat consistent, the lyrics have evolved over time. For instance, the second verse, in which a foam-throated narrator ends up in jail, does not appear in earlier "Alumni's" (compare 5/19/90, 12/7/90, or 2/14/91 with 10/17/85, 4/1/86, or 10/31/86). The first verse has changed as well, both with ad-libs and evolving lyrics (listen to 10/30/85 and 5/15/88, for example). One other notable feature in almost every version of "Alumni" is the appearance of "Letter to Jimmy Page," the distinctive driving instrumental that appears after the initial verse.

By the end of 1991 the band members tired of this song, and it has appeared only once in the subsequent years (4/15/94—one verse with the horns, although the band also plays an "Alumni Blues" theme during the horn introductions on 12/3/94). Other fine versions include 3/23/87, 11/3/88, 4/15/89, 7/13/91, and 7/15/91.

"Anarchy"

"Anarchy" is seven seconds of punk Phish. The band first introduced this song in 1985, and in fact, many phans find these introductions more entertaining than the song itself. On 10/17/85, for instance, Trey tells the crowd at Burlington's Finbar's "Here's one of our few punk songs. . . . This is a new one that we wrote since the last time you've seen us. It's called 'Revolution.'" Then Fish counts out one, two, three, four as the band pounds away for a half-dozen seconds while chanting "Revolution." "Actually we do have one other punk song," Trey then told the crowd, "and since you guys reacted so well to that one, we'll do this one, this one's called 'Anarchy.'" At which point Fish counts out the song, and Phish pounds away on the same chords for the same period of time while chanting "Anarchy." Phish performed three consecutive "Anarchy"s on 8/1/87.

"Asse Festival"

"Asse Festival" shares a relationship to "Guelah Papyrus" that is inverse to the one that "Landlady" shares with "Punch You in the Guy." Got that? Let me explain. "Asse Festival" debuted at Wetlands on 9/13/90. If you listen to that tape, you'll realize that this song strongly resembles the middle section of "Guelah Papyrus." The reason is that Trey incorporated "Asse Festival" into "Guelah Papyrus" when that song debuted five months later (although trivia buffs may wish to note that "Asse Festival" emerged for one more solo appearance on 4/27/91).

The song itself is a musical fugue, which presents both a melodic theme and variations on that theme. This work reflects the compositional exercises that Trey completed under the tutelage of Ernie Stires. As a result, he dedicates the version of this song on *Picture of Nectar* to his mentor.

"Asse Festival" raises some question of set list etiquette. Should you list "Guelah Papyrus" on a set list as "Guelah Papyrus"—"Asse Festival"—"Guelah Papyrus"? Initially, most phans did this, as they assumed that the band had simply placed "Asse Festival" in the middle of "Guelah" much as "The Man Who Stepped into Yesterday" engulfs *Avenu Malkenu* or "Alumni Blues" swallows "Letter to Jimmy Page." However, this practice eventually ended for most phans by the time *Picture of Nectar* appeared. Although a few phans who take their set lists *very* seriously continue to label the songs separately. (One of these maniacs even labels each part of "Fluffhead" individually—you should see the cramped handwriting on his J-cards.)

"Axilla (I)"

This is another Gamehendge song, one of the later additions to the saga of this majestic region. "Axilla (I)" (or "Axilla," as it was known before the advent of "Axilla II") focuses on events that occurred after Errand Wolfe has appropriated the Helping Friendly Book, as rebel forces once again conspire to liberate Gamehendge. "Axilla" describes the experiences of one of the participants on the front lines of the battle. (In this regard the song is similar to "Llama.")

"Axilla (I)" debuted at St. Michael's College in Colchester, Vermont, on 11/19/92, and the song inspired some furious headbanging from the start. The band continued to perform "Axilla (I)" through August 1993, at which point Trey decided that he no longer felt comfortable singing the lyrics (of which many are condensed into a few lines of music, plus the words are a bit heavy on the Dungeons and Dragons side). So rather than scrap the song altogether, he opted to modify the words when Phish entered the studio to record *Hoist*. The result was

"Axilla II"

This version of the song continues the tale of "Axilla (I)." The initial song ends just as the narrator feels the beam of an opponent's weapon dissolve his loins (ouch!). "Axilla II" picks up his story a while later as he sits by the pool and thinks back on that event. The lesson that he's learned? That time passes and there's no going back. This is quite possibly a metaphor for the thoughts that Trey experienced as the band entered the studio to record *Hoist*, an album that represents a break from the band's past efforts in the recording studio.

"Axilla II" was the last of the *Hoist* songs to appear live, at the Mullins Center, Amherst, Massachusetts, on 4/16/94. This version is similar to the original in that it doesn't contain the jam that leads out of the song on the album. On *Hoist*, of course, that jam also contains cryptic slowed-down words spoken by Trey. Many of the "Axilla II's" that Phish now performs contain that outro jam, although only some of these also feature the spoken section (for instance 11/20/94, where

Trey says "Don't shine that thing in my face Topher, I'm serious," referring to Chris Kuroda, the band's lighting director). Also, if you're wondering whether Phish ever performed "Axilla" after the introduction of "Axilla II," listen to 10/16/94.

"Bathtub Gin"

The *Lawn Boy* version of this song only hints at what it sounds like live. For instance, Phish often incorporates some jazz into this tune, such as "Rhapsody in Blue," which is quoted in the recorded version, or "Jump Monk," which appears on 4/24/94. "Bathtub Gin" debuted in the spring of 1989, although its explosive potential was not immediately realized. Listen to 5/26/89 or 5/28/89 for two of these early appearances. When you think you're ready to hear a "Bathtub Gin"'s "Bathtub Gin," do some deep breathing exercises and put on 8/13/93, recorded at the Murat Theater in Indianapolis. Once you've listened to that "Gin," you'll undoubtedly understand the wise words of John Wood, who, after witnessing a similarly satisfying "Gin" on 12/4/95, rubbed his belly and in the finest Homer Simpson tradition murmured, "Mmmmm, 'Bathtub Gin.'"

Photo credit: Bart Stephens

If you want to find a few additional "Gin"'s look in particular for 5/20/94 and 12/29/95 ("Gin"—"Real Me"—"Gin"). By the way, one final "Bathtub Gin" fact is that the lyrics to this song were composed by a friend of the band named Suzannah Goodman. If you can catch her on a good night and ask nicely, she's been known to sing this one with a phan or two.

"Big Black Furry Creatures from Mars"

You want Phish hardcore? You got it. This tune provides one of the band's few forays into this genre, and it lasts a hell of a lot longer than "Anarchy." "BBFCFM" debuted in August 1987 and has remained an uncommon treat over the years. If you're listening on tape, Mike's ever-changing lyrics and Fish's raging responses build to a frantic, noisy climax. If you're there in person, "BBFCFM" often becomes a spectacular production number. After Fish starts screaming, the stage often fills with fog and strobes while Trey runs around like a man possessed, swinging his megaphone or pretending to throw his guitar into the audience. Although you can't hear any of this on tape, the musical melee still proves eminently satisfying. Plus you get you to hear Fishman count out "one, two, three, four" just like Joey Ramone.

Some interesting versions of "BBFCFM" include 8/21/87, 5/3/91, 7/19/91 (with horn intros), 3/13/92 (in "Run Like an Antelope," some phans' all-time favorite), 7/6/94 (as a bookend to "Sample in a Jar"), 7/13/94 (with music to "Scent of a Mule") and 11/18/95 (as a bookend to "Acoustic Army").

"Billy Breathes"

This song debuted at the Cal Expo Amphitheater in Sacramento on 9/27/95, the first show of the fall tour. With "Billy Breathes" the band continued its efforts to expand its musical offerings and occasionally change pace and mood with a mellower composition. This song does not resemble one of the band's earlier ballads so much as it does a gentle lullaby.

"Bitching Again"

Although the Dude is not a member of Phish, he is closely affiliated with the group. So the Dude's songs will be included in this chapter instead of the next one, which examines Phish's cover tunes.

Phish and the Dude first performed "Bitching Again" at Amy Skelton's farm on 8/3/91. Some phans really despise this song, as they feel that it reinforces negative female stereotypes. Others say no, this song actually pokes fun at such stereotypes. (Why take the Dude seriously in this song if you're not going to take him seriously in any others?) To which the original group says yes, but nonetheless it reinforces stereotypes. This debate continues among phans. By the way, the woman who appeared onstage with the Dude at Amy's farm to sing this one (and who sings on the album as well) is Sofi Dillof, then Page's significant other, now his wife.

"Bouncing Around the Room"

Trey has often stated that he feels that "Bouncing Around the Room" contains some of Tom Marshall's best lyrics. As those lyrics suggest, this song began as a dream that Tom had and later wrote down. He sent the words along to Trey, who put them to music.

Phish debuted this song at Dartmouth College on 1/20/90, and it has remained a constant element in the band's set lists ever since. In some ways this was Phish's first radio song, as a few low wattage stations added this one to their play lists after the release of *Lawn Boy*. Some phans tend to gripe about "Bouncing" because (a) it doesn't vary much from version to version and (b) Elektra released this song to radio after it issued *A Live One*. Audience behavior makes this song particularly enjoyable in the live context, as it is always cool to see a few thousand phans bopping up and down in time with the beat.

"Brother"

"Brother" burst onto the scene on 9/25/91, appeasing many phans who longed for a new song with fewer words and more opportunities for improvisational jamming. Phish made the most of this one in a short period, performing "Brother" twenty-five times in the three months between its debut and New Year's Eve, 1991. The band continued to present this song through 7/16/92, after which

Phish abandoned it. The group revived it once, on 8/2/93, but it has not been heard in concert since. Many phans repeatedly question the band members about the possibility of reworking and reintroducing this one, as Phish did with "NICU" in 1994. Some favored "Brothers" include 11/30/91, 3/13/92, 3/24/92 (with trumpet), and 4/17/92.

"Buffalo Bill"

"Buffalo Bill" is one of the rarer Phish originals. This short, macabre song debuted as an encore at the SUNY Stony Brook show on 11/21/92. Since then the band has performed "Buffalo Bill" on only two additional occasions, 10/29/94 and 12/31/94. "Riker's Mailbox" is said to have resulted from a version of this song recorded at the *Hoist* sessions (see "Riker's" entry).

"Bundle of Joy"

This song did not debut as a portion of "Fluffhead," although Phish eventually incorporated it into that song. In fact, many of "Bundle of Joy" 's initial appearances take place as segments of "Harpua" (for example, listen to 8/21/87 or 8/29/87). By the spring of 1988, Phish had found a place for this song at the end of "Fluffhead" (listen to 3/11/88 or 5/14/88). Nonetheless, "Bundle of Joy" continued to make a few solo appearances through 1989 (for example, 9/12/88 and 10/20/89).

"Buried Alive"

Trey introduced this song at its debut on 9/13/90 as the product of "a very strange dream." Close your eyes and listen. It's easy to imagine "Buried Alive" as the soundtrack to a fevered reverie full of chase sequences and narrow escapes. "Buried Alive" has been a versatile song over the years, appearing as a featured number with the horns (7/24/91 and 4/4/94), as a song to perform with guests (2/6/93, with John Popper), as a segue into other tunes (particularly "Poor Heart"—for example, 12/31/92, 11/22/94, and 10/15/95), as a great song to tease (11/2/90 in "Possum"), and as the source of signals and quotes in its own right (listen carefully to 7/12/91 and 12/7/91).

"Camel Walk"

Jeff composed "Camel Walk," which Phish began to perform during the fall of 1985. Earlier versions of this song take advantage of Phish's dual guitars, resulting in a denser texture than "Camel Walk's" performed after Jeff left the band. Jeff sang lead on the initial versions of this song (10/17/85 and 4/15/86), with Trey taking over by the fall of 1986 (10/15/86, 3/23/87). Phish stopped performing "Camel Walk" in the spring of 1989 (2/24/89 may be the last version), then suddenly revived it in the middle of the first set at Sugarbush Summer Stage in Fayston, Vermont, on 7/2/95. The band has not yet played it again. By the way, if you're curious about the meaning of the song, find a copy of 4/15/86, where Jeff offers a bit of insight.

"Cars Trucks and Buses"

This one made its debut at Cal Expo on 9/27/95 (this was a big night for keyboard debuts, with "Keyboard Cavalry" following in its footsteps). "Cars Trucks and Buses" is a jazzy instrumental that some phans also feel sounds a bit like a Meters song. Almost everyone is happy with this addition, as it provides a new opportunity for Page to step up and dazzle. This McConnell composition also features two false endings, which have taken in more than a few distracted analog tapers over its short existence (for instance, 12/4/95). If you're curious as to the origin of the song title, look at the signs that greet you as you pull off the highway to enter a service area (and see the next page). You'll also want to hear the version of this song from the New Orleans Jazz Fest with Michael Ray on trumpet (4/26/96).

"Catapult"

One of the earliest "Catapult's" appeared at the Warfield Theater on 4/17/92 in the middle of "David Bowie." In fact, the song made

four such appearances within "Bowie" that evening, so that the set list reads "David Bowie"—"Catapult"—"David Bowie"—"Catapult"—"David Bowie"—"Catapult"—"David Bowie"—"Catapult"—"David Bowie." Cool, huh? Many phans would agree, although a few others think that this arrangement looks a lot better on paper. "Catapult" is Mike's creation, and Phish has performed this song infrequently over the past few years, most typically in the middle of "David Bowie." The "Catapult" on *Picture of Nectar* also features a snippet from a sound effects record, "Dr. Davis, Telephone Please," that occasionally appears in soap operas and can also be heard in the Sample's *No Room* disc. If you're looking to amass a "Catapult" collection, you'll want to include 4/21/92, 6/22/94, 7/16/94 (with an interesting exchange between Trey and Fish just prior to Trey's wedding), and 6/16/95.

"Cavern"

The one that made *Nectar* famous. Of course, it almost didn't. If Phish continued to perform the initial version, which debuted in the spring of 1990, the famous guy would have been someone named Penile Erector. Come to think about it, the cover of that album would have been a sight to behold (and no doubt banned at

Wal-Marts everywhere). That's right: The line about Burlington's favorite restaurant proprietor was added to Cavern soon after its debut, replacing "Penile Erector." At that time the band also decided to abandon an original verse that described dropping a knife-wielding brothel wife into manure (although the brothel wife returns on occasion—listen to 4/4/94). Tom Marshall wrote the lyrics to this song via E-mail with his friend Scott Herman, who is credited for his contribution on the liner notes to *Picture of Nectar*. Phish has performed many entertaining versions of "Cavern" over the years, including 4/6/90 (another early version), 7/11/91 (with horns), 7/15/91 (Trey asks the audience for help when he forgets the words), 8/17/92, 4/4/94 (horns), 6/24/94 (acoustic), 12/10/94 (lyric flub and cover), and 6/25/95.

"Chalkdust Torture"

"Chalkdust Torture" is David Letterman's Phish favorite. When Phish appeared on the *Late Show* in December 1994, Dave asked the band to play this song (and Phish obliged). "Chalkdust" debuted in February 1991 and has remained in rotation ever since. The lyrics to any song are open to many possible personal interpretations, any of which are valid, but "Chalkdust" supposedly recounts the narrator's experience at his in-laws' dinner table (think of Jezmund as a self-righteous, insecure, angst-in-his-pants narrator addicted to non sequiturs and it works). Here's another phun phact: Trey's vocals are slowed down on the version of this song that appears on *Picture of Nectar*. If you want to hear some interesting "Chalkdust"'s listen to 7/14/91, 12/7/92, 7/23/93, 8/9/93 (with "Who Knows"), 11/16/94 (a favorite of many), 12/10/94 ("Chalkdust" reprise), and 12/31/94.

"Clod"

Like "Bundle of Joy," "Clod" enjoyed a solo existence before being added to "Fluffhead." For a few of these "Clod's" listen to 12/6/86 and 8/21/87. By the spring of 1988 "Clod" was firmly entrenched in "Fluffhead" (listen to 3/11/88 or 5/14/88). Nonetheless, this song also emerged for some non-"Fluff" appearances on a few subsequent occasions through 1989 (for instance, 10/26/89).

"Colonel Forbin's Ascent"

"Colonel Forbin's Ascent" is an integral part of the Gamehendge saga. It recounts the efforts of Colonel Forbin to climb a mountain and find Icculus in order to ask for his aid against Wilson (for more on the Gamehendge song cycle see its entry in this chapter). "Colonel Forbin's Ascent," which debuted in the spring of 1988, is noteworthy because it is the only Gamehendge song that currently features narration whenever Phish performs it live. Phans close their eyes and allow Trey to carry them away from the venue and into Gamehendge to join Colonel Forbin's climb. This climb always culminates with the appearance of Icculus, who consents to release the Famous Mockingbird.

Early versions of "Colonel Forbin" do not contain complete narrations. In fact, prior to the spring of 1992, most contain no story (7/23/88, 5/28/89, and 11/2/90) or an abbreviated account of the events (5/16/91). By April of 1992, however, "Colonel Forbin" contains the creative stories that remain a hallmark of this song. Some of these include 4/16/92 (extended Gamehendge narrative), 4/21/92 (travel to Gamehendge through houseboat and hang glider), 5/2/92 (journey through space), 5/6/92 (through the earth), 11/27/92 (inside Fish's head), 12/31/92 (spaceship, with audience participation—see somewhat less Secret Language entry in chapter 4), 2/7/93 (peapods harvested turned into stew, ending up in baby's diaper), 10/5/95 (Matrix, where music comes from, overintellectualizing of birth process), and 12/1/95 (Tao of Physics—philosophy, science, religion, milk chocolate). Of course, there are many, many more. If you enjoy Trey's narration, you should seek out any version of "Colonel Forbin" since April 1992.

"Contact"

In case you haven't guessed, "Contact" is the sublime product of Mike Gordon's febrile (certainly not feeble) imagination. This is another

Photo credit: Brett Virmalo

song that is more enjoyable in person than on tape due to Chris Kuroda's keen lighting effects when the band comes around for the final chorus. Also, Trey and Mike will often lead the audience in a bit of arm-waving as well. Indeed, "Contact" presents one of Phish's more deadpan assaults against the conventions employed by certain live performers, as it tweaks both lounge singers and bombastic rockers. If you want to hear a few such "Contact" 's, listen to 4/14/89, 5/28/89, 4/5/90, 4/18/92, 11/28/92, and 8/9/93. Finally, to continue the NPR theme that began in this chapter with "All Things Reconsidered," "Contact" occasionally appears over the closing credits on the informative and amusing *Car Talk* NPR program, where Click and Clack often suggest that it is the worst song about an automobile ever written (Mike probably appreciates this high compliment).

"Crimes of the Mind"

The Dude's signature song. At least this is the song that he has performed most commonly on stage with Phish (five times—

8/3/91, 11/8/91, 8/9/93, 8/28/93, and 7/10/94). It is also the title song of his album, which he recorded with Phish in August 1991, although Elektra didn't release it until the fall of 1994.

"The Curtain"

Trey introduced this one at its debut on 8/21/87 as a song about Jim Bakker. Initially, "The Curtain" had a different instrumental segment after the verses, which was later torn from the song to provide one of the central riffs for "Rift." Some early "Curtain" 's that feature this ending include 8/29/87 and 5/25/88. Notable later "Curtain" 's, which some phans feel contain a "Reba"-esque concluding sequence, include 11/4/90, 3/13/92, 11/22/94, and 12/11/95.

"Dahlia"

This Dude tune made its debut at the Wetlands on 9/13/90. "Dahlia" is mislabeled on a number of J-cards as "Done Me Wrong," but the release of the Dude's album cleared this up. This song provides an interesting image of a woman in a bathtub smoking a cigar, but many phans feel it offers little else.

"Dave's Energy Guide"

Trey composed this song with "looks too much like" Dave Abrahams. The two worked on "Energy Guide" one summer while Trey attended the National New Guitar Workshop. (Trey's involvement with the workshop came full circle during the summer of 1993, when he appeared as an instructor—tapes of this appearance circulate.) The short instrumental piece bears more than a passing resemblance to King Crimson's "Discipline," which is why some phans label this song as "Crimson Jam" on their J-cards. In fact, the original title of this song was "Dave's Energy Guide (A Memo to Robert Fripp)." Fripp was one of Trey's early influences, as was fellow Crimsonite Adrian Belew.

One of the earliest appearances of "Dave's Energy Guide" in a

Phish set list is on 10/17/85 at Finbar's. Trey introduces this song after it emerges from "Mike's Song." "Dave's Energy Guide" is often not listed on tapes, as some phans don't recognize it and just assume it is part of a jam. For some distinctive "Energy Guide" 's listen to 3/23/87, 4/24/87, 7/23/88, or 8/6/88. Then pop 12/29/94 II into your tape deck and listen to the music at the end of "Bowie." Sound familiar? That's right, it sounds too much like Dave's.

"David Bowie"

Trey wrote the music and composed the lyrics (all four of them) to this song that Phish has performed since 1986 (10/31/86 is an early appearance). Although there are few lyrics to "David Bowie," there is much else to hear and enjoy. This song has long rewarded close listeners with numerous quotes and teases, for instance, 10/7/89 ("Fly Like an Eagle"), 10/20/89 ("Major Tom" introduction—Bowie in "Bowie"), 4/5/90 ("Bonanza" and others), 4/18/90 (the Jaegermeister song), 11/2/90 ("Mike's Song," "Divided Sky," "Lizards," "Foam," "Makisupa Policeman," and more), and 5/8/93 "(Jessica," "Get Back"). The opening to "Bowie" also has been the source of numerous signals, both before and after the group officially introduced them, for instance, 10/13/91 (signals plus some comments about Fish's love for his high hat), 10/31/91 (after "wait"), and 3/12/93. The song has consistently offered phans some outrageous improvisational jams, including 12/6/86 ("Bowie"—"Clod"—"Bowie"), 3/11/88, 10/26/89, 7/12/91 (with horns), 11/7/91 (with Aquarium Rescue Unit), 11/24/91 (with gift of bathrobes to crew), 3/6/92, 4/17/92 (with catapults aplenty), 11/23/92 (a different approach), 2/19/93 (with "Moby Dick" and vacuum), 6/18/94 ("Mind Left Body" jam intro), 7/15/94, and 12/29/94. Also, in case you're curious, with Phish's performance of "Life on Mars?" on 10/13/95 the group finally added a Bowie song to its live repertoire. The band has yet to complement this with a complete UB40 selection (the closest may be a few words from "Red, Red Wine" as on 11/3/88).

"Dear Mrs. Reagan"

Phish's only overtly political song made its debut in 1986. As you might expect, this tune did not outlast the Reagan presidency. Phish shelved it before President Bush won the election in November 1988. Most of the lyrics to other Phish tunes, particularly from this period, are subtle, bordering on oblique, which renders this selection all the more of an anomaly. This song rather bluntly suggests that Nancy Reagan wields all the power and encourages her to gun down her husband (so that George Bush can become president—as it turns out, Nancy wasn't needed for this task). If you want to hear "Dear Mrs. Reagan," look for 4/1/86, 4/15/86, and 4/24/87. In all of these versions Trey's vocal phrasings and enuciations emulate those of Bob Dylan, and at the 4/1/86 and 4/15/86 shows Trey later introduces Phish as the Bob Dylan Band.

"Demand"

The version of "Demand" that appears on *Hoist* raises some questions. What is the song that's dropped into the car tape deck and causes the driver to speed and crash? And what about the haunting Hebrew music that appears afterward—is that a prayer? Two fine questions. The jam you probably recognize as "Split Open and Melt." Phish is particularly proud of this version, which they originally performed at the Newport Music Hall in Columbus, Ohio, on 4/21/93. As for the Hebrew, that's not a prayer but rather the magnificent Israeli folk song *"Yerushalim Shel Zahav"* ("Jerusalem, City of Gold").

"Demand" first appeared at the Broome County Arena in Binghamton, New York, on 4/9/94. This version contained only the bare song itself without any of the accoutrements that appear on *Hoist*. All subsequent "Demand"s have followed this pattern except for the version that Phish performed during its *Hoist* second set on 6/26/94 at the Municipal Auditorium in Charleston, West Virginia. For a few additional "Demand"s, listen to 4/14/95 and 12/7/95.

"Destiny Unbound"

Highway Bill and Highway Jill first took to the road at Providence, Rhode Island's Living Room on 9/14/90. Mike wrote this song, which seems to reflect his work as a film major, as the lyrics present a twisted version of the buddy-road movie (the pair doesn't make it very far because the street isn't paved). Phans seemed to enjoy this one, but "Destiny" disappeared from Phish set lists in November 1991, possibly because certain people felt that this one sounded a bit too much like the Grateful Dead. Of course, this song also may have been put away so that Mike can tinker with it a bit. "Destiny Unbound" began as a work in progress that experienced some revisions along the way (for instance, compare 9/22/90 and 11/1/91). Other enjoyable "Destiny Unbound"'s include 2/7/91 and 4/11/91.

"Dinner and a Movie"

The Dude of Life contributed the lyrics to this song that Phish first performed in the fall of 1987. "Dinner and a Movie" has evolved a bit over the years. Early versions begin with the band's vocals (3/11/88 and 8/6/88). Later, Phish worked out the instrumental introduction (8/26/89 and 10/1/89). "Dinner and a Movie" is also one of the songs that received an entertaining makeover for the first Giant Country Horn tour (for instance, 7/11/91 and 7/15/91). "Dinner and a Movie" also has served as a fine segue into other tunes over the years, for example, 7/23/91 ("Gumbo"), 10/28/91 ("Stash"). Recently, Phish has performed the song much less, with only three appearances in 1994 and two in 1995.

"Divided Sky"

On occasion, when people attempt the difficult (and probably futile) task of identifying the quintessential Phish song, they often mention "Divided Sky" (along with "You Enjoy Myself," "David Bowie," "Mike's Song," "Guyute," and a few others). Why? Well, first of all, like many other Phish songs that phans enjoy, "Divided Sky" contains both an elaborate composed section as well as ample room for improvisation. The composed section is additionally interesting since as it includes one short segment that is then followed by its mirror image. (On *Junta* you can hear this for yourself beginning at 1:17.)

"Divided Sky" also is identified as a representative Phish song because it is related to the Gamehendge saga. As the liner notes to *Junta* indicate, "Divided Sky" was recited as part of a ritual by the Lizards in the years before the rule of Wilson. Trey has elaborated

on this in concert on a number of occasions (for instance, 4/30/89 or 7/8/94).

"Divided Sky" also is intimately related to another piece of the Phish mythos, the Rhombus. As related in chapter 1, Trey often met with his friends Tom, Dave, Aaron, and others at a large metal rhombus to compose music. It is said that Trey wrote the song "Divided Sky" at the Rhombus, a site that remains important to Trey and his friends. (Trey has discussed the Rhombus from the stage most recently on 6/23/95 and 12/1/95, where he offers directions on how to find it.) As a result, Trey has incorporated the real-life Rhombus into the Gamehendge story. As the *Junta* insert indicates, the "Divided Sky" ritual actually occurs on top of the Rhombus. Trey has, in fact, preceded some "Divided Sky" 's with a brief story about the nature of the Rhombus (for example, 12/7/89, 12/29/89, and 3/17/90).

Finally, "Divided Sky" contains a particularly Phishy segment where the band stops playing altogether (somewhat akin to the silent jam). At one point in the song the band begins playing softer and softer until it becomes hard to hear them unless you're right up front. Then they come to a complete halt. Trey often relates a particular experience of his when he had stopped and let the jam continue in his head only to hear the audience cheer at an appropriate moment for the music that Trey played in his mind. Ever since then Trey has tried to re-create that moment, pausing for an ever-expanding period of time so that phans can listen in their own heads for corresponding jams. This silent period has increased over the years—for instance, compare 9/13/90, 8/3/91, and 12/30/95.

Some versions of "Divided Sky" that many phans enjoy include 8/21/87 (the early version with an ending that mimics the song's opening notes), 11/5/88, 7/19/91, 11/19/92, 8/20/93, 6/24/94, 10/31/94, 7/2/95, and 10/31/95.

"Dog Faced Boy"

This one's a country-tinged tearjerker. The narrator is looking back and lamenting the love and friendship that he's tossed aside due to his deceitful, hurtful ways. And it's got circus freaks, too, which makes it a real winner.

"Dog Faced Boy," which appears on *Hoist*, did not make its initial concert appearance until nine shows into the 1994 spring tour at the Beacon Theater on 4/14/94. At that time the song was performed with Phish's acoustic lineup, which enhanced the doleful aspects of the tune. Since then the song has appeared infrequently, usually with the band on their electric instruments (for example, 6/16/95 or 12/16/95). On almost every occasion this one is said to bring a tear to the eye of Jonathan Fishman.

"Dog Log"

This phan phavorite (and soundman's choice) was inspired by the habits of Trey's dog Marley, aka Mar Mar. This one made its first appearance by 1985, with some enjoyable early versions, including 10/30/85, 4/15/86 (with a bonus Marley story), and 8/21/87. Although Phish has performed "Dog Log" less than a half-dozen times in concert since 1990, the song has been a pretty common one to sound check, partially because Paul really enjoys it. Lucky sound check listeners have heard a number of versions of "Dog Log," including a reggae version, a lounge lizard offering, and a funkier interpretation. Some of these have made it onto tape, with 12/6/91, 12/5/92, and 5/7/94 making the rounds.

When Phish performed "Dog Log" on 8/2/93 after a two-year absence, many phans hoped that the band would reintroduce it into its live rotation. This didn't occur and "Dog Log" enthusiasts had to wait until 12/11/95 for the song to make a surprising and triumphant return. On this night at the Cumberland County Civic Center in Portland, Maine, Trey announced that Phish was going to release an album composed of fifteen versions of "Dog Log." He asked phans to help out the band by remaining quiet as if it were a sound check and then joining together at his signal for a collective boo. Later in the set he asked them for a second take, and the audience members provided some appropriate screeches following a particularly oily version of the song.

"Done Me Wrong"
See "Dahlia."

"Don't Get Me Wrong"
Trey cowrote this song with John Popper of Blues Traveler. Some of the music is drawn from early versions of "Reba," in particular the segment between the last verse and the present bridge (on 10/1/89, for instance). "Don't Get Me Wrong" made its debut at the Capitol Theater in Port Chester, New York, on 10/6/90 with Popper on lead vocals and harmonica. Phish performed it live on only a handful of occasions, all of these with Popper's assistance (10/8/90 and 12/28/90). "Don't Get Me Wrong" is also notable because Popper joins Phish for a vocal jam at the song's conclusion (12/28/90 is the one to hear). If you're desperately searching for more versions of this song, a notable "Don't Get Me Wrong" quote occurs in "You Enjoy Myself" on 5/2/92.

"Down with Disease"

"Down with Disease," the first single from *Hoist*, first appeared live in its entirety at the Flynn Theater benefit on 4/4/94. However, you may not be aware that Phish performed a section of this song four months earlier on New Year's Eve. Pull out your copy of 12/31/93 and listen to the third set. (This show was broadcast and rebroadcast on WBCN in Boston, so crisp versions abound.) At midnight, after "Auld Lang Syne," Phish segues into this song and jams on it for a few minutes. They did this while camera crews recorded the event for the "Down with Disease" video.

The band members eventually expressed some reservations about the video, but they expressed none about the director's bass performance on this tune. Mike, the video director and bass player in question, rarely has an opportunity to perform a more traditional bass line in his work with Phish. "Down with Disease" offered him such an opportunity, and band and phan alike have praised his efforts.

Many stellar versions of this song exist. Ever since its initial appearance at the Flynn, it has become clear that the outro jam in particular offers many possibilities for the band. Some outstanding versions of this song include 6/24/94, 11/30/94, and 11/17/94. Many phans feel that the extended version of this song that Phish performed at the Saratoga Performing Arts Center on 6/26/95 represented a creative zenith in the band's interpretation of this song (the seamless segue into "Free" provides the punchline). The band may have agreed, as they elected not to perform the song again until 12/1/95. The version that follows on 12/12/95 also ranks in the select pantheon of DWDs.

"Eliza"

Trey wrote this instrumental for his girlfriend (now wife) Susan Eliza. It debuted in November 1990, after which the band performed the song roughly a dozen times before retiring it in the spring of 1992. Some of these versions include 11/17/90, 11/1/91 (Mike introduces the author as Ringo), and 4/21/92. Since this song now shares a name with Trey's young daughter, it is quite likely that the author will limit future performances of this song to her nursery.

"Esther"

There may be no Phish image more frightening than that of Esther and the Armenian man produced by Jim Pollock for the interior art for *Junta*. Look at the wide-eyed innocence of Esther and the smile on the face of the Armenian man. It's all the more tragic when one considers Esther's eventual fate.

But it wasn't always this way. The version of "Esther" that Phish introduced at Sam's Tavern in Burlington on 9/12/88 develops and ends quite differently. Esther isn't pulled into oceanic depths by an evil puppet. Instead, Esther is an archbishop's daughter (sort that one out for yourself). Also, the man, who is not identified as Armenian, says nothing about chopping off his legs and peeling off his socks; he just offers Esther a beautiful puppet. The story then follows the same general pattern, with a mob chasing her. However, in this version, Esther emerges from the water, runs back to the carnival, returns the puppet to its owner, and escapes. The old man is left to confront the mob that emerges from the water. Trey abandoned this version of the song because it wasn't creepy enough for him.

"Esther" is also worth noting because, technically speaking, this song and not "Down with Disease" was the first subject of a video produced for a Phish song. At the Somerville Theater in Somerville, Massachusetts, on 7/19/91 an animated "Esther" video was screened between sets. This video, based on the art of Scott Nybokken, had been produced by a computer graphics company located in Rhode Island. It has not yet resurfaced.

Finally, "Esther" was the subject of one of the subtlest (some would say lamest) Phish Halloween costumes. At the Glens Falls Civic Center on 10/31/94, a group of individuals arrived at the show dressed as . . . you guessed it, an angry mob of joggers.

"Faht"

Fishman wrote this number for the acoustic guitar, and on rare instances he'll play it alone onstage, accompanied only by some sound effects provided by Paul (for instance, 12/2/95). The original version of this song was called "Windham Hell," poking gentle fun at the record label that gravitates toward New Age music. All was well and good except that the owner of the label didn't appreciate the good-natured ribbing. So the band was pressed to find a new title for the song, and here's where the fun begins.

The fall 1991 *Phish Update* (now the *Doniac Schvice*), ran a story in "Fish's Forum" that the drummer wrote in a southern dialect. However, due to a typographical error the letter *f* replaced the letter *h* in the word "raht," changing the end of a sentence to "faht tuh the front door." Jon became quite disgruntled when he discovered the alteration, claiming that it changed the entire intent of the piece (for the better, I've heard from a few phans). Not so long after the incident the band needed to change the title of "Windham Hell" and Fish was away. Eventually they decided on "Faht" so that they could approach him and say, "Look, the record company made the same damn screw-up."

"Family Picture"

More from the Dude. The Dude of Life took the stage with Phish to sing this original composition at the Ivory Tusk in Tuscaloosa, Alabama, on 11/8/91. The Dude cleared the room on this evening. If you listen to the tape, you can actually hear far fewer people clapping at the end of this song, his third that day, than you can hear after "Jesus Left Chicago," which preceded the Dude's appearance. (Actually, "Family Picture" segues into "Crimes of the Mind," so listen then.) Some phans who recorded the show onto a DAT claim that if you listen really closely to their tape, you can hear the random gripes and grumblings of the bartenders who were losing tip money by the minute.

"Famous Mockingbird"

"Famous Mockingbird" relates the flight of the Famous Mocking-bird, enlisted by Icculus to retrieve the Helping Friendly Book for Colonel Forbin and his revolutionaries. For the full story on this song, soar over to the Gamehendge section or the "Colonel Forbin's Ascent" entry.

"Fast Enough for You"

When Phish first performed this song at St. Michael's College on 11/19/92, some unenlightened phans thought it was a prank. They kept waiting for the rapid shift in tempo. And they kept waiting . . . and waiting. . . . A ballad? From Phish? Plus the title made it sound like a joke, as if the band were asking listeners "Is this one fast enough for you?" A total goof? Well, no.

"Fast Enough for You" initiated a period of slower songs and more serious themes for the band. "Fast Enough for You," which commonly appears on set lists under the acronym "FEFY," suggests a moment in a relationship when someone fears that things may indeed be progressing too rapidly while the other individual strives to keep things moving. Serious stuff. So pay close attention to this one, breathe it in, and don't feel the need to use this tune for a midconcert bathroom break. By the way, the debut performance of "Fast Enough for You" also features Burlington resident Gordon Stone on pedal steel guitar, which he also contributes to the version of this song that appears on "Rift."

"Fee"

The heartwarming story of Milly's love for her weasel, Fee, ranks among many phans' favorite Phish songs. "Fee" appears on *Junta*, where Pollock's interpretation of his smiling face joins "Esther" in the insert. The song also appeared on the initial pressing of *Lawn Boy*, but it was later deleted when Elektra rereleased the album.

"Fee" is most noteworthy for three attributes. First, on 11/19/92

Trey began to sing the verses of this song through a megaphone. Many phans enjoy this effect in the live setting, although it has become hard to discern his vocals on tape and on occasion Trey has been plagued by a broken megaphone. (Nonetheless, many phans are happy to have the megaphone there just so Trey can run around with it during "BBFCFM"). Second, "Fee" shares a distinction with "Lizards" as the two Phish songs whose lyrics he most commonly forgets (for instance, listen to 10/14/89, 4/11/91, 4/19/92, or 11/29/95). Finally, "Fee" is one of the songs that employs the recurrent nipple-slicing motif (see the "Oh Kee Pah Ceremony" entry for more on this).

Phish began performing "Fee" in concert in August 1987. If you want to hear a representative sampling of "Fee" 's, listen to 8/21/87, 11/3/88, 6/16/90, 7/12/91, 2/3/93, 4/16/94, and 9/28/95.

"Flat Fee"

Phish has two "Fee" 's? Indeed. Trey acknowledged the confusion from the stage on 8/21/87, when he introduced them both and the band performed them back-to-back. Trey composed "Flat Fee" as one of his exercises with Ernie Stires. However, the "Flat Fee" 's that Phish performed in 1987 sounded very different from the way Trey had initially envisioned them, as he had composed horn charts for the song. So the band stopped performing "Flat Fee," only to revive it during July 1991, when the band hit the road with the Giant Country Horns. Phish performed "Flat Fee" at their first gig with the GCH on 7/11/91 at Battery Park in Burlington as Trey announced, "This song was written about six years ago, and it's been waiting to be played until this very day. . . . We never had the brass." Phish had the brass for the next three weeks, during which the group performed "Flat Fee" almost every evening before the song disappeared once again, with a potential revival looming at any future horn show.

Photo credit: Kurt Zinnack

"Flip"
See "Glide II."

"Fluffhead"
The song that we know as "Fluffhead" came to its current power and glory slowly through accretion. The initial version of this song, which the Dude of Life sang on 12/1/84, contained only the first part of the epic that you hear today. Other segments of the song entered the Phish universe and floated around for a while until they were slowly added. "Clod," "Bundle of Joy," and a section from "Lushington" were slowly incorporated into "Fluffhead" along with some new music until that song reached its current form in the

spring of 1988. If you want to hear the evolution of the song, then along with the initial version, listen to 10/15/86, 3/23/87, 4/29/87, and 5/15/88.

"Fluffhead" is such a favorite of many phans that set lists and J-cards are often marked "Fluffhead"! If you want to hear some of the versions that have earned the song this punctuation, listen to 6/20/88 (with a bonus "Bette Davis Eyes" and "Goodnight, John Boy"), 8/3/91, 11/20/92, 8/8/93, and 6/11/94.

Finally, one source of confusion is whether the Fluff comes to "my door" or "New York." Which is it? The answer is both, as you can hear on a number of occasions, for instance, 9/24/88, 2/20/93, and 7/14/94.

"Foam"

Phans often gripe when "Foam" is played right before or after "Runaway Jim." "They always do this," one phan complained at the Beacon Theater on 4/14/94. This is simply not true. Mark, if you're reading this, here's the evidence.

Phish does often perform "Foam" early in the first set. This is because it serves as an ideal warm-up tune. "Foam," which debuted at Hamilton College in Clinton, New York, on 10/12/88, is almost an entirely composed piece. Everything in this song is scripted except for the middle solo, which is written over changes (Trey composed "Foam," which reflects Ernie Stires's influences once again). As a result "Foam" enables the band members to start their fingers moving, to test their muscle memory and the like.

And now on to the statistics. . . . Ever since "Runaway Jim" entered the Phish lineup in May 1990, the likelihood that Phish will perform "Runaway Jim" next to "Foam" if it plays "Foam" is less than 30 percent. If you expand the inquiry a bit to ask what is the likelihood that the band will juxtapose "Foam" or "Runaway Jim" at a show where one of these songs appears, then the odds drop to less than 20 percent. Also, if you attended any given show during this period, the odds that you would see the band perform both of these songs side by side are less than 10 percent. Finally, if you were to consider how many times this pairing opens, the percentage drops to about 5 percent. There you have it. So next time you're at a show and someone next to you decides to mutter loudly, " They do this all the time," feel free to correct her. Or don't. Better yet, just sit back and enjoy the music.

"Fog That Surrounds"

For the full story on this song first read the entry for "Taste," as "Fog" is a reworked version of "Taste." The first incarnation of "Fog," the second of "Taste," occurred at Cal Expo on 9/27/95. Trey introduced the song with the comment that some phans "think you know this song but you don't." This became clear as Fish began singing new words to the "Taste" music.

The debut did not immediately win over the multitudes. First, many phans really liked "Taste." They had welcomed this new song over the summer and wanted to see the band open it up and start exploring it a little further. Instead, they found Phish tweaking the song and working out Fishman's vocals onstage. This led to problem number two, Fish's vocal cords. Of the four band members', Fish's voice tends to deteriorate the most quickly—just listen to some versions of "Amazing Grace" or "Sweet Adeline" from late in a tour. Also, the band's arrangement of "Fog" required him to enunciate some serious, thoughtful lyrics while simultaneously supporting the song's rhythm. During "Taste" he had been able to concentrate on his drumming while Trey sang the lyrics. One of the problems that soon arose with "Fog" was that it became hard to hear Fish over the band, so that some of these early versions sound much like Fish mumbling over some of the instrumental segments of "Taste" (for instance, listen to 9/30/95 or 10/2/95).

The band may have shared some of these thoughts because on 10/24/95 at Dane County Coliseum in Madison, Wisconsin, Phish debuted a second version of "Fog" (the third version of "Taste" if you're scoring at home). This one combined the initial "Taste" and the first "Fog" in a delightful musical melange. Trey opens the new version with a verse from "Taste," then Fish follows with a verse from "Fog," and then the pair sing alternating and simultaneous verses from the respective songs. The result is a fine culmination of the two earlier tunes (almost as if it had been planned that way from the start . . .).

"Free"

"Free" debuted at the Lowell benefit show on 5/16/95, and it quickly earned the allegiance of phans. "Free" has a lot to recommend it: (a) interesting water-based lyrics that feel integrally connected to the tenor and tone of the music, (b) a rousing sing-along chorus that features gorgeous harmonies, (c) cohesive yet exploratory improvisational jamming, (d) on most versions, Trey on his mini–drum kit taboot. Mike has referred to this one as a

Photo credit: Arch Stanton

southern rocker (presumably in the Lynyrd Skynryd tradition), and you can listen for such influences, but this is most distinctly a southern rocker as filtered through Burlington, Vermont.

Many of the versions of this song are eminently satisfying, but the best ones are must listens. Check out 6/16/95 and 6/26/95 in particular, along with 11/10/95, 11/22/95, 11/30/95, and 12/30/95.

"Gamehendge"

Gamehendge is the mythical land that serves as the backdrop to many Phish songs. Indeed, Trey has often indicated that the members of the band are traveling minstrels from Gamehendge (4/30/89, for instance). The original Gamehendge songs include "Lizards," "Tela," "Wilson," "AC/DC Bag," "Colonel Forbin's Ascent," "Famous Mockingbird," "Sloth," and "Possum." The saga has expanded over the years and now includes "Axilla (I)," "Axilla II," "Divided Sky," "Harpua," and "Llama," among others. The original Gamehendge songs appeared as part of Trey's Senior Study at Goddard College entitled "The Man Who Stepped into Yesterday."

Trey was inspired to create Gamehendge from a poem and a musical for children. The poem was Tom Marshall's fanciful "McGrupp and the Watchful Hosemasters," which Trey received in the mail and posted on the door to his room. The children's musical was *Gus the Christmas Dog*, which Trey had been writing with his mother. Indeed, Trey and his mother, an editor at *Sesame Street Magazine*, produced a number of songs together during this period that were published by the Children's Television Workshop, including "Timothy Tatter's Sad Gloomy Day" and "Quintin the Quackless Duck."

By the time Trey began to think about his Senior Study project, he decided to produce another musical work that adults could appreciate as well. In turn, he fashioned the Gamehendge song cycle, drawing from Tom's poem and from a tune he had written with Tom and Aaron Woolfe entitled "Wilson, Can You Still Have Fun?" The final project consists of a tape that includes the songs, tied together by Trey's narration between each song, along with an accompanying text that relates the origins of the work.

The story recounts the adventures of Colonel Forbin, who passes through a door into the land of Gamehendge where he meets the Lizards. These people had been enslaved by a mysterious figure named Wilson, an outsider, who had come to the land and read the Helping Friendly Book that the deity Icculus had given to the Lizards. Wilson took the knowledge from the book to enslave the Lizards and set himself up as ruler, and then he hid away the book. Colonel Forbin meets two of the rebels, Rutherford the Brave and Tela, the latter of whom instantly wins him over with her charm. Colonel Forbin returns with the pair to the rebel camp, where he greets their leader, Errand Wolfe, just as the forces learn that Mr. Palmer, Wilson's accountant who had been funneling money to the revolution, is to be hanged that afternoon. He also watches in horror as Errand has Rutherford strangle Tela, whom he reveals is a spy. The Colonel then decides to climb a mountain to ask the possibly mythical Icculus for help. It turns out that Icculus does exist, and the deity releases the Famous Mockingbird, who retrieves the Helping Friendly Book for the rebels. After Errand receives the book, he captures the Mockingbird, hires a figure named the Sloth to kill Wilson, and then sets himself up as the new dictator. The story ends with Icculus looking down on the events and smiling.

Trey carefully composed and integrated the Gamehendge songs. The opening song, "Lizards," for instance, begins in the middle of the action, in a manner inspired by Peter Gabriel's "Chamber of 32 Doors." Trey composed "Tela" with the intent that Page would sing it. This was the first song that Trey ever wrote for another vocalist, so he tried to tailor the song to make it musically and thematically comfortable for Page. Trey had to modify the Wilson lyrics a bit, removing his friends Mike Christian, Rog, and Pete from the original, replacing them with a line that Errand sings about his son Roger, who had been killed by Wilson. "Famous Mockingbird" is intended to convey a sound reminiscent of the classical composition "The Flight of the Bumblebee." "Possum" modifies Jeff's original lyrics to allow Icculus to provide his metaphoric account of events.

Phish has performed four complete Gamehendges and one near miss. The original, on 3/12/88, offers the complete original Senior Study saga. A second version that circulates from 10/13/91 collects a number of the Gamehendge songs in a random order with an incomplete narration (and without "Lizards"). On 3/23/93 Phish once again presented the entire story with narration but also with a few modifications. The band removed "Possum" from the end, replacing it with "McGrupp and the Watchful Hosemasters," an appropriate summary. Also, as with the next two versions, Trey cut out any mention of Tela's death due to spying. The two most recent accounts of the story, from 6/26/94 and 7/8/94, mirror the interpretation from 3/23/93 with some minor revisions. (On 6/26/94 Trey adds some Rhombus narration before "Divided Sky," which follows "McGrupp," and on 7/8/94 the story begins in the dentist's chair after Phish performs "N_2O.")

"Glide"

Phish premiered this song as an encore at its show at the Warehouse in Rochester, New York, on 9/27/91. Trey composed "Glide" along with Tom and Dave while in high school, and the song remained abandoned for many years until Trey pulled it out and Phish recorded it for *Picture of Nectar*. "Glide" was a common live song through 1994, but the band performed it only three times in 1995. Noteworthy versions include 11/30/91, 7/9/92 (the world premiere HORDE show, which also features a "Glide" reprise), 4/14/94, and 6/24/95.

"Glide II"

So far this song has made just one appearance in a live setting, at the Voters for Choice benefit on 5/16/95. While the word *glide* undoubtedly provided this tune's title, "Glide II" shares a more intimate relationship with "Guyute." How so? Pull out an early version of that song and listen carefully to the instrumental section in the middle. Then listen to "Glide II" from Lowell. Recognize anything?

"Golgi Apparatus"

Trey wrote this one in the eighth grade. Well, no, that's an exaggeration. He wrote this in the eighth grade with the help of a few friends, Tom Marshall, Bob Szuter, and Aaron Woolfe. You can imagine how this one might have developed: As the group headed home after school to play some Space Invaders or street hockey or even some music, someone just started making up nonsense rhymes about the subjects of that day's science lecture—lysosomes and golgi apparatus. In most cases, however, the story would have ended there and not eighteen years later, when one of the songwriters performed that song with his band as the show opener at a sold-out New Year's Eve show at the Boston Garden.

There's another side to this story as well. Trey lost touch with Aaron over the years, who may have learned that Trey performed in a band but didn't know that Phish performed "Golgi." Trey intended to invite him to a performance at New York's Marquee in 1990, and then perform the song to freak him out. As it turned out, Aaron had actually heard the song at a party a few months prior to the show, and had tried unsuccessfully to convince his acquaintances that he had written the song in the eighth grade.

"Golgi" contains an instrumental segment that also appears in another Phish song. Which song is it? Here's a hint: If you want a show in which both of these songs appear side by side, listen to 10/1/89. The correct answer appears in the other song's entry in this chapter.

"Guelah Papyrus"

"Guelah Papyrus" marks the incorporation of "looks too much like" Dave's mother into Phish mythos. Apparently, when Trey, Tom, and Dave were growing up, Mrs. Abrahams, Guelah, occasionally entered Dave's room to quiet the group. In a bizarre tribute to this memory, some of the song's lyrics describe this very situation.

"Guelah" debuted at the abbreviated Brown University show on 2/1/91 (the second set of this show ended after three songs due to a university curfew). "Guelah" has become an interesting song to see live, however, because it usually provides a showcase for some of Trey and Mike's choreographed high-stepping. Also, "Guelah" incorporates the "Asse Festival" fugue in between verses.

Okay, so here's a bit more trivia. You now know that Dave's mother appears in "Guelah," and you know that Dave is featured in "McGrupp," but what about his father? His dad appears briefly in "Sample in a Jar," dancing on a bed.

''Gumbo''

Phish debuted this song during the fall of 1990 (some early versions include 9/26/90 and 11/30/90). Trey composed the "Gumbo" music, but the lyrics were supplied by Fish, and they are blissfully dumb. This song took on a new dimension during the summer of 1991, when it become one of the featured numbers on the horn tour (for instance, listen to 7/12/91, 7/19/91, or 7/23/91). "Gumbo" was then put on hold for a little while until it finally returned on 4/16/93. After one more appearance the song returned to hiatus until 6/16/94, and the band has played it sporadically ever since. When the Giant Country Horns joined Phish for two shows during December 1994, "Gumbo" was available once again for the horns to sweeten. The version of "Gumbo" from A Live One was taken from one of these performances, 12/2/94.

''Guyute''

This song debuted on 10/7/94 and reminded many phans of some earlier Phish songs. "Guyute" offers some brief but intriguing lyrics, a long orchestrated section, and an opportunity for improvisation. Trey induced some additional smiles at the song's debut when he told the audience, "Now you have one more choice of things to go to Halloween as," in reference to the impending show. Phish performed "Guyute" through 12/29/94, modifying it a bit along the way (compare the two above-mentioned versions with 11/26/94, which is missing the second verse). The song then went into the shop for ten months until a slightly tweaked "Guyute" returned on 10/31/95. If you want to hear another later "Guyute," listen to 12/28/95, after which Trey proudly announces "Guyute, the holiday pig!" Finally, for a few additional brief "Guyute" appearances, listen to "Glide II" from 5/16/95 and find a copy of the of 9/11/94 Bad Hat performance or the 7/18/93 Phish soundcheck.

''Ha Ha Ha''

It probably won't surprise you to learn this song is Fishman's brainchild. "Ha Ha Ha" debuted at the Voters for Choice benefit on 5/16/95. The song returned sporadically over the summer and fall (for instance, 6/15/95 and 11/30/95).

''Halley's Comet''

Although Phish didn't compose this tune, they've certainly made it their own over the years. This song was written by Nancy Taube, who attended Goddard with our Phishly trio. Nancy was at a number of the early Vermont gigs and often was called upon to lend his vocals to this tune. (If you haven't heard his vocal stylings, they're well worth hearing—his voice is far more skewed than that of the Dude. Listen to 5/14/88.) However, after being called upon to do this time and time again, he finally balked, proclaiming that he was sick of the song and would stop joining the band to perform it. Phish took this to heart and stopped playing it as well, and this tune disappeared from their live shows in May 1989, allegedly never to return. Fans of "Prep School Hippie" and "Dear Mrs. Reagan" should take note that in this case "never" lasted four years.

"Halley's" returned to open the second set on 3/14/93. After this performance, "Halley's" remained an uncommon addition to Phish live shows. Some phans particularly enjoy the transition when the song's distinctive doo-wop introduction emerges from the "You Enjoy Myself" vocal jam (for instance, 5/8/94). Some other entertaining "Halley's" include 4/29/87 (tribute to Duke Ellington), 10/29/88, 8/6/93, and 6/25/95.

"Harry Hood"

Who is this Harry Hood? What does he have to do with Mr.
Miner? Why should I feel good about Hood? Those are all fine
questions.

Let's begin with Harry. HP Hood is a dairy formerly headquar-
tered in the Charlestown section of Boston. Hood was founded in
the late nineteenth century, and by the 1950s the company was
supplying milk and dairy products throughout New England. "You
can feel good about Hood" was the company's slogan and in fact
still appears on its milk products and trucks, for that matter. In the
mid-1970s the company began running a television ad campaign
featuring a ten-inch-tall Claymation milkman named Harry Hood.
In these ads, people would open their refrigerators and find Harry,
standing on a shelf, next to a quart of milk or other Hood product,
dispensing advice. Which indeed raises the question posed by
Phish: Where did Harry Hood go when the refrigerator door closed
and the light went out?

How does Mr. Miner fit into this? Was he a Claymation diary
farmer? No, but that's a good guess. According to Mike, Mr. Miner
once lived in a house that Fish, Page, and he later occupied. One
letter that arrived for this long-departed resident ended "Thank you,
Mr. Miner." Some phans give little credence to this story and believe the band sings this line before moving into a minor key.

"Harry Hood" debuted on 10/30/85, after which the band suggests that HP Hood should sponsor them. This song remains a
phavorite of many as Phish has performed a number of memorable
"Hood"'s in the intervening years. A chronological sampling of
some of these versions includes 10/31/88, 11/4/90, 11/30/91, 4/18/
92 (with "Linus and Lucy"), 12/28/92, 12/31/93, 4/8/94, 5/27/94,
11/12/94, 10/7/95 (a highly controversial "Hood," as it is unfinished,
following on the heels of 9/27/95, which some feel is the worst
"Hood" ever), and 12/30/95. The "Harry Hood" on A Live One first
appeared on 10/23/94.

"Harpua"

As the band members have stated numerous times, every great song starts with an oompah-pah. This one proves it. "Harpua" provides Trey with an opportunity to tell a story with sound effects supplied by the band, including a few bars of some obscure or outlandish song that you'd never think they'd play.

Let me set out the basic structure of the song as it appears at present. Following the oompah-pah and musical introduction, Trey begins to spin his tale. The story involves the mean old man who lives up a hill with his hungry dog Harpua. The old man and his dog live in a village that often is located in Gamehendge, at other times somewhere near the place that Phish is performing. Then Trey introduces Jimmy, a boy of indeterminate age (usually he appears to be around twelve or thirteen, although at times he's a little older, such as 11/28/92, when he's savoring his favorite beer or 6/30/94 when he's at a karaoke bar). Typically, Jimmy is listening to the radio or playing a record, and the band then launches into its interpretation of whatever Jimmy is hearing or seeing (for instance, at Waterloo Village on 7/23/95, Trey revealed that Jimmy was listening to ABBA's *Waterloo*, which the band performed through that song's first chorus). Next, Trey reveals the name of Jimmy's beloved cat, often after strumming really loudly to produce a tension-and-release effect as Trey screams the feline's precious name . . . Poster Nutbag! From here, the tale turns tragic as the cat gets outside, confronts "Harpua" the hungry dog, and meets his demise before the mighty jaws of "Harpua" (of course, it doesn't always happen that way—listen to 2/12/93 or 8/20/93). We then hear Jimmy and his father talking about the loss of Poster, and learn that Jimmy wants a dog as the band concludes the song with a snappy "Harpua" jingle led by Page's swinging keys. Of course, this description doesn't even begin to cover the magic and majesty that is "Harpua." You need to hear this one for yourself.

When you're seeking out copies of "Harpua," be forewarned that the song itself has evolved over the years. Early versions contain only the singing element of the story without any additional narration by Trey (8/21/87 and 8/29/87). Later versions relate the story of Harpua and the mean old man, but Jimmy is relegated to minor character status without the additional musical segment (5/25/88 but with "a poster nutbag named Cat"). Finally, by the end of 1989 the basic structure of the song as it is played today is intact.

Here are a few versions that might interest you: 10/14/89 ("In-A-Gadda-Da-Vida"), 3/11/90 (Purple Haze), 5/3/91 (Cam Neely), 10/28/91 (Telluride story), 4/22/92 (with Johnny Fishman), 5/9/92 (Smells Like Teen Spirit), 11/28/92 ("Jimmy Olsen's Blues"), 7/16/94 (Comet), 10/31/94 (Vibration of Death, War Pigs), and 5/3/94 ("Sunshine of My Life" and "Sunshine of Your Love"), 6/30/94 ("Karaoke Honky Tonk Woman" with guest audience vocalist), and 10/31/95 (Halloween "Beat It" tease).

"Horn"

"Horn" debuted in the spring of 1990. One early version took place at the Brewery in Raleigh, North Carolina, on 5/24/90. If you listen to that "Horn", or the version that followed on 6/16/90, you can detect the slight variations in the placement of the verses and the bridge from the version that developed and appears on *Rift*. Phish has performed the song with some regularity ever since, and some representative versions include 12/28/90, 3/14/92 (with "Follow the Yellow Brick Road"), 4/5/92 (with voice crack), 7/3/94, and 12/14/95. Some phans note a similarity between this song and the band's football theme (listen for that theme on 5/2/92).

"The Horse"

True or false: "The Horse" has always preceded "Silent in the Morning." False. Although "The Horse" has preceded "Silent" on most every occasion, 5/30/93 and 6/23/94 are two occasions on which "Silent" appeared without "The Horse." Has "The Horse" appeared without "Silent"? No, not yet.

One interesting story about "The Horse" involves album covers. The cover of *Rift* features a fine painting by David Welker that incorporates every song on the album with the exception of one, "The Horse." Some phans have spent time with a magnifying glass trying to spy a horse somewhere in the work, to no avail. Phish rectified this on *Hoist*, which finally features a horse (Amy Skelton's Maggie).

While "The Horse" typically proceeds according to pattern, listen to 4/14/93 or 5/8/93 for longer, variant "Horse" (the 4/14/93 version in particular contiains numerous teases and quotes). Also during the spring 1993 tour Trey performed most "Horses" on an acoustic guitar before plugging in for "Silent."

"I Am Hydrogen"

"I am Hydrogen" is the only part of "Mike's Groove" that Mike himself did not compose. Recently, "I Am Hydrogen" has been displaced a bit as the segue between "Mike's Song" and "Weekapaug Groove" (even though the word on the street had been that the three would always be played together). However, what you may not realize is that the early versions of "Hydrogen" appeared independently of the other two (for instance, 4/24/87 or 4/29/87 are two early appearances of the song that extend far longer than the "Hydrogen's" that appear today). However, by the summer of 1988 "Hydrogen" had become the creme filling in "Mike's Groove." Although most versions of this song have remained consistent in this particular capacity, listen to 11/28/92 or 4/21/94 for examples of two variants of "Hydrogen."

"Icculus"

"Icculus" is the all-knowing and all-powerful entity worshiped by the people of Gamehendge. Perhaps his greatest accomplishment is the authorship of the Helping Friendly Book. This song is a tribute to this supreme entity and his literary skills. Icculus differs from the other Gamehendge songs because it is not narrated by a character in that land but rather by the members of the band Phish as they discuss their warm and fuzzy feelings for Icculus. (Unless, of course, you accept the fact that Phish is indeed composed of four wandering minstrels from Gamehendge).

"Icculus" is an extended exercise in tension and release. Many Phish jams employ this technique, but "Icculus" is the lone Phish song that is based solely around this concept. "Icculus" develops slowly as Trey spouts a variety of comments about the band's worship of this deity. The song continues to build as Trey's voice and the band's performance become increasingly manic. Trey discusses the virtues of this mythic figure without actually mentioning his name until . . . finally . . . no, not quite yet . . . yes, finally Trey screams out the name Icculus. After this, the band sings a line and then dives into what sounds like will progress into a slick jam, but it ends after a few bars. Very entertaining, frustrating stuff.

"Icculus" has never been a common Phish song. Early versions of the tune include 4/1/86, 10/31/86, and 12/6/86. For a short span the band performed this song regularly within "Colonel Forbin's Ascent" and "Famous Mockingbird" (4/16/92, 4/24/92, and 5/2/92). Other noteworthy "Icculus"es are 8/3/88, 8/12/89 (wedding dedication with Fish on trombone), 10/27/94, and 10/31/95. Also, the version of this song on the rereleased *Junta* is from 7/25/88 and not 5/3/88 (see the "Sanity" entry for the full explanation).

"I Didn't Know"

This song is another tune composed by the enigmatic Nancy Taube. Phish premiered its interpretation of "I Didn't Know" in 1987. The song is notable for many accompaniments over the years. Nancy occasionally has joined the band for this song (5/14/88). Fish has contributed on trombone (9/27/95). Mike has joined on electric drill, with Trey on megaphone (6/15/95). Fish has played Madonna washboard (3/31/93). Mimi Fishman has added cymbals (4/8/94—she's introduced as Mimi Fizeck). Fish has performed on the lyrically appropriate oversized portrait of Otis Redding (2/5/93). Fish, of course, has contributed a vacuum solo as well (12/28/95). Other fine versions of this song include 8/3/91, 3/28/92 (a cappella), 4/17/92, and 6/14/94 (engulfing "My Sweet One").

"If I Could"

This is the first of Phish's ballads with lyrics credited solely to Trey. "If I Could" debuted at the Flynn Theater on 4/4/94, emerging from the end of "Down with Disease" much as it does on the album. The segue on the album provides an interesting juxtaposition of these two songs, which some phans appreciate, some find a bit jarring, some find curious, and some quickly ignore. That segue only emerged after the band agreed with Paul Fox's suggestion to cut a long introductory guitar solo (part of which reemerged on 7/1/95).

There are additional vocals on the *Hoist* version of "If I Could" that were supplied by bluegrass goddess Alison Krauss. Her band, Union Station, has won accolades ever since she began playing with them in her early teens. (Krauss is also a member of the Grand Ol' Opry, a Grammy Award winner, and most recently a producer of the Cox Family's latest records.) Phish had acquired a deep appre-

Photo credit: Jay Crystal

ciation of her voice while listening to a number of her tapes over the band's years on the road. As it turned out, Krauss was performing in Los Angeles with Union Station while Phish was in the area recording *Hoist*. So Mike attended her show and then waited backstage to ask her if she would perform "If I Could" with Phish. Krauss hadn't heard of the group, but Mike's winning smile won her over and she agreed.

However, her session was almost canceled due to fire. The great Los Angeles fire of that fall struck the night before Krauss's session with the band, and the recording studio at Woodland Hills was in direct line of the approaching flames. The next morning streets were closed off, and the band members smuggled Krauss through the barricades and into the studio. The results are worth the band's efforts, as her voice soars through the song (although some phans had a difficult adjustment to a "strange" woman's voice on their Phish album. Fish, in particular, was shocked at the levels of antipathy directed at Alison).

Phish had to modify its arrangement of "If I Could" in order to perform the song live. Some of the complementary vocals were eliminated while others were tuned down. Also, Phish opened up the song a bit more, extending and exploring the jam before the final verse (for instance, listen to 4/8/94 and 12/4/94). One other version of this song well worth hearing took place at the Starwood Amphitheater in Nashville, Tennessee, on 5/3/94 when Alison Krauss joined the band onstage to reprise her initial role.

"I'm in a Hole"

Phish first performed this song on 10/20/89 at The Front. It appeared in moderate rotation for a short while and then disappeared by the end of the year. Many Phans lament this fact, as "In a Hole" contains both amusing lyrics and catchy, head-bobbing music. Rumors abounded that Phish would resurrect this one after Trey fell into a hole before the Buffalo show and tore ligaments in his ankle on 4/10/94, but, alas, this did not occur. Of course, others wonder whether Trey didn't jinx himself in the first place by composing the song, and await news of a nipple slicing (another prominent theme in his music).

"It's Ice"

Trey has often complimented Tom Marshall's lyrics on this song, which recount a man's experience with his mirror image. Others turn the praise back onto Trey for composing such complementary music that captures the essence of those words so well. The members of Phish also collectively hailed this tune when it premiered at the Colonial Theater in Keene, New Hampshire, on 9/25/91, as it afforded another opportunity for Page to sing. Phans and band alike have encouraged Page to take more lead vocal duties and were happy that he added another song to his repertoire. Finally, the song is notable because Mike and Trey stepped onto Gliders for synchronized skating displays during many of the versions of "It's Ice" that Phish performed in 1993.

Some "It's Ice"'s that should please you include 3/6/92, 3/22/93 (pre-Gamehendge version), 3/22/93, and 7/1/95 (with vacuum and electric drill).

"Julius"

A number of phans were somewhat unhappy with the shorter, more traditionally structured songs on *Hoist*. Phish's goal was to take full advantage of the recording studio to produce songs that sounded like distinctive products of that environment and not just twelve takes of live songs performed without the support of a live audience. One of the successful products of this approach was "Julius." The Tower of Power Horns joined Phish in the studio for this song, and the group's majordomo flugelhornist, Greg Adams, composed the horn arrangements. The Ricky Grundy Chorale, Rose Stone, and Jean McClain also helped create an energy on "Julius" that is missing from most of the band's other studio efforts.

This song, which is about Julius Caesar, debuted at the Flynn benefit on 4/4/94 without the Tower of Power horns but with a new, all-powerful version of the Giant Country Horns, doubled in strength from their original trio to a sextet. If you enjoy "Julius," you'll also want to hear 4/15/94, 5/4/94, 10/31/94, and 12/3/94. Also, you may want to find a copy of the *Late Show with David Letterman* from 7/13/95, when Phish performed this song with Dave Grippo and the CBS Orchestra.

"Keyboard Cavalry"

Just when you thought the fun was over with the advent of "Acoustic Army," the band took it up a notch for this one. This is another song that debuted at Cal Expo on 9/27/95. As you may gather, this song is the keyboard analog to "Acoustic Army," with Jon, Mike, and Trey walking over to Page and performing a song on his various keyboards.

As a discrete song many phans prefer "Acoustic Army." However, that song interrupts the flow of the show, as it requires the band members to receive their instruments at the front of the stage. During "Keyboard Cavalry" Page remains at the piano while the three other members of the band walk over and join him, so the flow continues. Thus, listen to 11/21/95, with its fine seamless transition from "Mike's Song" to "Keyboard Cavalry." Other notable versions of this song include 10/8/95 (Phish opens the second set with this song, then closes it with a "Keyboard Cavalry" reprise) and 10/17/95.

"Kung"

Fish composed this chant, which was a rare occurrence for a long while but surfaced quite a few times during the fall of 1995. Occasionally Trey has indicated that one must repeat this chant in order to get to Gamehendge (for instance, 12/31/92, 3/25/93, and 6/26/94). Also, the speed and ferocity of "Kung" has changed according to the mood and the situation (for instance, compare 2/20/93 and 10/14/95). A few "Kung" 's worth hearing include 4/14/93, 8/7/93, 10/21/95, 11/25/95, and 12/30/95. Listen to a few of these versions and you, too, may become voraciously alternate and stage a runaway golf-cart marathon.

"Landlady"

Phish yanked this one kicking and screaming from the middle of "Punch You in the Eye." The group dedicated an early performance of this musical passage at Wetlands on 9/13/90 "to the spirit of Carlos." Many phans, however, were underwhelmingly positive to the arrival of this song. It wasn't that they didn't like this musical snippet; rather they feared that the arrival of "Landlady" signified the departure of "Punch You in the Eye." These fears escalated when "Landlady" appeared on *Picture of Nectar*, which many felt definitively signified the end of "Punch You in the Eye." However, as per usual, Phish confounded expectations when "Punch You in the Eye" returned on 2/5/93 with the "Landlady" section intact, a rarity in the history of Phish musical excisions. Nonetheless, long before the return of "Punch You in the Eye," "Landlady" won a measure of respect in phans' eyes, particularly after Phish performed a number of noteworthy versions of this song with the Giant Country Horns during the summer of 1991. Some fine "Landlady" 's include 7/11/91, 7/21/91, 4/4/94, and 12/2/94.

"Lawn Boy"

Phish at their schmaltziest, as Page stands up, takes the microphone into his hands, and croons to the masses. The 1991 Giant Country Horns tour transformed many phans' appreciation of this song, as the addition of horns brought out its jazzier elements, which at times even seemed to overpower the schmaltz (listen to 7/19/91, for example). By the way, if you own the original version of the *Lawn Boy* album as well as the rerelease, you'll discover that the rereleased version of this song is quite a few seconds longer (and thus slower) than the original.

Photo credit: Rich Luzzi

"Lengthwise"

A real tearjerker. Johnny B. Fishman's tale of an empty bed and modified sleeping patterns was recorded for *Rift* before Phish performed the song in concert (it joined "Fast Enough for You" and "The Wedge" in this distinction). By the way, if you listen carefully to the second version of "Lengthwise" on *Rift* you can hear a number of the album's songs compressed into a few seconds. As for live performances, the debut of this song at St. Michael's College on 11/19/92 sounds very different from the version on the album (and most subsequent "Lengthwise"'s), as it contains a distinct reggae flavor. Some other spirited versions followed. In particular, check out 2/4/93 (reprise in Harry), 2/6/93 (with ad-libbed lyrics about burning his hand on a lighter), 3/31/93.

"Leprechaun"

Perhaps because the band members recently had expressed that "Mike's Song," "I Am Hydrogen," and "Weekapaug Groove" would forever be played in that order, "Leprechaun" emerged during the summer of 1993 to replace "Hydrogen." However, it didn't start in that role. It had to be groomed for that position. Thus, in its debut on 7/15/93 the song served as the segue into "Runaway Jim." But on its next time out, two shows later at Wolf Trap in Vienna, Virginia, it occupied the sacred slot. "Leprechaun" also appeared between "Mike" 's and "Weekapaug" on 7/31/93 before the song mysteriously disappeared like its sprightly namesake.

"Letter to Jimmy Page"

This is the instrumental section that appears in the middle of "Alumni Blues." Trey has always acknowledged that Jimmy Page was an influence on him, and this song affirms his allegiance. Some phans assume that "Letter to Jimmy Page" is just a part of "Alumni," however, the two are separated most notably in the band's *White Tape*. Just as "Alumni" briefly resurfaced in 1994, so did "Letter to Jimmy Page." While hints of this song are occasionally heard in "Tweezer" 's, "David Bowie," "Mike's Song," and "You Enjoy Myself," Phish revived this song in its entirety at Ottawa's Congress Center on 7/6/94. Only a couple hundred people were there to hear this song at the most sparsely attended Phish show of 1994, which may have brought the band members back to yesteryear (a fact that is suggested by the "Cities" resuscitation later in the show). Many more phans heard "Letter" when it opened the second set at Jones Beach on 7/16/94.

"Lifeboy"

"Lifeboy began as a poem by Tom Marshall. Based on this, Trey and Tom collaborated to compose this ballad. Phish first performed "Lifeboy" in concert at the Portland Expo on 2/3/93. The band performed the song occasionally during 1993 before taking this song into the studio that fall.

The "Lifeboy" on *Hoist* is a modified version of the song that Phish had performed. First, the vocals are very different. Although Trey had dug deep for a climactic final chorus on many of the early live versions, in the studio he elected to perform the song as he thought the narrator would have sung it (closer to crying than yelling). In order to complement this mood, he abandoned the electric guitar, opting for an acoustic. Finally, the band threw a curve ball by asking Bela Fleck to perform on this tune. The banjo is generally not thought of as a somber instrument, requiring the New Grass Revival veteran to employ his wits to produce his subtle, successful effort.

"Lifeboy" has emerged in the post-*Hoist* era as a changed tune. Most notably, Trey's vocals have remained subdued on many versions. The music is more restrained, too, creating a darker and more disturbing version of the song. In order to hear some representative versions of this song throughout its Phish career, listen to 2/6/93, 7/15/93, 10/18/94 (with Bela), 6/8/95, 12/30/95.

"Lizards"

"Lizards" began its life as another song. Much of the melody is drawn from Trey's work with his mother on the *Gus the Christmas Dog* musical. Indeed, "Lizards" ' original title was "If I Were a Dog." This is particularly noteworthy because "Lizards" is the Phish song with the lyrics most commonly forgotten by Trey (with "Fee" a close second). Two notable such incidents are 2/7/91 (when Trey abandoned the song altogether) and 7/3/95 (Fish comments, "I think you need a teleprompter there Trey"). Some phans wonder why Trey flubs these straightforward narrative lyrics when he can remember the nonsense of "Tube." One possible answer is that every once in a while the earlier lyrics drift into Trey's head, and he has to bail or he'll start singing about dogs and not lizards.

"Lizards" is one of the songs from Trey's Senior Study. Indeed, along with "Possum," "Lizards" is the most commonly performed selection from "The Man Who Stepped into Yesterday." This fact does not seem to bother most phans, who enjoy flouncing around the room to the story of Rutherford the Brave. Some entertaining versions of the song include the Gamehendge narrations as well as 7/11/91, 6/23/95, and 12/31/95.

"Llama"

"Llama" is another Gamehendge song, although it represents a later era in the kingdom. As the liner notes in *Picture of Nectar* indicate, this song presents an account of one of the rebels fighting to restore the region to the life of tranquillity the Lizards once shared. However, he must do this with the help of some heavy artillery, which he fires during the song. "Llama" has appeared as a set opener and closer as well as a launching pad for exploration. Some of the versions in which Phish has really kicked the stuffing out of this song include 7/25/92 (with Carlos Santana), 8/21/93, and 10/18/94 (with Bela Fleck, acoustic beginning).

"Lushington"

If you're the kind of person who enjoys worming your way to the front of an arena to hold up a cardboard sign imploring the band to play a song that they are probably not going to play because of some silly sign, why not write "Lushington" on it. "Prep School Hippie" and "Dear Mrs. Reagan" are interesting but overrepresented in the dorky sign category. "Lushington" has inane lyrics over a galloping musical score (listen to 4/29/87 or 8/29/87, just before this song disappeared). Of course, "Lushington" still does exist in some form today; it can be heard as a portion of "Who Do We Do" in "Fluffhead." Nonetheless, phans want to hear the original, in all its nose-picking splendor. So if you're a cardboard-carrying, row-scamming, Magic-Marking nitwit, then give "Lushington" a chance. Thank you.

"Magilla"

"Magilla" and "Cars, Trucks and Buses" represent Page's two solo compositions performed by Phish. Trey's great respect for Page's craftsmanship on this tune is revealed by the fact that Bad Hat also performs "Magilla." In the latter situation the song is often sandwiched between tunes by Miles Davis and Duke Ellington.

"Magilla" premiered with Phish at the Wetlands on 9/13/90. Like "Landlady," this one has really shined with the addition of horns. For two pre–Giant-Country-Horns-assisted "Magilla" 's, hear 2/8/91 and 5/12/91; for some GCH-abetted "Magilla" 's, seek out 7/19/91, 4/4/94, and 4/15/94. Some other notable "Magilla" 's, featuring the song's author, the Chairman of the Boards, listen to 8/3/91, 12/6/91, 3/25/93, and 4/9/94. Phish has not performed "Magilla" since 5/4/94, as the band feels that its jazz tunes do not translate well into the larger performance spaces.

"Makisupa Policeman"

"Makisupa Policeman" is one of the earliest Phish songs and one that evolved out of some of the nonsense that Trey and his friends used to spout in their youths. "Makisupa" is the band's lone reggae original, and it certainly calls attention to itself as such. The lyrics to this one have been modified over the years, but all of them refer to the song's musical style (the narrator sounds like a deluded poseur trying to be Irie.) The words to this song have evolved over time as well (for a sample listen to 12/1/84, 10/14/89, 4/29/93, 10/22/95, 11/9/95, and 12/30/95). "Makisupa" disappeared for a while. Since then Phish's performances have ranged from quick tokes to dense, gnarly sessions (listen to 5/7/94, 7/2/95, 12/29/95).

"Mango Song"

Some phans are surprised to learn that this song debuted in the spring of 1989 (three early appearances are 3/30/89, 4/15/89, and 5/26/89, with slightly different arrangements than present "Mango"s). Many assume that this was a later tune because it quickly disappeared and resurfaced two years later on 2/1/91 to become a common Phish song during the spring. "Mango"'s appearance on *Picture of Nectar* has served to fool some phans as well. By the way, the song disappeared again for a period between 5/17/92 and 7/24/93, after which it has returned infrequently.

Now that we've cleared that up, want to move to the meaning of the song? Well, if you've read the *Picture of Nectar* liner notes, you know that this Anastasio-penned selection is about a waiter with an addiction problem. Apparently this scenario evolved from a film idea that Aaron Woolfe shared with Trey about a genius child in Vietnam born with mangled limbs ("Mangled" transformed into "Mango"). If you want to hear some fine "Mango"'s, sit down with a slice of grape apple pie and listen to 2/7/91, 8/20/93, and 12/17/95.

"The Man Who Stepped into Yesterday"

This title refers to two separate, related works. "The Man Who Stepped into Yesterday" is the title of Trey's thesis (see the Gamehendge entry). However the band also performs a song by the same name, which appears in the thesis during Trey's narration. Many phans feel that this music is among the most beautiful pieces that Trey has composed. Of course, in true Phishy fashion, the band juxtaposes this one with its chant of the Hebrew prayer *"Avenu Malkenu,"* which swiftly breaks a listener out of her reverie (for a few representative versions listen to 8/29/87, 8/26/89, 12/30/92, and 12/30/95). Ever since Phish began performing this song in late 1987, "TMWSIY" has sandwiched *"Avenu,"* with some notable exceptions (for instance, 2/4/93 and 11/19/94). By the way, on 8/29/87 Trey introduced this song as "The Man Who Stepped into a Pile of Yesterday."

"Maze"

Phish introduced this song to the phaithful at the Portsmouth Music Hall on 3/6/92. Since then it has continued to please as it provides a showcase for Page's talents. A number of impressive "Maze's" are eagerly traded and enjoyed by phans. Some believe that when the song emerges from *"Also sprach Zarathustra"* it particularly rages (check out 4/11/94 and 9/29/95). Other eminently worthwhile versions include 2/19/93, 8/12/93, 12/31/94, and 7/1/95.

"McGrupp and the Watchful Hosemasters"

This is the song that begat Gamehendge. Tom Marshall sent "McGrupp and the Watchful Hosemasters" to Trey as a poem, with no additional text. Trey placed this poem on the door of his dorm room, where it remained for a year or so before Trey decided to set it to music. In early versions of this song, Phish performs this music while Trey simply recites the poem (for example, 10/17/85). One big change occurred when Trey incorporated the music from "Skippy (the Wondermouse)" into "McGrupp" to provide an instrumental introduction (for instance, 12/6/86). Eventually Trey began to sing the words, and the jam at the end of the song took shape (5/15/88). As some phans have noted, part of the jam that emerges from "McGrupp" also appears in "Golgi Apparatus" (10/1/89 makes this abundantly clear).

The song itself takes places some years after the visit of Colonel Forbin to Gamehendge as a shepherd sits back and sings about the Colonel's adventures. The song is named after Colonel Forbin's dog, which sometimes confuses phans since Trey often neglects to include him in his Gamehendge narration. Nonetheless, this song indicates that McGrupp does journey through the door, and Trey just fails to describe the moments when he barks at the Unit Monster or chases the Multibeasts and Spotted Stripers around.

"McGrupp" can be seen as a coda to Trey's musical Senior Study. However, although this song helped to spark the whole saga, "McGrupp" was not submitted as part of Trey's original thesis. Thus "McGrupp" was not performed at the initial live performances of Gamehendge: 3/12/88 or 10/13/91. In more recent versions, Trey has interposed this selection in place of "Possum" (3/22/93, 6/26/94, and 7/8/94). Other fine "McGrupp's" include 2/7/89 (with trombone), 8/7/93, and 12/11/95.

"Mike's Song"

The decisions of many phans as to whether to attend any given show often rests on this simple question: When was the last Mike's?

If it seems like "Mike's Song" is due, many of these people will make the effort to get to the show. Why? So that they can watch the trampoline routine? Usually not, although the tramps are certainly an enjoyable part of the song. Most love to hear the intense, innovative performances that this song elicits from the band.

Since 1988 "Mike's" typically has led into "I Am Hydrogen" and then into "Weekapaug," a trio collectively known as "Mike's Groove" (for instance, 7/23/88, 4/5/90, and 12/31/91 [with "Wimoweh"], 2/15/93, 7/10/94, and 6/10/95). However, in the past few years

Photo credit: Arch Stanton

"Mike's" has led into a variety of different combinations as Phish has produced some stunning segues (for instance, 7/17/93, 8/11/93, 5/27/94, 7/2/94, 6/25/95, and 11/11/95). This is not to say that "Mike's" cannot be enjoyed on its own terms; for instance, listen to the band's set-closing "Mike's" on 12/31/95.

Phish first performed "Mike's Song" on 10/17/85, at which point Trey introduced the song as "Microdot." The initial "Mike's" has an additional introductory verse as well, which Mike occasionally has offered over the years (8/21/93 and 2/6/93). The Dude of Life performed the role of Mike on 5/12/91. Some other notable "Mike's" include 5/28/89, 10/31/90, 7/15/91 (with horns), 4/19/92, 8/17/92, 12/29/92 (with "On Broadway"), 12/31/92 (with "Auld Lang Syne"), 3/27/93, 8/2/93, 8/13/93, and 10/8/94 (with girls soccer team— "north, south, east, west—muppets are the best").

"Minkin"

"Minkin," which appears on Phish's *White Tape* demo project, is a commercial jingle composed for the painter Marjorie Minkin. She is the artist who has provided many of the band's backdrops. She also is the artist who provided the band's bass player, as Minkin is Mike's mom. Indeed, the very funny "Minkin" was composed by Mike. Listen to this one and then run out and buy your bite-size "Minkin," this week only.

"Montana"

The musical snippet that appears as "Montana" on *A Live One* was culled from a mammoth "Tweezer" that Phish performed on 11/28/94 in . . . you guessed it, Montana (Bozeman, to be more specific).

"Mound"

Phish first performed "Mound" at the Portsmouth Music Hall on 3/6/92. This song, in case you hadn't guessed, is the inspired work of Mr. Michael "Cactus" Gordon. Apparently, the song came to Mike in one mad rush. So he hummed what he thought the lyrics would sound like and recorded it. Later he transcribed the humming and changed some of the resulting nonsense words into a story. Some of Mike's original transcribed phrases appear in the booklet that accompanies *Rift*. Live versions of the song include some collective audience clapping led by Trey and Mike. A few representative "Mound's" include 11/27/92, 3/26/93, 4/25/94, and 12/2/95.

"My Friend, My Friend"

Phish first performed "My Friend, My Friend" at Portsmouth Music Hall on 3/6/92. For a brief period some confusion existed about the title of this tune, which the band first introduced as "Knife." By the time *Rift* was released, everyone learned the truth. One interesting story about this song relates to the studio recording of the *Rift* album. The band ensconced itself at White Crow Studios in Burlington during September and October of 1991 to record the album. In early October, as Phish finished work on "My Friend, My Friend," the group called local radio station WIZN to ask local phans for some assistance. Approximately one hundred people made it over to White Crow, where Phish instructed them on the fine art of screeching. Many takes later, the volunteers successfully completed the task, which made it onto the final version of the song.

"My Friend, My Friend" currently appears uncommonly in Phish set lists, often as a show opener. Some good versions of this song include 2/12/93, 5/5/93 (with Manteca), 4/10/94, 10/7/94, and 9/30/95.

"My Sweet One"

Ahhh yes, another traditional love song courtesy of Mr. Jonathan Fishman. Supposedly, he composed "My Sweet One" in one sitting at Mike's mom's house, although Fish denies that the object of the song is Marjorie Minkin. Indeed, Trey occasionally teases Fish from the stage about the subject: "Here's one Fish wrote about you-know-who. . . . We all know who this one is about" (2/7/91).

"My Sweet One" premiered on 9/9/89. The herbivore line in this song is among many phans' all time Phishy favorites. The song is also interesting to hear live, as many times the band will perform "My Sweet One" in its acoustic lineup (6/22/94 and 11/3/94, for instance). Some other fine "My Sweet One"'s include 2/19/93 (with Jimmy Herring), 6/14/94 (inside "I Didn't Know"), and 11/30/94.

"NICU"

"NICU" premiered at Portsmouth Music Hall on 3/6/92. The title of the song remains something of a mystery. Trey called this one "In an Intensive Care Unit" after the band first played it. "NICU" is certainly not an acronym for that phrase (although medic phans have noted that it is short for Neonatal Intensive Care Unit). However, "NICU" definitely is a play on the phrase "and I see you," which appears in the song. Nonetheless, most phans and some band members refer to the song with the title "NICU," so that's that.

Phish performed "NICU" twelve times between its introduction and 5/1/92. Then, to the disappointment of many, the band put this one away, unhappy with the arrangement. This wasn't a total surprise, since Phish had tinkered with this along the way (compare the initial version with 4/19/92, for example, at which point Phish had altered the speed of the song and modified the lyrics, adding some "dooh dooh dooh" lines). A number of phans hounded the group about this one, repeatedly asking them when "NICU" would return. The band members typically said that they intended to work on it a bit. A number of scoffing skeptics were proud to be proved wrong when Phish did indeed work on this song a bit and returned it to live rotation on 6/23/94. Since then Phish has played the song sporadically, and some fine versions include 7/1/94, 6/14/95, and 12/29/95.

"N_2O"

The return of "N_2O" represents the most surprising revival of an older Phish tune in recent years. The song was recorded on the *White Tape* but never performed live. "N_2O" remained inert until 6/25/94, when the band opened its show at Nautica Stage in Cleveland, Ohio, with this tune. This breakout really had phans scratching their heads (albeit happily so). However, the pieces seemed to fall into place on 7/8/94 at Great Woods, in Mansfield, Massachusetts, when show opener "Llama" drifted into this song, which in turn served as a vehicle for Trey to begin his Gamehendge narration (the story of Colonel Forbin begins as he sits in a dentist's chair). Phish performed the composition one more time over the summer of 1994 (7/16/94), and then returned "N_2O" to its prior state.

"No Dogs Allowed"

This song is pure Anastasio. Not pure Trey, but pure Anastasio. Trey collaborated on "No Dogs Allowed" with his mother, Diane. Indeed, as he mentioned from the stage at Wetlands on 10/26/89, "No Dogs Allowed" was one of the songs from the musical *Gus the Christmas Dog* that the two completed (Diane provided the words, Trey the music). Phish first performed "No Dogs Allowed" a handful of times in 1988–89 (7/23/88, 10/20/89, and 10/26/89). One of their friends persisted in requesting it thereafter (listen to 3/17/91).

"The Oh Kee Pah Ceremony"

"The Oh Kee Pah Ceremony" has two meanings in Phish circles. First, the phrase refers to the ritual itself (which has taken on a particularly Phishy twist). It also refers to the song that emerged from this ritual.

As anthropologically minded phans know, the Oh Kee Pah ceremony was a rite of passage for young men in certain Native American tribes. The ritual requires piercing part of the body, inserting sticks into the open flesh, and then suspending the initiate in the air solely by these sticks for a period of time. To see one version of the ritual, rent a copy of *A Man Called Horse* from your local video store and screen it at home. Since these flesh hooks often were inserted into the young men's nipples, "Oh Kee Pah Ceremony" is the fourth Phish song that refers to nipple slicing, along with "Fee," "Punch You in the Eye," and "Sloth."

Phish has developed its own version of the Oh Kee Pah ceremony that is less physically painful but not less draining. The band's ceremony requires seclusion in a confined area with instruments, amplifiers, and a few other cryptic implements of consumption and destruction. The product of one such ceremony appears on *Junta* as "Union Federal."

"Oh Kee Pah" first appeared in a Phish set list in 1987. Typically, "Oh Kee Pah" appears as a segue into other songs. Most commonly it leads into "Suzie Greenberg" (9/9/89, 7/23/91, and 4/15/94), other times it carries the band into "AC/DC Bag" (11/30/89, 5/12/91, and 6/9/95). Occasionally it leads into other songs. Lately, "Oh Kee Pah" has had few such opportunities. The band performed the song only twice in 1995.

"Poor Heart"

Phish first performed the woeful story that is "Poor Heart" on 5/10/91 at the Colby College Student Center in Waterville, Maine. Mike wrote this song, which partially draws on some unfortunate circumstances he experienced during his senior year at UVM. While he was working on his senior film project at UVM, someone stole his four-track recorder. This is one of the images that Mike entered into his journal and later worked into "Poor Heart."

Some phans have criticized "Poor Heart" over the years because they feel that the song does not vary dramatically from performance to performance (they often say the same about "Sparkle"). Phish brought this complaint to a crashing halt at the Charlotte Coliseum on 11/19/95 when it debuted a throttled-down version of the song. Given the song's lyrics, this slower "Poor Heart" sounded to some like a country-and-western drinking song, and to some ears it sounded quite reminiscent of the Grateful Dead. Four shows later, at the Hampton Coliseum in Hampton, Virginia, on 11/25/95, the great "Poor Heart" experiment reached its dramatic conclusion as the band embarked on a Poor Heartfest. Phish opened the show with the traditional, upbeat version of the song. The band then closed the second set with the decelerated version of the song. Then, as they returned for an encore, they teased both a really slow "Poor Heart" and a lightning-fast version before saying "Get it?" and launching into "Fire." The slower version has not yet reappeared.

Some other "Poor Heart" 's worth hearing include 11/19/92 (with Gordon Stone), 6/24/94 (acoustic), and 11/29/95 (with Bela Fleck).

"Possum"

"Possum" is the last remnant of Jeff's contribution to the band. He wrote this song and presented it to Phish in 1985. They began performing this upbeat number with Jeff singing lead. Over the years some phans have noted a resemblance between this song and Lynyrd Skynryd's "Swamp Music," and similarities do exist. However, Phish was not aware of these and continued performing the song after Jeff left the group, with Mike on vocals. Trey even played with this song a little bit and included it as the concluding number on his Gamehendge thesis (although "Possum" 's role in the Game- hendge story has been lessened as of late. While the song appears on Trey's thesis and in the first live Gamehendge on 3/12/88, "Pos- sum" has been dropped from the four subsequent live performances of the complete saga).

"Possum" has remained one of the band's more popular songs. It offers some ever-altering enunciations from Mike along with pun- ning lyrics and slick vamping. Lighting director Chris Kuroda has described some occasions when even he has been overwhelmed on this latter point (as the band brings it around one more time). Also, "Possum" has become a rich source of secret language signals. To hear all these elements of the song listen to 4/15/86 (Jeff on lead vocals, original lyrics), 11/2/90 (with "Buried Alive"), 4/27/91, 12/5/91, 4/5/92 (with "Crossroads"), 4/18/92 (with "Mind Left Body" jam), 5/17/92, 12/30/92, 2/6/93 (with John Popper), 7/22/93, 4/30/94, 5/27/94, 6/14/95, 6/26/95, and 10/29/95.

"Prep School Hippie"

Given Jerry Garcia's untimely passing in 1995, it is unlikely that Phish will perform this one again (although the band hadn't played this one since 1986). This song pokes fun at the prep school dead head phe- nomenon. The narrator is torn between his desire to wear tie-dyes or

Vuarnets, between the kegger at the frat and watching Jerry shake his . . . you get the picture. This song contains another clear Grateful Dead allusion, as the band breaks into a segment that mirrors the chorus of "Not Fade Away" (as the narrator looks forward to dipping into his trust fund). How often do you get to hear someone onstage yell "Trust fund!" before furiously fanning his guitar? If you want to hear this, listen to 10/30/85, 4/15/86, or 12/6/86.

"Prince Caspian"

When some phans first learn of Gamehendge, the story reminds them of C. S. Lewis's The Narnia Chronicle saga (the most famous of these books is *The Lion, The Witch, and the Wardrobe*). With "Prince Caspian," Trey made it clear that he is not afraid to acknowledge such influences as well. "Prince Caspian" debuted at the Delta Center in Salt Lake City on 6/8/95—a short, sweet tribute to the mythical prince (and eventual king) of Narnia. The band's harmonies on this song alone justify the price of admission on many nights.

"Punch You (Me) in the Eye"

When "Punch Me in the Eye" debuted in 1987, it was a very strange song. The original version was an interesting amalgam of musical styles with some bizarre lyrics about punching oneself in the eye. Trey soon put this one away and reworked it, transforming it into a Gamehendge song. "Punch Me in the Eye" relates the story of a man in a kayak who lands in Prussia. Wilson enslaves him and throws him in a tiny shack (but not before holding a piece of paper to his nipple). Fortunately, the kayaker escapes and makes it back to his land, from which he sings the chorus at Wilson.

The original title of this song was "Punch Me in the Eye." When Trey reintroduced it in the fall of 1989, he announced this title (listen to 10/26/89, for instance). However, almost every phan ignored Trey's introduction and called it "Punch You in the Eye" because that's what the chorus says. Eventually, Trey relented, and for most purposes the song goes by the second title. Besides, "PYITE" is a much cooler acronym than "PMITE."

"Punch You in the Eye" disappeared from live rotation soon after its reintroduction. During this time the "Landlady" section was excised from the song, and things looked bleak for the kayaker. But after four years of inactivity, the band revived "PYITE" on 2/5/93. Since then the song has appeared occasionally in set lists, to the great joy of everyone (except maybe Wilson).

Some fine versions of "Punch You in the Eye" include 12/30/93, 6/23/94, and 12/31/95.

"Reba"

Phish first presented the story of Reba at The Front on 10/1/89. This version differed a bit from the current one as it was a bit heavier on the bag-it-tag-it side and also included an extra instrumental section (that was soon excised and transformed into "Don't Get Me Wrong"). The premiere version did include the whistling reprise, which the band has started to omit in recent years (for example, 5/28/94, 11/20/94, and 10/21/95). All in all, "Reba" remains a phan phavorite due to its amusing, sing-along lyrics and the jam that typically follows those lyrics. Also, "Reba" is the Hebrew word for "fish." Phish has performed a number of enjoyable "Reba"'s over the years, including 9/16/90, 12/30/92 (with "I Walk the Line"), 4/9/94, 5/27/94, 6/24/94, 10/7/94, and 5/16/95.

"Revolution"

This song is not the Beatles' Revolution. In fact, this song has much more akin to Phish's "Anarchy." Listen to 10/17/85 in order to appreciate this bit of humor.

"Revolution's Over"

Phish backed the Dude of Life's rendition of this song at Wetlands on 9/13/90. There's not too much more that needs to be said about this one or about the Dude. Hmm . . . how about this: He's not extremely tall (unlike, say, Tom Marshall, with whom he is often confused in the minds of phans).

"Rift"

As you may remember, the current version of "Rift" contains a piece of music that originally appeared in "The Curtain." However, the original version of the song, which debuted at Baltimore's 8 × 10 Club on 2/25/90, does not incorporate that distinctive riff. Indeed, there is little distinctive about this version aside from the lyrics, which is why Phish performed this song a couple more times and then abandoned it. Two years later, on 3/6/92, the same Tom Marshall lyrics returned with new musical accompaniment drawn from "The Curtain." Actually, the band had made one slight adjustment in the words, removing the original song's final line. That line is easy to spot, however, as it appears on the inside cover of the *Rift* insert booklet. A few versions of "Rift" that people enjoy include 4/5/92, 7/15/93, and 11/25/95.

One version of "Rift" that many people did not enjoy took place at US Air Arena in Landover, Maryland, on 11/22/95. The band started into the song and reached the fifth line when Trey brought it to an abrupt halt. "We'd like to credit that last one to our drummer, Mr. John Fishman," he announced, identifying the culprit as Fish stood up and took a bow. Trey then made a point of counting out the beginning to "Free," which the band started. This, of course, demonstrated a disagreement that occasionally occurs because Trey, the former drummer, has his own ideas of how Fish should sound. Meanwhile, the drummer prefers to innovate, and this can become frustrating in a composed piece in which he and Mike are supposed to anchor the band. Fear not, however. This rift was mended.

"Riker's Mailbox"

Jonathan Frakes, Commander Riker of *Star Trek: The Next Generation* fame, plays trombone on this song, which appears on *Hoist*. Appar-

Photo credit: Kurt Zinnack

ently, Frakes, who played the trombone on a few *Star Trek: The Next Generation* episodes, lives next door to Paul Fox, the producer of *Hoist*. So Frakes was called in to play on the *Hoist* sessions. He did play on "Julius," but his performance on that song didn't make it onto the album (he was a bit overshadowed by the Tower of Power horns). However, some of his studio work did make it onto *Hoist*, and the result was "Riker's Mailbox." This short offering was pieced together from his work on another song. If you listen closely to this cut on *Hoist*, you can hear some words spoken backward that sound very much like "Olaffob." This suggests that "Riker's Mailbox" is from a version of "Buffalo Bill" that didn't make it to the album.

As for the story of the song title, apparently Frakes and his wife, Genie Francis (Laura of *General Hospital* fame), have a very interesting mailbox shaped like a cow. The cow's rear end faces out so that mail is inserted into the cow's butt. Apparently, the band members considered titling the album *Riker's Mailbox*, with a photo of Frakes and Francis, in their bathrobes standing in front of the mailbox, on the cover (or so the story goes).

"Runaway Jim"

In fine Phishy fashion, this song began as a little ditty sung by Trey and his hometown friends. Eventually, Trey added a few more verses, completed a musical arrangement, shared it with the band, and a new phavorite emerged. The group first performed "Runaway Jim" in the spring of 1990 (5/4/90 features an early Jim). The initial versions differed a bit from later ones, as they contained an extra verse that describes Jim's flight from home on the night he died. Phish has performed a number of notable versions of this song over the years, with some stellar ones appearing in 1995. A list of note-worthy "Runaway Jim"'s includes 8/21/93, 11/22/94, 6/16/95, 7/2/95, and 12/31/95 (which mentions original contributors Dave and Daubs).

"Run Like an Antelope"

On New Year's Eve 1993 and again in 1994, Tom Marshall took the stage to perform the very first lines that he wrote for a Phish song. No, not the chorus, which the Dude of Life supplied way back in the Space Antelope days at Taft. Apparently, Tom's first contribution was the "Marco Esquandolas" line. Many phans find this fact interesting because early versions of "Run Like an Antelope" feature some slightly different words (10/17/85 and 10/12/88, for instance, as the narrator seeks Spleef not Spike). Speaking of the words to this song, one thing that many phans enjoy about "Antelope"'s final triumphant lyrics is how well they express the feelings conveyed the music. Also on the subject of lyrics, any discussion of "Antelope" would be incomplete without a mention of its evil twin, "Roll Like a Cantaloupe." The music in "Cantaloupe" sounds just like the music in "Antelope," but at the end of the song the band chants "roll" instead of "run" while Trey describes a trip through the produce aisle. You really need to hear one of these versions; they're as twisted as you think (7/12/88, 3/11/90, and 11/4/91: "Walk into the supermarket. Watch the electronic door open magically as you step onto the black pad . . ."). Finally, "Antelope" is one of the songs that continues to feature secret language signals.

Some celebrated "Antelope"'s include 5/28/89, 8/26/89 (with trombone), 3/13/92 (with "BBFCFM"), 3/20/92 (with trombone), 5/14/92 (with *Spiderman* theme), 6/24/93, 8/7/93, 8/14/93, 8/28/93, 7/3/94 (with fireworks), 7/16/94, 10/29/94, and 10/24/95.

"Sample in a Jar"

When Trey announced the title of this song at its debut at the Providence Performing Arts Center on 2/4/93, many phans thought that they must have misheard him. Others praised the catchy new song about a urine sample. Of course, the principal image in the song actually is a metaphor that Tom Marshall says is akin to a butterfly pinned under glass. Also, that's Dave Abrahams's father, Elihu, a distinguished faculty member in Princeton University's Physics Department, dancing on the bed.

"Sample in a Jar" was the second single from *Hoist* released to radio. It received a fair share of airplay, although it never became the hit that some phans feared. Nonetheless, many still attack this one because it did appear on the radio and because the band doesn't melt this one with extensive improv. Still this song has its share of supporters as well, who enjoy the lyrics, the melody, and Trey's guitar work at the end. Some enjoyable versions include 4/16/94, 10/20/94, and 11/8/95.

"Sanity"

Here are two stories about the "Sanity" that appears on the rereleased version of *Junta*. First, when Elektra announced that it would rerelease *Junta* on two discs, it became clear that some additional space needed to be filled on the second disc. The band was psyched to hear this and decided to add some live versions of a few songs. While Phish was making this decision, the band was touring out west in the vicinity of phan-phriend-Phish.net goddess Shelly Culbertson. One day Shelly gave the group a tape to hear that included the versions of "Sanity" and "Icculus" that Phish eventually decided to include on the album. However, the tape that the band passed to Elektra had two different shows on either side. This is why the booklet that accompanies *Junta* identifies "Sanity" and "Icculus" from 5/3/88 and not from the correct date of 7/25/88.

The second "Sanity" story relates to that particular breed of phan who truly resents newer aphishionados and does everything to exaggerate the distinctions between old phans and newbies. In 1989, after Phish had performed "Sanity" for a few years, the band decided to speed up the pace of the song. The group decided that it wasn't happy with the results and stopped performing the song for a while. So when *Junta* was rereleased, a number of phans who remembered the faster version from 1989 were heard to complain rather loudly because the version on *Junta* didn't sound like it did "in the good old days." What these people didn't realize was that the song did sound like it did in the good old days—the good old days before they started seeing the band.

After "Sanity" returned in the spring of 1992, the song went into hiatus once again to return on only three occasions, most prominently during the third set at the New Year's Eve show on 12/31/95. Other notable "Sanity"'s include 10/31/86, 8/21/87, 2/7/89, 5/26/89, 3/20/92, 5/17/92, and 6/24/94.

"Scent of a Mule"

Mike composed this epic tale of extraterrestials and mule dung, which Phish debuted at the Flynn Theater on 4/4/94. Live versions of this song are notable for a duel between Page and Trey. In case you haven't seen it, the duel begins in the break before Mike sings his final verse. First Page then Trey take turns soloing from a common theme using as many various elements and implements as possible. Trey, for instance, often brings a foreign object into the ring (such as his original shrunken Languedoc-crafted guitar). At the completion of this challenge, the whole band joins in for some spirited Eastern European folk music before Mike sings his final verse. It is very entertaining in person although some phans feel that it drags a bit on tape. Memorable "Scent"'s include 10/18/94 (with Bela Fleck), 11/20/94, 6/9/95, and 12/30/95.

"Self"

The Dude doesn't care about anyone except himself. Apparently Phish cared enough about him to let him perform "Self" at Wetlands on 9/13/90. In fact, they care enough about him to have entered Archer Studios with him in 1991 to arrange and record his funny little songs. They do and do for the Dude, and this is the thanks they get.

"Setting Sail"

If you listen to Fish introduce "Setting Sail" at Jones Beach on 7/15/94 you'll him hear him say that it's the debut performance of this Tom Marshall sing-along. In an official, structured sense this may be true, but find a copy of the 4/20/91 University of Rochester show and listen to the vocal jam that emerges from "You Enjoy Myself." Sound familiar?

"Silent in the Morning"

Phish introduced "Silent in the Morning" at Portsmouth Music Hall on 3/7/92. Some phans immediately abbreviated "Silent in the Morning" on their set lists and J-cards as "SITM." This raises some questions of set-list acronym philosophy. Some phans do not use "SITM," as they feel that the acronym of a song should reflect that song in some way. For instance, "PYITE" ("Punch You in the Eye"): cool acronym, cool song. "BBFCFM" ("Big Black Furry Creatures from Mars"): bizarre acronym, bizarre song. "Scent of a Mule" raised some problems because it shares the same first letters as "Split Open and Melt," but many phans felt that "SOAM" better captures the essence of "Split," while "Scent" seems more appropriate for the newer song. Similarly, "SITM," just doesn't strike a respondent chord with many phans, who prefer to identify the song as "Silent" on their set lists.

"Silent in the Morning"'s lyrics make it a live phavorite, particularly when the band returns to a previous venue or performs on the same noteworthy date that it had in the past. For instance, listen to the crowd cheer when Trey sings the line about the same thing happening last year on 12/31/94. If you're curious as to whether "The Horse" has always preceded "Silent," the answer is no: listen to 5/30/94 and 6/23/94. For other fine "Silent's" listen to 11/19/92, 2/3/93, 8/12/93, and 12/29/94.

"Simple"

This song premiered as a work in progress at the Warfield Theater on 5/27/94. The lyrics came from Mike's journal and had traveled with him for a few years. Mike also contributed his ideas for the music, which many phans hear hinted at in earlier versions of "Mike's Song." The versions of "Simple" that appeared over the summer of 1994 reflect Phish's efforts to fine-tune this one (for instance, 6/17/94 and 6/24/94).

An additional feature of this song is its versatility. The song can be performed very straightforwardly as a "simple" exercise in vocal harmony (for instance, listen to the version on *A Live One*). However, when the band sees fit, the "Simple" jam can become a bit more open-ended, with an extended foray into the improvisational realm (for instance, 10/31/94). Additionally, "Simple" can serve as a great segue between songs (6/22/94 [surrounding "Icculus,"] and 7/2/94). It's a floor wax and a dessert topping! The one thing that Phish hasn't let "Simple" become is a horn song. Indeed, the fact that the lyrics boast a saxophone is the principal reason why the band hasn't added one to the mix during Giant Country Horns appearances (although the band did allow Cameron McKenney to give it a shot on 11/28/94).

"Skippy (the Wonder Mouse)"

The Dude sang the original version of this song at Phish's Nectar's debut on 12/1/84. The Dudely lyrics are complemented by some Trey-composed instrumentation that you may recognize. If you listen to the initial "Skippy (the Wonder Mouse)" or the version from 10/30/85 with Trey on lead vocals, you'll recognize the music from "McGrupp and the Watchful Hosemasters." Trey decided to abandon the wonder mouse's tale by 1986 and use the tune to complete "McGrupp."

"Slave to the Traffic Light"

This is one of the oldest Phish songs. The lyrics are by none other than the Dude of Life, who apparently has had his share of trying experiences at stoplights adjacent to zoos at city limits. The earlier versions do not spiral to a screaming conclusion with the same authority as the current ones, but the basic progression is there. Phish performed this song only a few times between August 1989 and August 1993, including a "Slave"-less gap from 10/27/91 to 8/6/93. The song's return in August 1993 took place, appropriately, at the Cincinnati Zoo show. The version of this song on *A Live One* is from 11/26/94. Along with this version be sure to check out 12/1/84, 10/30/85, 10/15/86, 7/23/88 (with horns), 4/22/90, 3/17/91, 12/30/93, 4/9/94, 10/31/94, 11/7/94, 12/3/94 (with horns), and 11/29/95 (with Bela Fleck).

"Sleeping Monkey"

Phish debuted this song as its lone encore at Portsmouth Music Hall on 3/6/92. This information surprises some phans who assume that "Sleeping Monkey" is an older Phish song. Perhaps they feel that singing about reviving a sleeping monkey on a train in falsetto with a "Home on the Range" melody and "Hey Jude" conclusion is the mark of a younger band. To Phish's immense credit, that's not true. If you want to hear some fine "Sleeping Monkey" 's, check out

3/14/92 (with John Popper), 2/20/93, 10/31/94, and 6/26/95. By the way the central image of this song is a metaphor for uhhh . . . erhhh . . . the word flaccid comes to mind.

"Sloth"

This pounding tune relates the story of the meanest man in Gamehendge, who eventually assassinates the evil Wilson (so that Errand Wolfe can become the evil Errand). It's also one of the four songs in Phish's nipple-piercing trilogy. Some representative versions of this song include 5/15/88, 4/18/90, 10/31/91, 12/28/92, 8/12/93, 12/7/94, and 12/31/95.

"Sparkle"

"Sparkle" made its glittering (one might say sparkling) debut at the Colonial Theater on 9/25/91. Phans tend to split on this one. Some absolutely love it: it starts them up and dancing. Others gets really down on it for the typical critical phan rationale—not enough variety from version to version. One slight variation on this view are those who say, "Well, all that's true but at least it's short." Before reaching a conclusion on such matters, it is useful to sit down and listen to a number of versions in chronological order: 10/19/91, 7/25/92, 6/30/94 (with redrum), 8/21/93, 10/3/95, and 12/31/95 will do.

"Split Open and Melt"

Phish first performed "Split Open and Melt" in the spring of 1989. Early versions of "Split" feature a rare Fish drum solo (4/15/89 or 4/30/89, for instance). The version that appears on *Lawn Boy* is notable because Phish added horns into the mix, their first such recorded venture. The band has altered its approach to this song quite a bit over the years. Trey has stated that for a while he didn't quite know what to do with it, and then one night (4/21/93) at Newport Music Hall, Columbus, Ohio, the band really hit its stride. This version of the song appears in "Demand" on *Hoist*. Phans champion different periods of this song. Some particularly enjoy the versions from 1991 to 1993 with extended exercises in tension and release. Others prefer some of the 1994 and 1995 versions in which the band works from a theme and then launches into a period of structured improvisation without the prevalent tension-and-release aspects. Still others point to the horn tour as the apogee of this song and remark that the band elected to record this song with horns, which must count for something. Some fine "SOAM"'s that reflect all of these preferences include 10/20/89 (horns), 7/13/91, 4/16/92, 12/30/92, 8/12/93, 5/13/94, 6/11/94, and 12/28/95.

"Spock's Brain"

This song's debut at the Lowell benefit show on 5/15/95 proved quite entertaining. When Fish took center stage to perform his new rendition of the Velvet Underground's "Lonesome Cowboy Bill," he asked the crowd if they wanted to know the song titles. Phans responded enthusiastically in the affirmative. When it came time to reveal the name for this song, Fish was a little hesitant, asking the other band members if he could do so. In response Trey stated that a Voters for Choice benefit was a appropriate place for an audience vote, offering four choices: "The Plane," "The First Single," "Israel," and the runaway, landslide winner, "Spock's Brain." Trey then admitted that tune had been written for the "Spock's Brain" episode of *Star Trek*. To remind you, this is the episode in which a woman beams on board, knocks out everyone and steals Spock's brain to use as an energy force for her planet. The *Enterprise* gives chase to her while Bones comes up with a method so that Spock's brainless body can be controlled. Kirk, Bones, Scotty, and the debrained Spock beam down and eventually confront the woman and reclaim the brain. As it turns out, a race of powerful women, the Eymorgs, who live underground, are using the brain as an energy supply to satisfy all the needs of the Morgs, who live above ground. Rest assured however, it all ends happily.

The song, like the brain, disappeared over the fall of 1995.

Photo credit: John Richter

"Squirming Coil"

This song incorporates quite a bit of imagery from other Phish songs. The Jimmy who goes off to camp may very well be "Harpua" 's Jimmy. The Tannis root could be the same root that the people of Gamehendge harvest before making their pilgrimage to the Rhombus to sing "Divided Sky." Indeed, that very same root might be the one that Colonel Forbin clutches as he climbs the mountain. But no, that's not "Icculus" in there; it's Icarus, the mythological figure who covered himself with wax and feathers and flew in the air until the sun melted the wax and he tumbled to earth. "Icculus" is much too wise for such shenanigans.

"Squirming Coil" premiered at Dartmouth College on 1/20/90.

Since then many phans have taken particular pleasure from set-closing "Coil" 's as Fish, Mike, and Trey often exit the stage, leaving Page alone for an extended solo (particularly since Page began touring with his baby grand in February 1993). Some notable "Coil" 's include 10/4/91 (with "Linus and Lucy"), 5/17/92 (with happy birthday to Page), and 10/31/94. The "Squirming Coil" on *A Live One* is from 10/9/94.

"Stash"

Phish premiered "Stash" at Wetlands on 9/13/90. At that first performance Trey introduced the song by noting, "We told you we're gonna give you a lot of new songs. . . . This one's called 'Stash.' You're gonna like it." Trey's a wise man because phans did indeed like it. The song features a number of memorable musical passages, interesting time signatures, and some fantastic improvisational sequences. Some of the chord progressions are drawn from Charles Mingus's "Jump Monk."

Oh yeah, and cool lyrics, too. Many a phan has attended a show while dangling his stash. And the question that serves as the song's refrain has become a mantra to many others. As regards these lyrics, Tom Marshall has stated that some of his songs provide consistent themes while others collect sounds and images. "Stash" falls into the latter category, which is not to say that this detracts from the song, as "Stash" remains a feast for the ears.

The song has a few additional features in concert. First, you get to watch Trey wail up at his cohorts asleep in the trees. Second, some audience participation has evolved as phans have come to interject their own rhythmic clapping at the appropriate musical cues (originally many phans snapped their fingers, but this doesn't carry well in arenas).

A number of excellent "Stashes" exist. Check out 7/15/91 (with horns), 5/2/92, 11/20/92 (with "Linus and Lucy"), 4/14/93 (with "Kung"), 8/21/93, 5/13/94, 7/16/94, 11/14/95 (with "Manteca" and "Dog Faced Boy"). By the way, the "Stash" on *A Live One* is from 7/8/94.

"Strange Design"

Another debut from the Voters for Choice benefit on 5/16/95. Fishman introduced this song as "Ahhhh, Page, Sing" reflecting a desire on the band members' parts to hear Page sing more lead vocals. The song's working title was "Companions," which sums up the lyrical content quite well. Some fine versions of this song include 7/1/95 and 12/31/95.

"Suzie Greenberg"

This song was introduced onto the band's playlist in 1987. The Dude of Life contributed to this song, and he currently performs it with his band. "Suzie Greenberg" turned a corner during the summer of 1991, when Carl Gerhard composed a horn chart and the Giant Country Horns performed on it. Once phans heard "Suzie" with horns, it became hard for many to imagine that the song wasn't written with a horn chart. Also, a number of phan-favorite one-liners have emerged from Fishman's mouth ever since he began his screaming during the "neurologist" line in 1991. For some fine "Suzie"'s with all of these elements listen to 3/21/91, 7/23/91 ("Have you seen junior's grades?"), 8/17/92 (a cappella intro), 6/11/94, and 7/13/94 (with "Slave to the Traffic Light").

"Taste"

The band debuted this song on 6/7/95. Over the course of the summer tour, "Taste" continued to win its supporters, particularly as the band began to explore the possibilities held within. Sadly, "Taste" came to a premature end in September when "Fog That Surrounds" stole its music. Some of "Taste"'s lyrics returned in the reworked "Fog" that appeared on 10/24/95. If you're a sentimentalist and wish to hear some fine versions of "Taste" in its earlier glory, check out 6/9/95, 6/23/95, and 6/30/95.

"Tela"

"Tela" is one of the compositions in Trey's Gamehendge thesis. Trey has stated that this tune represented a breakthrough in his songwriting craft as it is the first song that he composed with another singer in mind, Page. As a result, this freed him to explore the possibilities of Page's vocal range while also taking the keyboardist's personality into consideration so that he would be comfortable with the song. The results have pleased many phans.

"Tela" has undergone some modifications over the course of its history. To hear these changes, seek out 3/12/88, 6/20/88, 12/8/89, 1/28/90, 5/3/91, 5/6/93, 6/11/94, and 11/24/95.

"Theme from the Bottom"

Phish first performed "Theme from the Bottom" onstage at the Voters for Choice Benefit on 5/16/95. "Theme" picked up its converts quite quickly as it boasts fish imagery, fine vocal interplay, and, of course, an extended jam (that some phans feel is a bit reminiscent of "Reba"). "Theme" quickly escalated in the hearts and minds of phans so much that it became a pleasing encore choice by midsummer. Some recommended "Theme"'s include 6/29/95, 7/1/95, and 12/28/95.

"Tube"

"Tube" first appeared at the Wetlands show on 9/13/90 offering a skewed story with a funky beat. The song also offers applause for Robert Palmer at its end. (Palmer's "Sneaking Sally through the Alley" was an early Phish cover tune.) "Tube" has made infrequent appearances over the years. To hear some of these listen to 11/4/90, 12/5/91, 4/19/92, 11/20/92 (with "Buried Alive"), 4/12/93, 6/26/94, 10/13/95 (in honor of Trey's birth in Texas), and 12/11/95 (in appreciation for booing and screeching during "Dog Log").

"TV Show"

The Dude informs us that life strongly resembles a television program that should have been taken off the air long ago. When "TV Show" debuted at the Ivory Tusk in Tuscaloosa, Alabama, on 11/8/91, plenty of people in attendance directed that sentiment to the Dude.

"Tweezer"

"Tweezer" debuted during the spring of 1990 (an early performance took place at J. J. McCabes in Boulder, Colorado, on 4/5/90). Trey introduced this song as " Tweezer So Cold," although by the time *Picture of Nectar* came out, the title had been shortened to "Tweezer." This song evolved out of a sound check that Phish performed on 12/31/89. The band also worked on this one onstage a bit before presenting it as an independent tune (listen before "David Bowie" on 2/25/90). A number of "Tweezer" 's have acquired legendary status among phans. Some of the longer ones, clocking in at over thirty minutes apiece, include 5/7/94 (essentially a "Tweezer" second set as other songs drift in and out of "Tweezer"), 11/2/94 (this one appears on *A Live One*), 11/28/94, 6/14/95, 6/22/95 and 11/30/95. Other versions worth hearing include 9/16/90, 4/27/91 (with "Sweet Emotion"), 7/12/91 (with horns), 11/19/92 (with "BBFCFM" quote and "Ring of Fire"), 2/20/93, 5/6/93, 5/17/94, 7/9/94, 12/1/94 (with "Norwegian Wood"), and 12/2/95.

"Union Federal"

The "Union Federal" on *Junta* is from one of Phish's Oh Kee Pah ceremonies. The bass line four minutes and thirty seconds into the song is from "Under Pressure."

Vibration of Life

The Vibration of Life is not a song, it is more akin to "Kung." Phish has created the Vibration of Life on numerous evenings by pro-

ducing a rhythm of seven beats per second. Typically Trey introduces the Vibration of Life by explaining that "everything we see
and hear is a vibration . . . the theoretical glue of the universe is
seven beats per second. So if Mike and I can conjure up a vibration
of seven beats per second it should put you in tune with the universe and fill you with great energy." If you want to be energized,
find yourself a copy of 4/16/94 or 11/30/94 (among others). Or
depending on your mood you may want to hear 10/31/94, which
features the Vibration of Death.

"The Wedge"

"The Wedge" was the only song on *Rift* that wasn't road-tested
before the release of the album. In fact, "The Wedge" was a last-
minute addition concocted by Trey and Tom Marshall while the
band was working on the final mixes of the album. The band decided to hold back this one during the 1992 fall tour in order to
work out its live arrangement. Phish grew dissatisfied with the initial
version, which premiered on 2/3/93, and soon abandoned it. A re-

worked version made a brief return at Red Rocks that summer on 8/20/93. (This was inevitable, as when you go to Red Rocks you quite literally take the highway to the great divide in the stones.) But then the song disappeared again for nearly two years until the band performed a shorter "Wedge" on 6/7/95.

"Weekapaug Groove"

Weekapaug—where is it and what is it? Weekapaug is a small seaside community on the southwest tip of Rhode Island. It is one of the small townships that collectively are known as Misquamicut. The town is pretty mellow during the winter, but a number of people have summer homes there. "Weekapaug Groove" is the band's tribute to that region (for instance, listen to 2/7/89).

What's so great in Weekapaug? What happened there? Listen to the words of the song, which describe efforts at making connections with members of the opposite sex. Beyond that? Listen carefully and leave it to your imagination.

While Phish has performed "Mike's Song" without "Weekapaug" and "Weekapaug" without "I Am Hydrogen," you'll be hard-pressed to find a complete "Weekapaug" without a corresponding "Mike's." A number of noteworthy "Weekapaug"'s have appeared over the years. Check out 7/23/88, 11/8/91 (with "Slice of Pizza" and "Bucket of Lard"), 5/14/92 (with "Wait"), 11/19/92 (with "Price of Love"), 2/4/93 (with "Push th' Little Daisies"), 12/29/92 (with "Maria"), and 12/31/95.

"Weigh"

Mike composed this song after watching the wonderfully twisted Martin Scorsese film *After Hours*. It began with a guitar lick that Mike composed while attending the National New Guitar Workshop. "Weigh" debuted at Portsmouth Music Hall on 3/7/92, and Phish has performed the song infrequently ever since. A representative sampling of "Weigh"'s includes 11/23/92, 2/20/93, 12/30/93, 5/20/94, 6/7/95, and 10/22/95.

"Wilson"

Trey composed the original version of this song, entitled "Wilson, Can You Still Have Fun," with Tom Marshall and Aaron Wolfe. This song served as one of the blueprints for Trey's Senior Study. He modified the lyrics slightly and included the song in the original Gamehendge saga. The band has performed the song consistently ever since. One recent variation is the audience chant that has become frozen into the song due to its appearance on *A Live One* (that "Wilson" is from 12/30/94). Some other interesting "Wilson"'s include 8/21/87, 9/24/88, amd 12/31/91 (with electronic swearing device), 4/15/94, and 12/9/95 (with Beavis and Butthead noisemaker).

"Wolfman's Brother"

This is the only song on *Hoist* with a songwriting credit for the entire band plus Tom Marshall. For the *Hoist* version, Greg Adams and the Tower of Power horns came on board. While crediting players, one should not forget Greasy Fizeek on "Shirley Temple." "Greasy" is Fish's alias, and under his picture in the *Hoist* booklet he is credited with drums and "Shirley Temple." His "Shirley Temple" work can be found on this song.

"Wolfman's Brother" debuted at the Flynn Theater on 4/4/94. Following this initial performance the song somewhat fell by the wayside. Perhaps the band was unhappy with its arrangement of the song without horns. At any rate, "Wolfman's Brother" appeared only seven more times over the course of the year.

Here's one more "Wolfman's Brother" tale. As the story goes, Mike was anxious to open the final set of the 1995 summer tour on 7/3/95 at Sugarbush with this song. Trey, on the other hand, wanted to revive " Timber" as the set opener. Eventually, Mike gave in and " Timber" opened the set. Cut to the opening show of the fall 1995 tour at the Cal Expo Amphitheater on 9/27/95. First song, first set? "Wolfman's Brother."

Another "Wolfman's Brother" worth hearing begins as an a cappella "You Enjoy Myself" vocal jam and then goes electric (4/26/96).

"You Enjoy Myself"

"You Enjoy Myself," which often appears in set-list shorthand as "YEM," has thrilled and confused phans since 1985. A solid ten-minute version of the song appears on *Junta*, although if you desire a bit more bang for your buck, check out the twenty-three-minute "YEM" on *A Live One*. An additional intriguing "YEM" graces many of the *White Tape* variations. This version consists of a forty-five-second a cappella snippet of the song's opening bars, which the band currently performs with instrumentation.

Trey wrote "YEM" following the summer that he and Fishman spent in Europe. As the story goes, Trey and Fish were hanging out in Italy, bumming and busking, when they made the acquaintance of a friendly native. Although the Italian man spoke only a few words of English, and Trey and Fish spoke fewer words of Italian, the three of them were inseparable, spending a few days together on the streets and in the cafés. At some point toward the end of this period, the man threw his arms around the pair and earnestly proclaimed, "When I'm with you, you enjoy myself!" Trey later incorporated this wisdom into the song.

The tune's great enigma is its lyrics. "What are they saying in 'You Enjoy Myself'?" has been posed on so many occasions and in so many newsletters that Phish-netters have come to abbreviate the whole query as WATSIYEM. Indeed, in the group's 1993 newsletters this question is asked and answered (of sorts) no less than twenty-four times. Most people seem to agree that the words sound something like "wash your feets, they drive me to a frenzy." While the line itself has changed from time to time, the likely answer to the WATSIYEM question is "wash uffizi, drive me to Firenze." What does this mean? Well, it means both something and nothing. While the words themselves are gibberish of a most Phishy nature, they refer to Trey and Fish's Italian experience. "Washa uffizi" is supposed to sound like "wash your feets." During the time that Trey and Fish lived as wandering minstrels, they experienced few opportunities to bathe, so their feet stank (as is the tendency of wandering minstrels). However, Uffizi also is the name of an art gallery in Florence, and Firenze is the Italian name for that city. So, to put it all together, the line is a pun that refers both to smelly toes and to this particular art gallery that Trey and Fishman often visited while in Italy (indeed, when the Uffizi Gallery was bombed in May 1993, the band expressed its condolences in the newsletter).

Phish has had a lot of fun with the WATSIYEM question. For instance, in the February 1993 newsletter, Mike answered this query, "Water your team, in a bee hive, I'm a sent you." Then, at the first show of that spring tour (2/3/93, at the Portland Expo in Portland, Maine), Phish performed "YEM" and inserted Mike's answer. In the next newsletter Mike recommended that fans listen to the tape of the Portland show and further "explained" that the phrase means "Yes, I'll play, but no, I won't raise." Some other answers to WATSIYEM that the band has offered over the years include, "Watch out, fin, see?," "Wanton in a key, I live, and me for horse-rent," and "Waschusett Fiji is sun-hives to floor antsy."

"YEM" is noteworthy for a few additional reasons. First, the instrumental segment leading up to the lyrics typically extends longer than ten minutes and often is downright explosive (for instance, check out 11/23/94 at the Fox Theater, St. Louis, which includes the Vibration of Life and a "Frankenstein" tease). Also, "YEM" is one of those songs during which the band brings out its trampolines if the occasion seems fit. Furthermore, "YEM" is interesting because it ends in a vocal scat jam that is often either haunting or hilarious, and at times a bit of both. The words in the vocal jam vary from show to show but the results are usually quite entertaining (for instance, listen to 10/31/91, with its "pizza" theme, or 3/14/93 in Gunnison, Colorado, which contains a twisted "We Will Rock You"–"We Are the Champions Welcome to the Machine" theme). Finally, "YEM" is important because on at least one occasion Trey has indicated that the complicated arrangement of this song was one of the factors that helped to drive Jeff from the band.

Phish has performed many notable "YEM" 's, including 4/15/86, 3/23/87, 10/31/88, 3/30/89, 5/26/89, 5/28/89, 6/5/90, 10/19/91, 10/28/91, 11/24/91, 4/5/92, 4/17/92, 7/25/92 (with Carlos Santana), 5/5/93 (with Aquarium Rescue Unit), 5/4/94 (with horns) 5/13/94, 5/28/94 (with vacuum and Les Claypool), 6/11/94, 6/18/94, 6/30/94, 10/24/95, 10/31/95, 12/9/95, and 4/26/96 (with "Wolfman's Brother" vocal jam).

3 if i only had a brain

Phish often inserts teases, quotes, hints, and snippets of songs within its other songs. Some of the more notable teases and quotes that Phish has performed within its own compositions are mentioned within individual song entries in chapter 2. However, here is a sampling of songs that the band has quoted along with the date of the performance. Find each tape and seek out the actual quote on your own: "Andy Griffith Theme" (8/26/89), "Bang a Gong" (3/18/93), "Beat It" (10/21/95 and 10/29/95), "Black and White" (5/3/94), "Breathe" (10/25/95), "Cannonball" (5/7/94), "China Grove" (5/17/92), "Dream On" (12/30/93), "Fly Like an Eagle" (10/7/89), "Frosty the Snowman" (11/14/91), "If I Were a Rich Man" (8/26/89), "Linus and Lucy" (10/4/91, 11/20/92, and 4/18/92), "Psycho Killer" (5/23/94), "Push Th' Little Daisies" (2/4/93), "Rock and Roll All Night" (2/20/93), "Smoke on the Water (8/14/93), "Sweet Emotion" (4/27/91, 5/3/91, and 5/7/94), "Tequila" (8/6/93), "Who Knows" (8/9/93), "Whole Lotta Love" (3/1/91), "Wimoweh" (12/31/91), and "You Shook Me All Nite Long" (4/20/89).

"All Along the Watchtower"

This Bob Dylan classic is not a Phish live staple, but it's a favorite of the Dave Matthews Band. So when the DMB joined Phish on-stage for the encore at the Lawrence Joel Veterans Memorial Coliseum in Winston-Salem, North Carolina, on 4/21/94, a dual-band jam segued into a collective performance of this tune, with Dave supplying lead vocals and everyone else providing some enthusiastic musical interplay.

"All Blues"

If you're a Miles Davis fan, you'll be pleased with Phish's effort on this one. As you may remember, in his Senior Study, Page identified Bill Evans as one of his three major musical influences. Evans, of course, played piano on the original "All Blues," which appears on Miles Davis's *Kind of Blue* album. *Kind of Blue* presents five spectacular improvisations by an all-star star cast that features John Coltrane, Julian Adderly, Paul Chambers, and James Cobb. In turn, Page emulates Evans as he leads Phish through this one in the version of the song that circulates from the Front on 2/6/89.

"Also sprach Zarathustra"

Richard Strauss composed this selection, which appears as the theme to Stanley Kubrick's 2001: A Space Odyssey. The song was retrofitted for Phish performance during the summer of 1993. The band debuted this song, with appropriate accompanying fanfare (fog, lights, etc.), to open the second set at the Mann Music Center in Philadelphia on 7/16/93. The band members must have enjoyed the totality of this experience, as they presented the 2001 theme in each of the next nine shows.

The 2001 theme typically segues into a handful of Phish originals (the four most common are "Run Like an Antelope, "Mike's Song," "David Bowie," and "Maze"). Many phans believe that whenever Phish performs "Also sprach Zarathustra," the version of whatever song follows receives an extra boost of energy. "Maze" in particular is said to benefit—listen to 4/11/94 or 9/29/95. Some other notable transitions include 2001 into "Slave to the Traffic Light" (8/20/93),

2001 into "Halley's Comet" (6/24/95), and for an interesting role reversal "Theme from the Bottom" into 2001 (11/19/95). One additional momentous 2001 that doesn't translate as well onto audio tape occurred at the Boston Garden on 12/31/94, when the band performed this song as the JUMBO hot dog, Coke, and fries were lowered to the stage.

"Amazing Grace"

Phish first performed "Amazing Grace" over the airwaves on WBCN in Boston on 1/28/93. Later that night the band also sang "Amazing Grace" at Boston's Hard Rock Cafe in order to celebrate the release of *Rift* (after which the band donated Fish's original vacuum to the restaurant—see above). Phish then performed this song five days later at the opening show of its tour on 2/3/93 at the Portland Expo in Portland, Maine.

Although almost every version of "Amazing Grace" has been a cappella, there have been two notable exceptions. In particular, on 5/8/93, the closing night of the spring tour at the University of New Hampshire Fieldhouse, Phish followed its a cappella rendition of this song with a moving instrumental version. This also occurred at the Five Season Arena in Cedar Rapids, Iowa, on 10/20/95.

"*Avenu Malkenu*"

"*Avenu Malkenu*," which means "Our Father, Our King" in Hebrew, is a solemn prayer usually associated with the holiday of Yom Kippur. The band has performed this song since 1987, always tucked within the watchful guise of "The Man Who Stepped into Yesterday." Three additional notes about this song. First, when the band performed "*Avenu Malkenu*" on 4/18/92 during the holiday of Passover, Trey informed phans that "Mike 'Cactus' Gordon will now perform a Happy Passover bass solo." Second, this song was the subject of many dedications to many cousins on 12/30/92. Finally, on a more somber note, Phish performed "*Avenu Malkenu*" on 11/9/95 at the Fox Theater, the first Phish show to occur after the tragic assassination of Israeli President Rabin.

"Auld Lang Syne"

Phish has performed an instrumental version of this song at midnight during each of its New Year's Eve shows since 1989. The consensus favorite version is 12/31/92, which burst through "Mike's Song" to set a standard for years to come. Phish also has teased the song in some of its pre–New Year's Eve shows over the past few years as well (for instance, listen to the "You Enjoy Myself" on 12/30/92). However, the band topped itself in 1995 when it slipped "Auld Lang Syne" quotes into each of the three pre–New Year's Eve performances.

"Baby Lemonade"

"Baby Lemonade" continued Fish's string of Syd Barrett favorites. Fish debuted this song at the Colonial Theater in Keene, New Hampshire on 3/11/92. For complicated and enigmatic reasons he immediately abandoned this tune thereafter. If this leaves you unsatisfied and you want to seek some solace in Barrett's original, you may find it on the Barrett album.

"Back in the USSR"

With the opening notes of this song, Phish began its odyssey into the White Album on 10/31/94 at the Glens Falls Civic Center. So far Phish has relived this moment only once, performing "Back in the USSR" as an encore at the University of California–Santa Barbara Event Center on 12/6/94.

"The Ballad of Curtis Loew"

Here's another one that got away. "The Ballad of Curtis Loew" is a Lynyrd Skynyrd tune that first appeared on that band's *Second Helping* album (the same album that features "Swamp Music," the song that inspired "Possum"). Phish began playing this song in 1987 and continued to play it semiregularly until its hasty departure in 1990. "Curtis Loew" returned in 1993 to make three triumphant appearances (two of which took place at celebrated shows—3/14/93 and 8/2/93—which suggests a tie between such exceptional performances and the band's return to its roots). "Curtis Loew" also is noteworthy as light board operator Tim Rogers occasionally joined the band on harmonica for this tune (3/11/88, for instance).

"Bell Boy"

Phish performed this song as part of their *Quadrophenia* set at the Rosemont Horizon on 10/31/95. The band coerced a member of their crew to sing this one. They also coerced him to walk onstage in a bell boy costume while carrying some luggage. He did, but he also brought a fifth of whiskey on stage, took a deep swig before his performance, and then drained it before collecting his luggage and leaving.

"Bike"

"Bike" is one of Fish's older Syd Barrett covers, as he premiered this song in 1987. Phish's drummer has often stated that people have to talk him into performing many other songs but that he really enjoys the ones by Syd Barrett. If you'd like to hear the original version, it appears on Pink Floyd's debut album, *Piper at the Gates of Dawn*.

"Blackbird"

Page sang this one as part of Phish's White Album set on 10/31/94. He sang it again at the Jesse Auditorium in Columbia, Missouri, on 11/22/94.

"Blue Bossa"

Phish performed this Blue Note jazz standard at Pete's Phabulous Phishfest on 7/23/88. "Blue Bossa" was written by trumpeter Kenny Dorham, although this song is more closely associated with Joe Henderson, who has performed and recorded it a number of times over the years, often with Dorham.

"Blue Sky"

The circumstances under which Phish played this Allman Brothers Band song are very interesting. On 8/12/89 the band consented to provide the musical entertainment at the wedding of two friends. Phish performed "Blue Sky" for the newlyweds' first song.

"Bold as Love"

Phish premiered "Bold as Love" in the fall of 1988. The song is a Jimi Hendrix composition from the Jimi Hendrix Experience's second album, *Axis: Bold as Love*. When Phish began performing the song, it was one of the band's few tunes featuring Page on lead vocals. Phish continues to play "Bold as Love," although the song became an infrequent treat after 1989. Indeed, for reasons known only to Phish, the band performed this song exactly five times a year in 1993, 1994, and 1995. Someone must have skipped a notation because they played "Bold as Love" six times in 1992. By the way, on all twenty-one occasions over these four years the song appeared as an encore. If you want to hear some representative versions of this tune over the course of its Phish career, listen to 11/3/88, 11/19/92, and 6/24/95.

"Boogie On Reggae Woman"

Recognize this one? It's a Stevie Wonder classic from *Fulfillingness' First Finale* (and later *Original Musiquarium I*). The members of Phish always have had a deep admiration for Stevie Wonder, particularly his work from the seventies. When asked what album they would prefer to play before the 1994 Halloween vote, Wonder's *Innervisions* was one of their choices. If you want to hear a version of this song that Phish performed between 1986 and 1988, find yourself a copy of 4/29/87 or 3/21/88.

"Brown Eyed Girl"

Here's an interesting guest appearance. Not by Van Morrison, the author of this song, but the original Parrothead himself, Jimmy Buffett. He joined Phish onstage at the Auditorium in West Palm Beach on 11/16/95 to lend his vocals to "Brown Eyed Girl."

"Caravan"

"Caravan" is a composition by Duke Ellington and his trombone player Juan Tizol. Sir Duke used to feature this number with his orchestra, although Irving Mills also contributed lyrics to the song, which some performers have opted to incorporate. (Ella Fitzgerald recorded a few such versions, and "Caravan" also appeared with lyrics in the Broadway musical *Sophisticated Ladies*.) Phish has opted for the instrumental version, ever since it began to perform "Caravan" on 1/20/90. This song reflects the influence of Page, who identified Duke Ellington in his Senior Study as one of his three greatest influences. The whole band certainly respects Ellington; Phish has performed a number of his compositions over the years and commemorated Duke's birthday from the stage on 4/29/87. As you might expect, some of the more enjoyable versions of "Cara-

Photo credit: Rich Luzzi

van" have occurred with horn assistance (for instance, 7/15/91 or 12/2/94). By the way, Phish has performed this song much more infrequently in recent years because they feel that it doesn't translate very well into larger venues.

"Carolina"

"Carolina" is another song that the band debuted at Dartmouth on 1/20/90. The members of Phish actually took barbershop quartet lessons in order to master the genre. It's much trickier than it looks, with separate mouth positions required to produce particular sounds. On one occasion Mike was walking through the parking lot before a show and spied some photos taken by a phan named Rich Luzzi. Mike spent some time with Rich, trying to figure out what he had been singing in each particular shot based on the position of his mouth. Phish continues to perform "Carolina" and other a cappella numbers, so you can conduct your own study of this phenomenon at a future show.

"Cities"

This is one of the songs that often identifies those individuals who haven't seen Phish in a long while. If you mention the band to someone or see somebody at a show and she inquires "Do they still play 'Cities'?" you can safely identify her as someone who hasn't been attending the meetings. "Cities" is a Talking Heads song from their *Fear of Music* album. One of Phish's early performances of this song appears on the tape of their first Nectar's show, 12/1/84. "Cities" remained a common Phish song through 1988, when it suddenly disappeared. Phish revived the song at the Congress Center in Ottawa on 7/5/94 (the same show that features the return of "Letter to Jimmy Page"), but as yet the song has not made another appearance in a Phish set list.

"Cold as Ice"

Most phans know that the band performs "Hold Your Head Up" as "Henrietta's Theme" (because Fish really doesn't like that song). What you may not know is that for a short period during the spring of 1992 the band replaced "Hold Your Head Up" with Foreigner's "Cold as Ice" because Fish really doesn't like that song either. In fact, it appears that Fish really, really doesn't like that song. Listen to 4/18/92, when the band plays "Cold as Ice" for a bit too long and Fish tries to stop them. ("Okay, I think we get it . . . I apologize for that"). Or listen to 4/21/92, when he displays his displeasure: "Sad isn't it?" By the end of the tour, "Hold Your Head Up" had returned, quite possibly because some of the other members of the band were having difficulties swallowing "Cold as Ice."

"Communication Breakdown"

Trey and Fish have long identified Led Zeppelin as one of their favorite bands when they were growing up. So some phans are surprised that Phish does not perform additional Zeppelin tunes along with "Good Times, Bad Times." In January 1990 the band offered "Communication Breakdown," which appears on Led Zeppelin's eponymous debut. Sadly, the band soon dropped this one, although occasionally one can hear it at a sound check.

"Come Together"

On 12/8/95 at the Cleveland State University Convocation Center, Phish performed this song as its first encore "for a special person that we're going to send some love out to." This day marked the fifteenth anniversary of the tragic slaying of John Lennon. Phish followed "Come Together" with "A Day in the Life" before making a solemn exit.

"Corrine, Corrina"

Phish performed "Corrine, Corinna" somewhat frequently from 1986 to 1988. This is a traditional song, arranged most notably by blues guitarist Taj Mahal on his *Natch'l Blues* album. An interesting version of this song appears on the recently released Rising Sons sessions (a short-lived group that Taj formed in 1964 with Ry Cooder). To hear Phish perform "Corrine, Corrina," check out 3/23/87 or 2/6/89.

"Cracklin' Rosie"

Phish debuted this song at the Portsmouth Music Hall on 3/7/92 to the immense pleasure of Diamondbacks (Neil Diamond fans) everywhere. "Cracklin' Rosie" is a "very special" Fishman song, which he performs with visual aids—cymbals with three mystical letters painted inside. What do those letters read? The answer is "B-A-H." And while you can't see them when you listen to a tape, now you can find a version of this song and play along at home (4/22/92 is a particularly "memorable" version, as Trey notes from the stage).

"Crossroads"

"Crossroads" was written by the man whose name is most closely associated with Mississippi Delta blues, Mr. Robert Johnson. It is said that Robert Johnson went down to the crossroads to make a pact with the devil in order to play as well as he did. Sadly, if this is true, the devil received early payment, because Johnson died a mysterious death at age twenty-six. Phish first performed a few improvised versions of this song in 1992 and 1993 (for instance, in "Possum" on 4/5/92 and in the middle of "Mike's Song" on 5/8/93). For a somewhat more polished version, listen to 10/25/95 or 12/9/95. Trey's vocals won't make you think that you're at the Three Forks in Greenwood, Mississippi, but this one is worth hearing nonetheless.

''Cry Baby Cry''

Many Beatles fans thought that "Cry Baby Cry" was one of the standout numbers during the White Album set on 10/31/94. Many held out hope that Phish would make this song a permanent part of their repertoire. These wishes have been realized on two occasions, 11/22/94 and 6/16/95, when Phish responded with fine renditions of this song.

''Cryin' ''

Fish attempted this Aerosmith tune once, then sadly abandoned it. If you want to hear the original version of this song, check it out on Aerosmith's *Get a Grip*. Like many misbegotten youths who grew up in the 1970s, the members of Phish absorbed their share of the Toxic Twins. In fact, the band has quoted Aerosmith on a number of occasions (most notably on 12/30/93 and 5/7/94). On 9/29/95 at the Greek Theater in Los Angeles, Fish walked to the front of the stage, lyrics in hand, and did his best with this one. In this case I suppose his best just wasn't good enough (at least not for him— it was plenty good enough for many phans).

''Daniel (Saw the Stone)''

"Daniel (Saw the Stone)" is a traditional spiritual that Phish performed repeatedly to the great joy of many during the summer of 1993. However, they dropped it at the end of the summer. Indeed, the appearances of "Daniel" serve as bookends to the summer 1993 tour. Phish first performed the song on 7/15/93 at the Cayuga County Fairgrounds in Weedsport, New York, on the opening night of the tour and last played it as an encore on 8/28/93 at the Greek Theater in Berkeley, California, on the closing night of the tour.

"A Day in the Life"

Phish has a special feeling for the land and people of Colorado. Telluride took them in over the summer of 1988, and the band subsequently toured extensively within the state in 1990 and 1991. Since then, Phish has tried to work up something special for each of its return visits. In the summer of 1995 the product of this effort was the debut of this classic Beatles song from *Sgt. Pepper's Lonely Hearts Club Band*. Phish's version is a faithful interpretation of the song; in particular, listen to the ending. Over time some phans have complained that it is too faithful to the Beatles, as it does not vary much from version to version and lacks improvisation. If you want to hear this one for yourself, 6/10/95 and 12/30/95 are certainly representative.

"Diamond Girl"

The inimitable Seals and Croft took this one all the way up the charts to number six in 1973. The inimitable Dude of Life took this one all the way up the Southeast Expressway to Matthews Arena in Boston on 12/31/92. He walked onstage pushing a lawn mower, wowed the phans with this one, and walked offstage.

"Doctor Jimmy"

A number of phans chuckled when they realized that Phish was playing *Quadrophenia* on 10/31/95 because they knew that this song was on it. Phans of "Harpua" are left to wonder whether the young boy in that tale will grow up to become Doctor Jimmy (possibly a veterinarian, certainly not a sociologist or a neurologist).

"Donna Lee"

"Donna Lee" is a Charlie Parker song that has fallen by the wayside. Parker played alto saxophone, which is the featured instrument in the original "Donna Lee." So when Phish began to perform this song, it sounded quite a bit different, as Trey transposed Bird's alto lead to his guitar (for instance, listen to 6/30/89 when he encourages the audience to "sing along" or 4/5/90). This song sounded a bit more reminiscent of the original when Phish performed it with the Giant Country Horns (7/12/91). Either version would be welcome nowadays to those many phans who also appreciate the genius of Charlie Parker.

"Don't Pass Me By"

Mike interpreted this Ringo Starr composition at the Glens Fall Civic Center on 10/31/94. Given Mike's musical propensity, it may come as no surprise to you that he goosed this one a bit to give it a bluegrass feel. Although it's unclear what Ringo would have thought, most phans seemed to enjoy it.

"Don't You Wanna Go"

Phish debuted this traditional gospel song at the Voters for Choice benefit on 5/16/95. Many phans think the lyrics make for a terrific show opener ("Come on children . . . don't you wanna go?"), although Phish performed it sparingly over the summer and fall. Another fine version is 6/14/95.

"Don't Want You No More"

"Don't Want You No More" is a Spencer Davis song that Phish picked up secondhand. The version of this song that Phish performed from 1984 to 1985 emulates the version that appears on the Allman Brothers Band first album. Phish played this instrumental at its first Nectar's gig on 12/1/84.

"Dooley"

If you've ever seen episodes of the *Andy Griffith Show* that feature the Darling family, then you've seen the authors of this song. "Dooley" was composed by Mitch Jayne and Rodney Dillard, two members of the Missouri Ozarks bluegrass artists the Dillards. Phish performed "Dooley" with the assistance of Reverend Jeff Mosier on two occasions—first during the 11/19/94 Bloomington parking lot jam and then the next night at the Dane County Exposition Center. If you enjoy the bluegrass side of Phish, you should acquaint yourself with the Dillards (who also wrote the "Old Home Place").

"Drowned"

Phish performed this song quite admirably and faithfully during its *Quadrophenia* set at the Rosemont Horizon on 10/31/95. However, if you really want to hear the band make this one their own, listen to Phish's second live performance of "Drowned" two months later, when it returned to open the second set of the New Year's Eve show at Madison Square Garden.

"Eyes of the World"

This of course is a Jerry Garcia–Robert Hunter composition. It is also one of the songs that initially helped to pigeonhole Phish as a Dead cover band, even though this was far from the truth. Grateful Dead songs represented a very small fraction of the tunes that Phish performed during its first few years of existence. Nonetheless it was often easier for people to compare Phish to the Dead than to make the effort to articulate how the band's many varied influences have come together to produce a cohesive whole. If you want to hear Phish perform this song, give a listen to 12/1/84 or 4/1/86.

"Fire"

This song has been in the Phish repertoire almost from the start. The earliest commonly circulated tape, Nectar's 12/1/84, contains a

version of "Fire," a Jimi Hendrix original from *Are You Experienced?*
As for the 12/1/84 version, one of the aspects of Phish that many
phans enjoy is their irreverent attitude and playful take on conventions. On almost every occasion that the Grateful Dead played
"Scarlet Begonias" after the spring of 1977, the song segued into
"Fire on the Mountain." This became so common that the pair of
songs were often linked on Grateful Dead set lists as Scarlet>Fire.
Phish performed its own version of Scarlet>Fire during their early
years, however while the "Scarlet" was the Dead's "Scarlet Begonias,"
the "Fire" was Jimi's "Fire" (and then just in case anyone missed the
gag, they typically played "Fire on the Mountain"—so their set lists
read Scarlet>Fire>Fire).

Phish has performed a number of stellar versions of "Fire." For
instance, listen to 11/3/88,
3/22/93, and 12/12/95. A
few other "Fire"'s sound
great on tape but were better appreciated if you were
there. For instance, at the
Cincinnati Music Hall on
6/21/94, "Fire" opened the
second set after the first set
was cut short due to a fire
alarm. Also, at Roseland Ballroom in New York on 2/6/93,
John Popper returned to the
stage with Phish as they
emerged for their encore
and broke into this song.
Then they abruptly halted,
and Trey said, "Mike Gor-
don on the bass, ladies and
gentlemen," suggesting that
Mike was the cause of the
problem. They started the

Photo credit: Arch Stanton

song once again, Mike hit a few bum notes, and the band stopped. "Sorry," Mike offered. "Okay, ladies and gentlemen," Trey responded, "we're going to get Mike off the bass; we're going to bring Noel Redding out here to play." And so they did. The original bassist from the Jimi Hendrix Experience, whom Phish had met the night before at the Ritz Power Jam, came onstage to join Phish and Popper for a raging "Fire."

"Fire on the Mountain"

Mike is Phish's biggest Grateful Dead booster—in particular he admires Phil Lesh. Squinting phans have often spotted a picture of Phil Lesh on Mike's amp.

During the spring of 1993, just before their Laguna Seca Daze gig, Phish collectively attended a Dead concert. Numerous phans spotted the group before the show in the parking lot when both Fish and Amy (of farm fame) bungee jumped from a crane run by an enterprising entrepreneur. When Phish returned to the West Coast to play at Shoreline Amphitheater in Mountain View, California, in the fall of 1995 following Jerry's death, Trey dedicated "I'm Blue, I'm Lonesome" to Jerry, since Shoreline was the last place where Fish, Page, and he had seen Jerry perform (Mike had continued to see the Dead after the Shoreline show).

Although Phish stopped performing "Fire on the Mountain" by the end of 1985, phans occasionally hear Phish hint at this song in a number of their jams (most recently, about ten minutes into "Drowned" on 12/31/95).

"5:15"

Many phans felt that this song marked the second set musical highlight during the band's performance of *Quadrophenia* at Rosemont Horizon on 10/31/95. The Giant Country Horns had been flown in to sweeten the mix and to better replicate the original sounds of the album. This tune made it worth the trip.

"Fixin' to Die"

This song, written by Booker T. White, appears on the debut albums of both Bob Dylan and the Aquarium Rescue Unit. Reverend Jeff Mosier sang lead when Phish premiered this song as the last of four acoustic encores at Hara Arena in Dayton on 11/7/94. Trey took over principal vocal duties when Phish performed this one a second time without the Reverend's able assistance at the Evergreen College Recreation Center in Olympia, Washington, on 11/30/94. Both of these versions sound surly and inspired, which is exactly the way this song should sound.

"Foreplay/Long Time"

The members of Phish spent their formative years of radio exposure in the 1970s. Jon, Mike, Page, and Trey were eleven to fourteen years old in the fall of 1976 when "More than a Feeling" introduced the rest of America to Boston. That band's album sold millions of copies, and there came a time when you couldn't walk down the street without spying some kid wearing a T-shirt with the album-cover art spaceship lifting off from his chest. As a result it was not surprising that Phish decided to debut a version of these songs at Stabler Arena in Bethlehem, Pennsylvania, on 10/7/94. However, what did surprise some was the arrangement. Phish performed this quintessential product of 1970s electric music in an acoustic format with Fish on washboard, Mike on banjo, Page on upright bass, and Trey on acoustic guitar. To some phans this arrangement emphasized the enduring quality of the songs; to others it was a goof.

"Frankenstein"

This Edgar Winter song made it all the way to number one in 1973. Eighteen years later it became a showpiece for the Giant Country Horns, many of whom had enjoyed it on the radio as they were growing up. "Frankenstein" closed the second set of the first GCH show at Battery Park in Burlington on 7/11/91, and it continued to close sets or appear as an encore throughout the tour. Sadly, following its final performance with the GCH on 7/26/91, "Franken-stein" disappeared for nearly three years. Thankfully, Phish brought it back at Red Rocks on 6/11/94, and the band has continued to perform it ever since. Some notable recent non-horn-assisted "Frank" 's include 7/8/94 (sandwiched within "You Enjoy Myself"), 10/31/94, and 12/31/95.

"Freebird"

On 7/15/93 at the Cayuga County Fairgrounds in Weedsport, New York, Phish irrevocably altered the nature of their a cappella per-formances. With their rendition of "Freebird" they moved away from the traditional barbershop quartet songs into uncharted waters. They also set in motion a chain reaction, whereby someone yells "Freebird" whenever they move to the front of the stage. Of course, this isn't to say that some audience members weren't yelling this already—pull out a copy of 4/14/89 and listen to the yelps before "Contact" (or on 2/5/93 before "Amazing Grace," for that matter).

Trey introduced the first "Freebird" on 7/15/93 in a manner sim-ilar to Ronnie Van Zant on Lynyrd Skynyrd's *One More from the Road* album. On that fateful Weedsport evening Trey asked "What song is it you want to hear?" before Phish presented its a cappella ar-rangement of the song. In this interpretation the band doesn't just sing the vocal sections, they also produce the noises of the instru-ments (for instance, listen to 7/24/93, 8/8/93, or 4/23/94).

If you're a "Freebird" fan, you may want to hear an electric "Free-bird" effort from Nectar's on 3/6/87. Ninja Mike Billington supplies vocals while Phish halfheartedly backs him.

"Funky (Breakdown)"

"Funky (Breakdown)" is a song by Burlington's late, lamented insect-loving ragers, Ninja Custodian. Two of the Ninja boys, Magoo and Mike, have appeared onstage with Phish a number of times over the years. Phish performed "Funky (Breakdown)" on a couple of occasions in 1989.

"Funky Bitch"

Phish first performed this Son Seals song in 1987. At that time they performed this tune with some regularity, but by 1993 in order to hear it you had to attend their sound checks. This remains the case today, and avid sound check listeners have heard innumerable "Funky Bitch"es performed in a variety of styles. Some phans continue to request this song, a fact that Trey noted from the stage before the band performed it at Great Woods in Mansfield, Massachusetts, on 7/1/95. To hear some fine versions of this song check out 8/21/87, 7/25/92 (Carlos Santana trades licks with Trey), 2/19/93 (with Jimmy Herring), 12/11/95 (with Warren Haynes), and 11/22/94 (a favorite of many phans). Don't ignore the original artist either—give a listen to Son Seals's version on his recently rereleased *Live and Burning* album.

"Ginseng Sullivan"

In case you haven't listened to talk radio or entered a holistic nutrition center lately, you may not know all the magical properties of ginseng. This root's got a lot going for it! Phish rode the crest of this wave when they introduced this song into their repertoire at Club Eastbrook in Grand Rapids, Michigan, on 8/11/93. Norman Blake wrote Ginseng Sullivan and it appears on his *Home in Sulpher Springs* release. If you don't have an 8/11/93 tape, you might want to seek out 4/13/94 or 6/21/94, both of which include the gripping tale of woe that is "Ginseng Sullivan."

"Glass Onion"

It turns out that the walrus was Paul Languedoc. Also, many phans have listened to the White Album without hearing the lyrics about Guyute the pig. Phish set the record straight on both of these matters on 10/31/94.

Photo credit: Brett Virmalo

"Gloria"

From the moment that Gloria Steinem walked onstage to introduce Phish at the Lowell Memorial Auditorium on 5/16/95, some phans had a suspicion about this one. At the conclusion of the show, Phish started a somewhat tentative "Gloria" while Ms. Steinem herself walked on stage to wave and clap. If you want to hear Trey and Page perform a more thorough "Gloria," check out Blues Traveler sets from The Front on 9/8/90 and from Laguna Seca Daze on 5/30/93.

"Going Down Slow"

Trey introduced this song after the debut performance of "Stash" at Wetlands on 9/13/90 with the words, "We want to thank you for checking out all the new songs we're doing . . . and we're gonna do some more." Of course, to many phans "Going Down Slow" was not a new song—it was written by Jack Dupree and appears on Duane Allman's *Anthology* album. But Phish's version of this song skips along at a much quicker pace than Duane's. Indeed, many phans were pleased with the appearance of this one, as it indicated that Phish's affection for the Allman Brothers Band had not sub-sided. Sadly, Phish's affection for their arrangement subsided, and this song went away quickly.

"Good Times, Bad Times"

On 12/8/95 after viewing Jimmy Page's pants in the Rock and Roll Hall of Fame, Trey dedicated this song to Led Zeppelin—"one of my favorite bands growing up." "Good Times, Bad Times" is one of the few covers that Phish has performed consistently over the course of its career. If you want to sample a number of these, then take a walk through Phishtory and listen to 12/6/86, 6/23/89, 4/12/91, 2/21/93 (bluegrass version with Jeff Mosier), and 6/23/95 (with John Popper).

"Golden Lady"

As you already read in the "Boogie On Reggae Woman" entry, the members of the band indicated that they would have liked to play Stevie Wonder's *Innervisions* as their Halloween 1994 costume. A week and a half earlier, on 10/20/94 at the Mahaffey Theater in St. Petersburg, Florida, they took matters into their own hands with their version of "Golden Lady," a song from this album. Although "Golden Lady" has made the rounds at a sound check or two, it has not returned to show-time performance since that evening.

"Great Gig in the Sky"

Although Fish loves Syd Barrett, he also enjoys the work of Barrett's ex-bandmates as well. He made this abundantly clear when he de-buted this song from Pink Floyd's *Dark Side of the Moon* album at the Western State College Gym in Gunnison, Colorado, on 3/14/93. If you've seen this song live, you know that Fish's interpretation is Phish drama at its highest, with plenty of strobe lights and vacuum. The strobes don't translate very well onto audio tape, but it's possible to hear some bombastic versions of "Great Gig in the Sky" on 8/11/93 (sandwiched between "Mike's Song" and "Weekapaug Groove") or 5/2/94 (as a show opener).

"Have Mercy"

The version of "Have Mercy" that Phish performs is the one popularized by international reggae stars the Mighty Diamonds. Phish does not play the Paul Kennerly–penned "Have Mercy" that the Judds took to number one on the country charts. After a number of memorable performances of this song in 1986, "Have Mercy" disappeared for nearly seven years and then started to emerge in the middle of other songs. To hear the full range of "Have Mercy's," first pick up 4/1/86 or 10/31/86 (with Jah Roy) and then listen to 2/20/93 ("Weekapaug Groove") or 11/12/94 ("Down with Disease").

"Hello My Baby"

After a two-year lull, Phish added a new song to its a cappella repertoire on 9/27/95. "Hello My Baby" was popularized in the 1970s by enigmatic folk singer Leon Redbone. Many phans are happy to have this additional selection as an a cappella possibility, particularly with the two new microphones introduced during the summer of 1995, which maintain the intimate feel of the band's acoustic or a cappella performances while still carrying the music to the back lawns of amphitheaters.

"Help Me"

"Help Me" was composed and originallly performed by Chicago harp master Sonny Boy Williamson. Phish performed this song with the assistance of present-day windy city blues man Sugar Blue at the Aragon Ballroom on 4/10/93.

"Helter Skelter"

Phish performed "Helter Skelter" as part of its Halloween costume on 10/31/94. The song has returned just once, opening the 11/17/94 show at Hara Arena in Dayton.

"High Heel Sneakers"

"High Heel Sneakers" is a classic slice of blues written by Robert Higgenbotham and performed by a number of artists over the years, including Jerry Lee Lewis, Stevie Wonder, José Feliciano, and the Grateful Dead. Phish performed this song at Atlanta's Fox Theater on 4/23/94, aided by the capable hands and nimble fingers of Merle Saunders. The result is a real treat, so find yourself a copy of this show (which also features a guest appearance by Colonel Bruce Hampton during the second set).

"Highway to Hell"

"Highway to Hell" debuted at the Front on 10/1/89. Since then Phish has performed this homage to AC/DC on multiple occasions. One entertaining version of this song took place at the Broome County Arena on 4/9/94. On that evening, after the band performed "Amazing Grace," a number of phans up front began to chant "AC/DC Bag" over and over while the band members retrieved their instruments. Trey turned to the crowd and cupped his hand near his ear as if he were straining to hear them. Then he smiled and said, "We'd like to play one for these people down here." At which point Phish presented them with a smoking AC/DC cover.

"Hold Your Head Up"

The story behind this song is that Fishman really hates it—it is one of the songs that really gets under his skin. At some point during a mideighties practice session the band started into an impromptu version of this song, which Fishman immediately brought to a screeching halt. The other members of the band apologized, promised not to play this song again, and then launched into . . . another version of "Hold Your Head Up." Same result (well perhaps louder screeching). So it went for a long while as Mike Page and Trey continued to bombard the beleaguered drummer with the chorus to this song. Phish repeats this practice nowadays on most occasions when Fish steps out from behind his kit to bask in the solo limelight.

On most of these occasions Trey provides Fish with a nickname as well. A list of these includes Hankrietta (11/13/91), Henrietta Tubman (4/5/93), J. Edgar Hoover (12/7/89), Little John, Friar Tubbs (3/5/93), Lizard Queen (7/12/91), Moses Brown, Moses Heaps, and Moses De Witt (5/15/88), Moses Yastrzemski (2/7/89), Phil Collins (2/25/90), Showboat Gertrude (10/19/91), Sultan of Swat (7/21/91), Tommy Dorsey (4/19/92), Tubbs the Beast Boy (11/19/92), Yo Yo Ma of Vacuum Cleaners (4/17/92), and Zero Man (9/13/90).

"Hold Your Head Up" didn't become "Henrietta's Theme" until 1989; however, the band

Photo credit: Kurt Zinnack

teased this one a few times at earlier shows. For instance, both 8/21/87 and 5/14/88 contain "Hold Your Head Up" riffs along with comments from Trey indicating that Argent is Fish's favorite band. Although "Cold as Ice" briefly supplanted "Hold Your Head Up" in the spring of 1992, "HYHU" remains the musical weapon of choice to bug Fishman (along with "La Bamba"—listen to 11/1/91).

"Honey Pie"

Phish performed this song at the Glens Falls Civic Center on 10/31/94 as part of their White Album set. The band members take turns singing the introductory lines, and before Mike takes over, Trey modifies the lyrics to incorporate Mike's nickname: "If she could only hear Cactus, Cactus would this say. . . ."

"Hoochie Coochie Man"

On 4/10/93 at Chicago's Aragon Ballroom, Phish welcomed local blues artist Sugar Blue onstage to play harmonica and sing, among other songs, this piece of hometown blues by Willie Dixon.

"How High the Moon"

"How High the Moon" is a jazz standard that a number of artists have performed over the years. Charlie Parker and Duke Ellington, for example, have versions of this song among their recorded works. Phish performed this song on a few occasions; for instance, listen to 4/22/90 or the version in the middle of "Colonel Forbin's Ascent" and "Famous Mockingbird" on 3/8/93.

"I Am the Sea"

Phish recreated the sounds of this song to introduce its album selection at the Rosemont Horizon on 10/31/95. After the opening "Thriller" tease faded, Phish drifted into this one, beginning its Halloween costume set of 1995.

"If I Only Had a Brain"

Fish provides lead vocals on this song, the chapter's namesake, which Phish started performing in the spring of 1989. "If I Only Had a Brain," of course, is the Scarecrow's theme from *The Wizard of Oz*. One of the interesting things about this song is the way that it seems to reflect reality, as Fish often seems to forget the words (listen to 4/14/89, which is particularly bad in this regard, and note

Photo credit: Jay Crystal

Trey's comments). Of course, some phans think that Fish only pretends to forget the words as a sort of performance art. That's your call to make—listen to 10/1/89, 5/4/90, 11/14/91, or 10/25/94. One other reason to seek out a version of this song is that Fish usually gargles a verse or two through his vacuum cleaner.

I Know a Little"

"I Know a Little" is a Lynyrd Skynyrd song that appears on that group's *Street Survivors* album. Phish performed this song a few times in 1988. Listen to 5/25/88 for an example.

"I'll Come Running"

Mike sang this song as the band's encore at the Lowell Memorial Auditorium show on 5/16/95. "I'll Come Running" is a Brian Eno song from *Another Green World*. The band members had been singing the praises of this album for a while before this show, so phans weren't totally surprised at the song selection, although some were surprised by the arrangement. Others remain baffled by the fact that the band has not performed it since.

"I'm Blue, I'm Lonesome"

Phish debuted this James B. Smith song with its acoustic lineup at the Hill Auditorium at the University of Michigan on 11/16/94. This show marked the beginning of Reverend Jeff Mosier's week of bluegrass tutorship, and he joined Phish on banjo for each performance of this song through 11/22/94. After a break during the summer of 1995, the band resumed playing this song during the fall (10/13/95 and 12/12/95, for example). If you enjoy Phish's rendition of "I'm Blue, I'm Lonesome," you may want to hear Bill Monroe perform this one. Another version that might interest you appears on the *Bluegrass Reunion* album with David Grisman, James Kerwin, Herb Pederson, Red Allen, Jim Buchanan, and Jerry Garcia (although Jerry doesn't play on "I'm Blue, I'm Lonesome"). Trey dedicated this song to Garcia at Shoreline Amphitheater on 9/30/95.

"I'm So Tired"

Phish performed this one as part of its Halloween costume on 10/31/94. This song remained dormant for a while before Phish played it again on 11/18/95. Some phans think they pulled it out on that second evening to express a bit of exhaustion on their part.

"It's No Good Trying"

Fish debuted this Syd Barrett song at Hampshire College in Amherst, Massachusetts, on 12/7/90. Three weeks later John Popper joined him onstage to add a bit of harmonica to it. By the dawn of the new year this song had disappeared. If you want to hear Barrett's version, check out the *Crazy Diamond* box set.

"I Walk the Line"

Johnny Cash wrote this song, which Mike sang for a few months. Phish debuted its version of this song at the Palace Theater in

Albany on 11/20/92. Sadly, the band stopped playing this tune on 3/9/93.

"I Wanna Be Like You"

This song is taken from the Disney cartoon adaptation of Rudyard Kipling's *The Jungle Book*. Fish premiered this song at the Flynn Theater in 4/4/94. It is well worth listening to this version along with the one eleven days after at the Beacon, because Fish's interplay with the Giant Country Horns is very funny (as is his narration). After hearing these versions, go out and rent the film: That King Louie can swing.

"I Wish"

Stevie Wonder wrote and recorded "I Wish" for his *Songs in the Key of Life* album. Phish performed this bit of funk in the 1984–86 period. You can find this song on 10/30/85.

"Jesus Left Chicago"

Texas's premier power trio, ZZ Top, wrote this song, which appears on their *Tres Hombres* release. Phish has performed this song a few times a year since 1988 (with 1995 as the exception; they played it only once, on 10/31/95). Some interesting versions of this tune include 5/14/88, 11/8/90 (with John Popper on harmonica), 7/24/91 (with the Giant Country Horns), 3/5/93, 8/26/93, and 10/31/95 (with Dave Grippo).

"Johnny B. Goode"

When Chuck Berry recorded this song for Chess Records in 1958 he probably didn't have Johnny B. Fishman in mind. Nonetheless, it's reasonable to assume that Mike, Page, and Trey did think of Fish when they tucked this song into a "Tweezer" at the Nissan Pavilion in Gainesville, Virginia, on 6/17/95. Phish performed the song again, inside "Bowie," on 7/3/95. The third time's the charm here, though, as you'll hear if you listen to the "Johnny B. Goode" that appears as the lone encore at Madison Square Garden on New Year's Eve 1995.

"Jump Monk"

This song sometimes is labeled as Gamehendge jazz because it appears on the commonly circulated 3/12/88 Nectar's Gamehendge set right before "McGrupp and the Watchful Hosemasters." Phish couldn't have known it at the time, but by performing this Charles Mingus tribute to Thelonious Monk right before the Gamehendge set, they sent many a phan down the path to a jazz education. Trey continues to perform "Jump Monk" with Bad Hat and a quote from this song occasionally surfaces in "Bathtub Gin" (4/24/94 for example).

"La Grange"

Another ZZ Top song that Phish continues to perform. Like "Jesus Left Chicago" the original version appears on the group's *Tres Hombres* album. Some fine versions of this song include 2/8/91 and 8/7/93 and 12/29/95 (with Mike's bass teacher Jim Stinnette).

"Light Up or Leave Me Alone"

Phish performed this Traffic song from *Low Spark of High Heeled Boys* at Ian Maclean's farm in Hebron, New York, on 8/21/87. You can also find this song on 5/14/88 and 7/25/88.

"Life on Mars?"

Phish premiered this song at the Will Rogers Auditorium in Fort Worth on 10/13/95. "Life on Mars?" is drawn from David Bowie's *Hunky Dory*.

"Lively Up Yourself"

"Lively Up Yourself" is classic Bob Marley, from his *Natty Dread* album (it also appears on *Songs of Freedom*). Phish performed this song on 4/21/92 at the Redwood Acres Fairgrounds in Eureka, California, with Fish on vocals and Mike on vacuum (his debut). Immediately after this they felt obliged to apologize for their interpretation.

Photo credit: Brett Virmalo

"Lonesome Cowboy Bill"

Fish sang "Lonesome Cowboy Bill," which is a Velvet Underground classic from *Loaded*, on 5/15/95, 6/7/95, and 6/10/95.

"Love You"

"Love You," AKA "Honey Love," is a Syd Barrett tune that originally appeared on *The Madcap Laughs*. Phish's drummer added this one to his expanding catalog of Barrett tunes in 1989 and has continued to perform it ever since (although he played it only once in 1995, on 12/8/95). A number of interesting "Love You" 's have appeared over the years, in particular 10/31/90, 5/17/92 (with birthday monologue), 11/28/92 (with a long vacuum solo and some fine high hat action from Trey), 12/30/92 (another solo), 2/19/93 (with Jimmy Herring and birthday presents for Fish), 8/8/93, and 11/17/94.

"Loving Cup"

"Loving Cup" is a Rolling Stones song from their opus *Exile on Main Street*. When Phish first performed this song live on 2/3/93 at the Portland Expo, Trey announced that Page had refused to play it live until the band toured with a piano. Page still has the piano, so Phish continues to perform this (for example, 8/8/93 and 12/9/95). What a beautiful buzz . . .

"The Maker"

"The Maker" is a Daniel Lanois song from his fine *Acadie* album. Lanois is probably less known to many as a recording artist than as a record producer, perhaps most notably for his work with U2. "The Maker" is a song that the Dave Matthews Band occasionally performs. When DMB opened for Phish at the Oak Mountain Auditorium in Pelham, Alabama, on 10/15/94, Phish invited them onstage for the encore. A jam between the two bands segued into this song.

"Manteca"

"Manteca" is a Dizzy Gillespie–Chano Pozo–Walter Fuller composition that Gillespie often performed with his big band. Gillespie's versions usually contained a meaningful snippet of lyrics at the start, typically "I'll never go back to Georgia," referring to the racial prejudice that Gillespie and his group experienced while performing in that state. His version typically extends for six to ten minutes, far longer than the ones that Phish performs. To hear Phish's version of this song, listen to 9/16/90, 11/14/95 (in the middle of "Stash"), or 4/18/92, which features a "Manteca" reprise.

"Melt the Guns"

"Melt the Guns" is an XTC song from *English Settlement*. Many phans feel that this is a weird song choice, as XTC does not produce the type of music that one normally associates with Phish (although

Paul Fox, the producer of XTC's *Oranges and Lemons*, also produced *Hoist*). Phish's version of "Melt the Guns" can be found on 4/29/87.

"Memories"

Phish first performed this a cappella number at the Somerville Theater on 11/17/90. Since then Phish has rarely sung this one because the band grew dissatisfied with their performance. During a 12/7/91 Middlebury College "Memories" sound check, which appears with most versions of that tape, the band can be heard saying that the song has "gotten all the way up to the level of sucked." "Memories" last appeared in a Phish set list on 7/6/94.

"Minute by Minute"

Fish performed this late-era Doobie Brothers song at Wetlands on 9/13/90. Phish abandoned this tune after the attempt.

"Moose the Mootch"

"Moose the Mootch" is a Charlie Parker bebop composition that he first recorded for Dial Records in 1946. Bird watchers will be pleased to note that Phish performed this song with the Giant Country Horns on 7/12/91.

"Mustang Sally"

This really is a rock-and-roll classic, no matter how many times you've heard your local neighborhood bar band butcher this one. Wilson Pickett offered this song to the world in 1966 as the follow-up to his "Land of 1000 Dances" single. To hear Phish play "Mustang Sally," seek out 10/15/86 or 8/29/87.

"My Generation"

Phish performed this song as its encore at the Rosemont Horizon on 10/31/95. The band elected to perform the Who's electric rocker

Photo credit: Adam Hartman

with acoustic instruments (and afterward destroy some of those instruments onstage). Phish also quoted this song in the middle of the second set "Tweezer" on 6/22/95.

"My Long Journey Home"

This song has confused phans a bit. Some refer to it by this title, some label it "Two Dollar Bill," and some call it both names, depending on the evening. "My Long Journey Home" is the title that most bluegrass artists use for this traditional song. Bill Monroe and his brother Charlie recorded this song in the mid-1930s when they began their careers as a performing team. Phish started performing it with Reverend Jeff Mosier on 11/16/94 and have continued to play it with their acoustic lineup (for instance, on 11/25/95).

"My Mind's Got a Mind of Its Own"

Phish premiered this Jimmy Dale Gilmore song at the Portsmouth Music Hall on 3/7/92. Mike sings this one, which is not a novelty tune but rather a meaningful foray into someone's personal psyche. To hear Gilmore's original version, check out his *After Awhile* album. To hear Mike and the band perform it, listen to the above version, 2/20/93, or 12/4/94. As for a set-list abbreviation, at least one demented phan prefers "MMGAMOIO," although most use "My Mind's."

"Nellie Cane"

"Nellie Cane" premiered at the Mann Music Center on 7/16/93. This is a traditional song that Phish performed frequently, then abruptly abandoned. "Nellie Cane" appeared fifteen times in 1993, twenty-eight times in 1994, and zero times in 1995. For some fine versions listen to 8/21/93 (with Bela Fleck), 4/5/94, or 11/17/94 (with Reverend Jeff Mosier).

"Ob-La-Di Ob-La-Da"

Yes, this song is on the Beatles' White Album, and Phish played it on 10/31/94 at the Glens Fall Civic Center. But this was not the first time that Phish had played this song live onstage. On 5/6/93 at the Palace Theater in Albany, Phish performed the melody in the midst of an intriguing transition from "Mike's Song" to "Rocky Top."

"The Old Home Place"

This song had a very auspicious debut. "The Old Home Place" premiered on 6/26/94 at the Municipal Auditorium in Charleston, West Virginia, after Phish had performed one set of Gamehendge and one set of *Hoist*. This song was written by Dean Webb and Mitch Jayne, two of the original members of the Dillards. Phish

Photo credit: Rich Luzzi

never performed this song live onstage with Reverend Jeff Mosier, perhaps because they already knew this song and didn't need his guidance, although they did play it with him during the 11/19/94 parking lot jam. Unlike on the other Dillards song that Phish has performed, the band typically remains plugged in when they play "The Old Home Place" (for instance, 11/10/95 or 12/7/95).

"On Your Way Down"

"On Your Way Down" appears on Little Feat's *Dixie Chicken* album. Phish began performing it during a short period of Little Feat obsession during 1988–89. You can hear this one on 7/23/88 and 4/15/89, for instance. In case you were unaware, Little Feat traces its roots back to Frank Zappa and the Mothers of Invention, which may have endeared the group to Phish. Founding Little Feat members Lowell George (vocals, guitar) and Roy Estrada (bass) began their careers as Mothers (although Estrada had left the band by the time they recorded *Dixie Chicken*).

"Paul and Silas"

This song has proved confusing for phans and band members alike. "Paul and Silas" is a rollicking bluegrass tune with call-and-response verses. It is often labeled on set lists as "All Night Long" (the song opens with the line "Paul and Silas bound in jail, all night long" repeated three times). "Paul and Silas" is a traditional song that has been arranged by a number of bluegrass pickers, most notably Earl Scruggs. Phish first performed the song at Wetlands on 9/13/90, and it has appeared on set lists intermittently ever since. Two of the stronger versions of "Paul and Silas" are 7/22/93 in Stowe, Vermont, with Gordon Stone on banjo, and 4/12/93 Iowa City, Iowa.

The story would end here, if not for the fact that when Phish first started playing the song in 1990, the band pieced together its version from a recording that did not list the lyrics or even the title. As a result, Phish began performing the tune with its own slightly mangled lyrics under the announced title of "Hall in Solace." The band's version opened, "Hall in solace, bound in jail, all night long." The alternate lyrics mystified bluegrass aphishionados for quite some time, and these phans speculated as to whether or not the band was parodying the song. At some point in 1992, one of these troubled individuals expressed his confusion to Trey, who somewhat sheepishly admitted the band's error. Phish soon reintroduced the song into its repertoire with the traditional lyrics, but it's worth checking out one of the earlier versions, such as 9/13/90 or 5/4/91.

"Peaches En Regalia"

It would be wrong to suggest that "Peaches En Regalia" is the quintessential Frank Zappa song because Zappa's music is so wonderfully eclectic. What can be said is that "Peaches" was probably the first Zappa composition that yanked on the ears of the American public. "Peaches En Regalia" appears on *Hot Rats*, which is a fine introduction to the music of Zappa if you're interested. Phish first performed the song in the mid-1980s (for example, 10/31/86 and 7/23/88). After Frank passed away in late 1993, Phish opened their next live show at Bender Auditorium in Washington, D.C., on 12/28/93 with "Peaches," and Trey quotes it throughout the evening on 12/31/93.

"Phase Dance"

The Pat Metheny Group was one of Trey's early influences. Indeed, as the story goes, on at least one occasion Trey presented some of the Metheny's collaborations with pianist Lyle Mays to Ernie Stires for approval (Stires was not blown away). Phish performed the Mettheny/Mays composition "Phase Dance" in 1987. The original version can be found on the Pat Metheny Group as well as on that band's double-live *Travels*. The most commonly circulated Phish performance of "Phase Dance" appears on the 1987 *Pledge Party* tape.

"Pig in a Pen"

"Pig in a Pen" is a traditional bluegrass song. It appears on *Old and in the Way* with Jerry Garcia, David Grisman, Peter Rowan, Vassar Clements, and John Kahn. Phish premiered this song on the last night of the band's memorable three-show Roxy Theater run in Atlanta on 2/21/93. It should come as little surprise that Atlanta native Reverend Jeff Mosier joined Phish onstage that night for this song. Phish later performed "Pig in a Pen" with Mosier on 11/16/94 and 11/19/94.

"Purple Rain"

If you missed this one, you missed something all right. Fishman debuted this poignant love song by the artist formerly known as Prince at the Mann Music Center on 7/16/93. Fish's interpretation of this one confused and horrified many of those people in attendance. Some phans enjoy "Purple Rain" because it is one of the few Fishman songs that the band tends to segue into without stopping to perform "Hold Your Head Up." For example, listen to 12/30/93, where "Weekapaug Groove" flows into "Purple Rain."

"Pusher Man"

"Pusher Man" is a Curtis Mayfield song. If you want to hear this one in its original context, find the *Superfly* soundtrack. Phish performed this song after Fishman stepped to the front of the stage to sing "Love You" as an encore at Denver's Gothic Theater. Trey explained that they replaced "Hold Your Head" with "Pusher Man" on that evening because it is a song that Fish likes.

"Quadrophenia"

Phish performed the song and the entire album of this name at the Rosemont Horizon on 10/31/95. The band had contacted Who vocalist Roger Daltrey about the possiblity of lending his talents to Phish on this evening, but most phans agree that Page did an admirable job in his place. The songs that Phish performed on that evening that have not yet reappeared on a set list include: "Bell Boy," "Cut My Hair," "Dirty Jobs," "Dr. Jimmy," "5:15," "Helpless Dancer," "I Am the Sea," "I'm One," "Is It In My Head," "I've Had Enough," "Love Reign O'er Me," "Punk Meets the Godfather," and "The Rock."

"Quinn the Eskimo"

If you want to hear Phish's take on this Bob Dylan song, you can find it on a couple of moderately circulated tapes, for instance 4/1/86 and 8/1/87 (soon after which they stopped playing this one). Both the Grateful Dead and Manfred Mann have joined Phish in covering "Quinn the Eskimo." (Manfred Mann's Earth Band took the song to number ten on the pop charts in 1968.)

"Revival"

"Revival" was written by Dickey Betts and appears on the Allman Brothers Band's album *Idlewild South*. Phish performed this song for a short period of time in 1985–86 with Jeff singing lead. Indeed, the band played a few Allman songs during this time, as the Anastasio-Holdsworth guitar attack proved conducive to the dual guitars of the ABB. You can find "Revival" on the 10/30/85 Hunt's tape.

"Revolution #1"

Phish performed the album version of this one (not the single version that Michael Jackson sold to Nike) during the White Album set at the Glens Falls Civic Center on 10/31/94.

"Revolution #9"

Phans will forever associate this song with Jon Fishman's triumphant return to full frontal nudity at Glens Falls on 10/31/94. The band closed its White Album set with this song, re-creating as many of the sounds that appear on the album as possible. While it was interesting to watch and listen, the experience never inspired the primal fear of the Beatles' version. Until Fish lifted his dress over his head, that is. . . .

"Ride Captain Ride"

This is another of the lost Page songs. A Tampa band known as Blues Image recorded the original version of this song, which climbed the charts to number four in 1970. Phish first presented their interpretation of this song in early 1987 and shelved it by the end of 1989 (listen to 3/23/87 or 5/28/89). "Ride Captain Ride" returned twice in December 1992 at The Spectrum in Toronto on 12/12/92 and at Symphony Hall in Springfield, Massachusetts, on 12/30/92.

"Rocky Raccoon"

Okay, now let's see how well you've absorbed your Phishtory. The question is, When Phish performed this song at the Glens Falls Civic Center on 10/31/94 as part of its White Album set, the band altered two letters in the lyrics—how and why? Here's a hint: When

Photo credit: Kurt Zinnack

you listen to the song, pay particular attention to the third-person pronouns. Got that? Okay, then, here we go. . . . The correct answer is that the band changed the word "her" to the word "him" in the line about Nancy. And why did they do this? For Nancy Taube, the him who wrote "I Didn't Know" and "Halley's Comet."

"Rocky Top"

"Rocky Top" was written by Country Music Hall of Fame songwriters Boudleaux and Felice Bryant. A number of artists have recorded this song, including Chet Atkins, Roy Clark, and the Osbornes. Phish began playing this one in the late 1980s and continues to perform it today (most typically as an encore). For some representative versions check out 12/7/89, 5/12/91 (with horn), and 7/20/91 (with horns). By the way, a final fun fact: "Rocky Top" is one of the Aquarium Rescue Unit's favorites—listen to 11/7/91, where Trey sends this one out to them.

"Satin Doll"

"Satin Doll" is one of Duke Ellington's better-known compositions. He composed the music for this one while his friends Billy Strayhorn and Johnny Mercer added the lyrics. Page has sung these lyrics with Phish on a few occasions beginning in 1988 (9/12/88 or 2/25/90, for instance). The band revived the song on 4/12/93 at the

University of Iowa's Student Union Ballroom and dedicated it to Trey's grandmother, who had danced with his grandfather in that very room to the sounds of the Duke Ellington Orchestra. After all, "I wouldn't be here if my grandmother hadn't danced on this very floor with my grandfather to Duke Ellington, and neither would you."

"Scarlet Begonias"

Some phans tend to get a bit worked up when they learn that Phish performed a few Grateful Dead covers in their early years. They want to find copies of these early tapes "to hear Trey kick Jerry's ass." If you find yourself in this category, let me warn you, ass-kicking you will not find in these 1984–85 shows (remember, Trey had only been playing guitar for about four years at this point). What you will find is a clever but otherwise standard take on this tune, although the Scarlet>Fire>Fire idea hints at much of what is to come.

"Shaggy Dog"

Phish debuted this Lightnin' Hopkins tune in 1986 and played it infrequently up until 1992, when it disappeared from live shows. "Shaggy Dog" reappeared once on 10/29/95. If you want to hear Hopkins's original, you can find it on a number of his releases, including one entitled *Shaggy Dog*.

"She Caught the Katy and Left Me a Mule to Ride"

Yes, that's the complete title of this song, which is a Taj Mahal tune. The song appears on a *The Best of Taj Mahal* album if you want to sample his earlier, more traditional blues work. While Taj receives credit as the author of the song, many more people associate it with the Blues Brothers, who performed it onstage and on two of their albums. Phish played "She Caught the Katy and Left Me a

Mule to Ride" in 1986, and it disappeared from set lists a year later. If you want to hear some versions, check out 12/6/86 or 4/29/87.

"Shine"

Tom Marshall joined Phish onstage to sing this one at Madison Square Garden on 12/31/95. Tom appeared in the middle of "Colonel Forbin's Ascent" while Trey began flaunting the band members' other jobs as the creators of time. In order to demonstrate this ability, Tom momentarily returned the arena to 1994, when this Collective Soul song was a ubiquitous radio hit.

"Skin It Back"

"Skin It Back" was the second of three Little Feat songs that Phish introduced and abandoned by the end of the 1980s. The song first appeared on Little Feat's *Don't Fail Me Now* album. If you want to hear Phish perform "Skin It Back," check out 8/21/87 or 7/25/88.

"Sneaking Sally through the Alley"

This song was the title track to Robert Palmer's debut release. "Sneaking Sally through the Alley" is a noteworthy Phish song because it contained the earliest version of the Phish vocal jam. Listen to 5/25/88 or 7/12/88, for instance, and you'll find some interesting stuff going on. "Sneaking Sally" has not been heard from since this time period, although Robert Palmer does make a guest appearance in the song "Tube."

"Somewhere Over the Rainbow"

A number of jazz artists have performed this song over the years (perhaps most notably Chet Baker), so it shouldn't surprise you to learn that Phish has elected to give it a shot as well. Two fine versions are 8/17/92 and 4/20/94, with the Dave Matthews Band.

"Spanish Flea"

This song was written and performed by Herb Alpert and the Tijuana Brass. Alpert, by the way, is the man who cofounded A & M Records with Jerry Moss in 1962. His many other musical accomplishments include writing "Wonderful World" for Sam Cooke. If you listen to Phish's version of this song on 12/1/84, you may recognize it as the theme to the *Dating Game*. The "Spanish Flea" on 12/1/84 is also interesting because the Dude of Life introduces the entire band, including Jeff and Marc.

"Sparks"

Prior to 10/31/95, "Sparks" was the only Who song that had appeared in Phish's live repertoire (except for a few teases and quotes). This song is an instrumental from *Tommy*. Phish began playing this song in 1987 (listen to 3/23/87, for instance). In the years since, "Sparks" has returned in the middle of some particularly creative jams while the band evaluates its next move. For instance, listen to 8/7/93, 8/14/93, or 5/7/94. As an added bonus, if you are fortunate enough to see Phish perform "Sparks," Trey usually will throw in a Pete Townshend windmill or two.

"Suspicious Minds"

Mark James wrote this song for Elvis Presley, who recorded it in 1969. "Suspicious Minds" became his first number-one song on the pop charts in seven-and-a-half years. The Fine Young Cannibals also took a stab at this one in 1986. However, you've never really heard this song if you haven't heard it crooned by a man with a scratchy, tour-ravaged voice wearing a dress and a cape. Phish debuted "Suspicious Minds" at the Shoreline Amphitheater on 9/30/95 and performed it throughout the fall. Listen for Page, by the way, who keeps many of these versions interesting.

"Sweet Adeline"

"Sweet Adeline" was the second a cappella number the band performed, following "Carolina" by a few months. The band's arrangement of this song, as Trey informs a German audience on 6/23/92, dates back one hundred years. The only slight variations that you'll sometimes find in the band's interpretation hinges on whether Fish pauses before singing his "my Adeline" line toward the end of the song. If he does hesitate, the audience typically cheers, thinking that the song is complete, so Phish must wait out that interruption. For instance, contrast 12/5/95 (pause) with 12/9/95 (no pause). One noteworthy "Sweet Adeline" took place on 5/16/92 at Boston's Orpheum Theater, where the band performed the song without any amplification in its largest space to date. ("I'd like to see Metallica try that," Trey says in thanking the audience for remaining quiet.)

"Swing Low, Sweet Chariot"

Phish has performed an instrumental version of this traditional spiritual a number of times over the years. For a few examples of "Swing Low, Sweet Chariot" in its glory, listen to 10/31/86, 10/20/89, or 11/16/94 (with vocals).

"Take Me to the River"

Phish performed this song on 11/21/95. "Take Me to the River" appears on the Talking Heads' *More Songs about Buildings and Food*, although it was written by Al Green. In the mid-1970s the Reverend Green retired from popular music to become a minister at the Full Tabernacle Church in Memphis. Indeed, avid readers of the *Doniac Schvice* may remember the time that Fish abandoned his "Forum" responsibilities to go off to Memphis in search of Reverend Al (who, for what it's worth, also was elected to the Rock and Roll Hall of Fame).

"Take the A Train"

Although Sir Duke didn't write this one, "Take the A Train" became one of Duke Ellington's signature pieces. The song was composed by his longtime collaborator and the pianist in many of his orchestras, Billy Strayhorn. Phish has performed a number of memorable versions of this song over the years, many of which have drifted off into other jazz standards before returning to "A Train." For a representative sample listen to 4/29/87 (on Duke's birthday), 9/24/88, 11/7/91 (with scats by Oteil Burbridge), 11/14/91 (with a holiday message), 8/17/92, and 4/13/94.

"Tennessee Waltz"

Phish has performed this song a few times with some assistance. Fiddler Dick Solberg and acoustic guitarist Jeff Walton joined Phish at the Palace Theater in Albany on 5/6/93. Reverend Jeff Mosier helped them with this one on 11/16/94 and 11/19/94 (during the parking lot jam, not the show). Pee Wee King and Redd Stewart wrote "Tennessee Waltz," which has been interpreted by many artists over the years, including Roy Acuff and Patti Page.

"Terrapin"

"Terrapin" is another of Fish's Syd Barrett covers. The original appears on Barrett's *The Madcap Laughs*. To hear some "Terrapin"s check out 9/12/87, 4/30/89, 1/27/90, and 7/1/94. By the way, the version of "Terrapin" on 12/29/92 has a very long trombone solo.

"Three Little Birds"

"Three Little Birds" is a Bob Marley song from his *Exodus* album. It is also another song that the Dave Matthews Band performs. So it should not surprise you to learn that Phish performed this song with Dave Matthews on guitar and Leroi Moore on saxophone when Phish played in their home region at Nissan Pavilion in Gainesville, Virginia, on 6/17/95.

"Timber (Jerry)"

Josh White and Sam Gary composed this song, which guitarist-vocalist White first recorded in the 1930s. Folk blues singer Odetta picked this one up in the 1960s and performed it quite often in concert (you can hear her version on *The Essential Odetta* and a couple of other recordings). Phish played the song for a while in the 1980s then shelved it after 6/16/90. "Timber (Jerry)" made a brief reappearance on 12/30/92. After this point, word surfaced that the band did not intend to perform the song again. However, Phish brought it back for the local phans at Sugarbush on 7/3/95 and continued to play it through December. If you want to hear some early performances of this song, check out 8/29/87, 9/12/88, or 2/7/89.

Photo credit: Rich Luzzi

"Time Loves a Hero"

"Time Loves a Hero" is the third Little Feat song that Phish played and then dropped during 1988–89 period. You can hear two of Phish's few performances of "Time Loves a Hero" on 10/31/88 and 4/15/89. Little Feat's original appears on its album of the same name.

"Touch Me"

"Ladies and gentlemen, the Lizard Queen . . . Henrietta!" So cried Trey a few times during the 1991 summer horn tour introducing "the fourth member of the Giant Country Horns" just before Fish offered his interpretation of this song. "Touch Me" is from the Doors' *Soft Parade* album. If you want to hear this one, check out the song's debut, 7/11/91, and its revival on 12/3/94.

"Tush"

Yes, Phish played this one, too—a ZZ Top smash from *Fandango*. In particular, listen to 12/6/86, when Trey introduces it as a Barry Manilow song. If you're a big fan of "Tush," you may also want to hear 8/1/87.

"Uncle Pen"

"This a Bill Monroe tune that we learned specifically for the trip out west. . . . We're just going to miss the bluegrass festival in Telluride," Trey announced from the stage at J. J. McCabes in Boulder on 4/5/90 before performing this song. "Uncle Pen" salutes Pendleton Vandiver, Bill Monroe's uncle and musical mentor. The members of Phish particularly enjoy this tune because two of the traditional songs mentioned in the lyrics, "Soldier's Joy" and "Boston Boy," are also performed within the song itself. Phish continues to play "Uncle Pen," for instance on 6/23/92, 3/5/93, 5/6/94, and 10/13/95.

"Undone"

Until Phish covers Rush, Canadians will have to be happy with the Guess Who. Mr. Johnny B. Fishman made his neighbors to the north very happy by lending his vocals to this song on a few occasions (although on 12/7/89 he attributes the composition to Frank Sinatra).

"Walk Away"

Joe Walsh and his bandmates in the James Gang recorded the original version of this song, which appears on *Thirds*. Phish has performed "Walk Away" since 1988, with Page doing a very credible Joe Walsh (7/23/88 and 11/3/88). Some of the more interesting versions emerge from other songs, most typically "Tweezer" (for instance, 2/20/93, 4/30/93, 7/22/93, and 5/7/94, but also hear 8/14/93, where it appears in "Run Like an Antelope").

"When Something Is Wrong with My Baby"

This song originated as a moving soul 45 recorded by Sam and Dave. Phish performed the tune briefly in the spring of 1993, then stopped. If you want to hear "When Something Is Wrong with My Baby," listen to one of the versions that Phish performed as an encore, either 4/25/93 or 4/30/93.

"While My Guitar Gently Weeps"

When considering the Beatles' White Album one cannot ignore the estimable contributions of George Harrison. Phish made this clear with its interpretation of this song at the Glens Falls Civic Center on 10/31/94. (Trey's guitar solo stirred more than a few phans who had started to nod off due to the show's late start.) Phans who hoped that this song would return didn't have to hold their breaths for very long because "While My Guitar Gently Weeps" closed the first set of the very next show on 11/2/94 (it was the only White Album song performed that evening). Phish has performed a number of mammoth versions of this song since then, with some notable ones taking place on 6/14/95 and 12/11/95 (with Warren Haynes). As one final point, many phans abbreviate this song as "WMGGW," while others prefer to write "Guitar" as their shorthand. Those in the latter category think "Guitar" captures the essence of the song much better than "WMGGW" (and many have an obsession with vowels).

"Whipping Post"

Phish initially covered this song faithfully, with Jeff singing lead and exchanging some guitar riffs with Trey. After Jeff's departure Trey assumed vocal duties, with Mike and Page compensating for the lost second guitar. The song endured a final change and a greater indignity when Fish began to contribute lead vocals and a vacuum solo to it. No, the true indignity took place on 10/28/91, when Fish made his debut on fretless guitar during "Whipping Post." The band has performed this song only three times since then (12/6/91, 12/5/92, and 4/20/93). For a sampling of Phish "Whipping Post"'s listen to the above versions along with 11/23/85, 12/6/86, 5/25/88, 11/3/88, 2/7/89, and 6/5/90 (with a "What I Am" quote).

White Album

Phish performed the Beatles' White Album as its Halloween costume on 10/31/94. The band performed every song on the album except "Birthday" (they quoted a bit during the Brad Sands cake ceremonies) and "Good Night" (Paul played the original version as outro music when the band left the stage after the second set). The White Album songs that Phish has not played since that evening include "The Continuing Story of Bungalow Bill," "Dear Prudence," "Don't Pass Me By," "Everybody's Got Something to Hide Except Me and My Monkey," "Glass Onion," "Happiness Is a Warm Gun," "Honey Pie," "I Will," "Julia," "Long, Long, Long," "Martha My Dear," "Mother Nature's Son," "Ob-La-Di, Ob-La-Da," "Piggies," "Revolution #1," "Rocky Raccoon," "Savoy Truffle," "Sexy Sadie," "Wild Honey Pie," "Yer Blues."

"Who by Fire"

"Who by Fire" is a Leonard Cohen song that Phish has performed just once, on 4/23/94 at the Fox Theater in Atlanta. Colonel Bruce sat in for this one, which may explain the admirable yet curious song selection. "Who by Fire" appears on Cohen's *New Skin for the Old Ceremony* release.

"Why Don't We Do It in the Road"

Fish had the good fortune to sing this one (surprise, surprise) as part of the White Album set at the Glens Falls Civic Center on 10/31/94. Unlike most of the other White Album tunes, the band continued to perform this song, on 12/10/94 and 6/25/95.

"Why Don't You Love Me"

On 3/23/87 at Nectar's, Phish performed a funked-up version of Hank Williams's "Why Don't You Love Me." Many phans feel that this arrangement has a Red Hot Chili Peppers feel to it. Elvis Costello recorded a more traditional version of this song on his *Almost Blue* release. Williams's original can be found on *Best of the Early Years*.

"Wild Child"

Lou Reed fans will want to hear the band's take on this one. "Wild Child" appeared on Reed's album of the same title and also on the *Walk On the Wild Side* greatest hits collection. Phish speeds this one up a bit and also adds a brief jam behind Trey's vocals which emulate Reed's own phrasing. You can find a version of "Wild Child" on 9/8/88.

"Wind Beneath My Wings"

Oh, the tears that were shed on the night that Phish performed this song. "Wind Beneath My Wings" is the "don't you know that you're my hero" song from *Beaches*. On 11/28/95 at the Civic Coliseum in Knoxville, the band brought out Colonel Bruce Hampton, retired, who sat onstage and read a newspaper while Fish belted this one out in his honor. Listen to the other band members' comments after this one and prepare to weep.

"Wipeout"

The Surfaris rode this California classic all the way to number two in 1963 and then jumped on board again for a return trip up the charts to number sixteen in 1966. What the Surfaris failed to do, and what any rational person would realize needs to be done, was to add a vacuum cleaner solo into the mix. Fortunately, that's why we have Phish. At the Capitol Theater in Port Chester on 4/27/91 they finally added the bit of Electrolux that the Surfaris had missed. Phish also performed a bit of this song to open the second set at Northwestern University on 4/15/91, alas without the vacuum solo.

"Ya Mar"

This one made it into the Phish repertoire thanks to a few afternoons that Mike spent poolside with his father in the Bahamas. The band that entertained the Gordons was a local calypso group called the Mustangs. Mike enjoyed listening to them, and he purchased a copy of their tape. Sadly, when he listened to it he discovered that the studio versions of the songs he had enjoyed had been altered, as the producer had added a profusion of keyboards. The only song that approached the version that Mike had enjoyed in the pool was "Ya Mar," which joined the live Phish gumbo 1987. A number of entertaining versions of this song have appeared over the years, many of which contain bonus "Oh Kee Pah"s. For instance, listen to 6/20/88 (with Jah Roy), 8/3/91, 4/29/93, or 6/25/95.

"Yerushalim Shel Zahav"

This haunting Israeli folk song, which translates as "Jerusalem, City of Gold," was written by Israeli folk legend Naomi Scheimer-Sapir. The song relates the hope for a Jewish homeland despite the wars and wandering experienced by the Jewish people over the years. "Yerushalim Shel Zahav" debuted in haunting harmony at the Mann Music Center on 7/16/93. This is also the song that appears in "Demand" on *Hoist*. (The band re-created that version of the song at the Municipal Auditorium in Charleston, West Virginia, on 6/26/94.) Other versions of this song to hear include both 7/23/93 and 7/2/94, when it appears in "Mike's Groove," and 6/30/94, when Phish performs it in "You Enjoy Myself."

"Won't You Come Home Bill Bailey"

Dr. Jack McConnell has joined Phish onstage once a year since 1993 to sing this song and join his son, the Chairman of the Boards, for a bit of boogie-woogie piano. If you want to hear the McConnells in action, listen to 7/28/93, 4/22/94, or 11/18/95.

4 secret language

ome parts of the Phish experience you just can't hear on tape. Actually, in many cases you can hear something (because the audience is going berserk), but you can't determine the source of their merriment or horror. This chapter will help to identify some of those mysterious moments and to recall some of them, if you witnessed any of the events described here. In recent years Phish has started to cut back on some of this behavior for fear that it has overshadowed their music. However, many phans feel that rather than overshadow the music, these actions have complemented it and enhanced their concert experiences, particularly because much of the behavior reinforces the special bond that exists between Phish and its phans.

Blades

On 9/28/91 Phish performed in Buffalo, New York, at a venue known as the Rink, which was built to accommodate roller-skating. Given the fact that Trey is an avid hockey fan and player, it may not surprise you to learn that his wheels were spinning as he approached this gig. As the band completed "I Am Hydrogen," Trey strapped on some in-line skates and grabbed a wireless guitar. As the momentum built in "Weekapaug Groove," he stepped off the stage and started into the crowd, skating and soloing (inducing only one minor injury in the process).

Big Ball Jam

The big ball jam was inspired by the band's experience at the Earth Day show in Eugene on 4/22/92. Audience members had brought a number of large bouncing globes to the show and began punching them up and down, which in turn inspired the band to begin playing somewhat haphazardly in synch with the balls.

When Phish emerged to open its fall tour nearly seven months later at St. Michael's College on 11/19/92, the band had given that initial germ of an idea a bit more focus. Pete Schall brought four large inflated orange balls to the stage and distributed them to the audience, with no further word from the band except, "This is a special song we wrote for Pete—it goes something like this." Then, as the balls were knocked about by the audience members, the band responded musically, based on the impact and nature of each audience jab. Admittedly, the initial big ball jam (BBJ) ended a bit awkwardly, as the audience kept one of the balls. Eventually, however, the segment would come to conclude with the band members linking arms with Pete at the front of the stage, producing a giant hoop into which intrepid audience members could toss the balls.

"You've just taken part in the first big ball jam," Trey announced to the appreciative phans at St. Michael's after the inaugural effort. Then he explained the theory of the jam, which would "allow the audience to jam the band for that period of the show." When the audience decided that they were done, they could return the balls to the stage. As for the crowd's initial efforts, Trey said, "I thought that was some good jamming . . . pretty good."

Future audiences had additional chances to jam the band. The BBJ took place at a few more shows during Phish's tour over the next few months, although not without the occasional mishap. Paul was struck at the sound board and Chris was hit at the light board at least once apiece. The whole idea made the tapers pretty nervous as well. In turn, the band wasn't sure if they would retire the BBJ after that brief November–December run. However, at the Portland Expo show that opened the band's late winter–spring tour on 2/3/93, a phan cried out, "Give us the balls!" when Fish stepped up for "Terrapin." So they did, with Fish on vacuum and Trey on drums. As of late, however, due to the larger arena sizes (and due to an influx of new ideas) the balls have gone on hiatus.

The Chess Game

The members of the band have long entertained themselves on the road with some friendly (and unfriendly) games of chess. The fall 1994 edition of the *Schvice* reported the dramatic conclusion to the McConnell-Fishman series in which Page captured the twenty-third and decisive game after three consecutive tournament victories by Fish.

Ever willing to break down the traditional walls between band and phan, Phish channeled their love for the game into an entertaining and innovative interactive competition. When the band emerged out west to begin their fall 1995 tour, a large chessboard with Velcro pieces appeared behind Page. At Shoreline Amphitheater on 9/30/95, Trey introduced the concept to the audience and explained how the game would operate. In its final version, when Phish took the stage at the beginning of the show, the board was lowered and Page made the band's moves. The audience members then huddled at the Greenpeace table during the set break to select collectively a move that an audience representative would then reproduce onstage before the second set. Now, as you may note, there was some disparity here—the band was able to think about its move for an entire day while the audience had about an hour (followed by some fevered debates and occasional browbeating at the Greenpeace table).

A few of the chess moves provided some interesting musical interludes. For instance, listen to the initial chess moves, made on

9/30/95, and you can hear the band jamming on a "White Rabbit" theme. During the next show, 10/2/95 at the Seattle Arena, listen for the distinctive sound of "Night Moves." The band also provides musical accompaniment to the start of the second game on 11/16/95 at the Auditorium in West Palm Beach.

As you might imagine, the chess game also provided a few additional moments of random entertainment. On Halloween, for example, after a furious debate at the Greenpeace table, the audience chess mover, a tour rat named Squirrel, who appeared in costume before his hometown crowd, was so overwhelmed with the moment and the gravity of his responsibility that he looked at the board and blanked out. Listen to Trey laugh and the audience jeer as he announces, "The Wookie is incapable of making a move, so we'll skip the audience chess move tonight," initiating a flurry of comments by the other band members. Another interesting exchange took place at the Mullins Center shows. On the first night the audience chess mover was the University of Massachusetts's basketball mascot, the Minute Man. Undaunted by this, the band met Dick Vitale before the next night's show ("that's right, bay-bee") and tried to convince him to come onstage to make their move. Sadly, Dickey V. had to leave to prep for the UMass–Wake Forest game that took place at the Mullins Center on the next night, so Page performed the move as usual. Incidentally, Trey did dedicate "Lizards" to their new friend, and Dickey V. had some kind words to say about the band during ESPN's coverage of the basketball game the next night.

In case you fixate on wins and losses, here are the chess game results. The audience opted to topple its king at the Sundome in Tampa, Florida, on 11/15/95, conceding the first match to the band. When a second game began at the Auditorium in West Palm Beach on the next night, audience forces mobilized. As the tour headed north up the East Coast, some phans tried to commit to making it to the Greenpeace table during the set break (as opposed to just watching the audience move and griping about it). The band grew a bit bold (and perhaps a bit cocky), ultimately electing to concede on New Year's Eve and knotting the series at one game apiece.

Photo credit: Arch Stanton

Gig Jigs

Okay, okay, this title is made up. But in order to identify all of the onstage behavior that doesn't translate onto tapes, the various choreographed and spontaneous dance moves that the band members perform can't be ignored. For instance, Trey and Mike often perform a brief stepping routine during "Guelah Papyrus." The pair also present an occasional samba during "Landlady" and "Punch You in the Eye," which they have taught to the audience (for instance, 2/5/93 during "PYITE," the "Punch You in the Eye" storm dance). In a similar spirit, Trey and Mike have been known to drop onto their backs for a synchronized ballet–bicycling demonstration during "I Am Hydrogen." Finally, sometimes the duo slip into a weird pattern whereby they walk to and fro diagonally from their respective traditional spots in a manner that seems simultaneously purposeful and random.

While on the topic of limber stage behavior, here are a few more things to look for (or to listen for if you enjoy hearing some mis-placed cheering on a tape): Trey occasionally runs around like a man possessed while Chris pounds the strobes during "BBFCFM." (On a really wild night he'll pick up his megaphone, start swinging it around, and pretend to throw it into the audience. On a wilder night he may do the same with his guitar.) At other times, Mike and Trey involve themselves in what appears to be a twisted vari-ation on the elementary school recess favorite, freeze tag. Some-times Fish will emerge from behind his drum kit to play along, while Page in particular hangs back and saturates the stage with noise.

The Gliders

The Gliders were exercising devices that people could step on to slide back and forth while remaining stationary. Trey and Mike did just that when the band incorporated the Gliders into their stage presentation in late 1992. Of course, the two songs ready-made for this invention were "Glide" and "It's Ice." The imagery of the latter song proved to be the more common source for Glider action, since Trey, the lifelong hockey player and fan, had an opportunity to showcase his skills. However, this is not to downplay the subtle grace and beauty provided by the gliding Michael Gordon.

Macaroni and Cheese Dinner

Phish has tossed boxes of macaroni and cheese into the audience on a few separate occasions. This practice began at an early Slade Hall show at UVM. A few years later, on the occasion of the band's last Vermont Halloween spectacular at Goddard College, the group also distributed boxes of mac and cheese. A great horned Trey joined with Page, Mike, and Fish to hand store brand boxes of macaroni and cheese to the masses. The band then jammed with the audience during the "David Bowie" intro while the audience members kept the beat along with their new treasured holiday treats. Also, many a phan enjoyed the food product in the early hours of the morning at the end of this crowded, exhausting show.

In the spring of 1994 the band repeated the experiment, throwing boxes into the audience at the Warfield Theater on 5/27/94, the final night of a three-show run. The events leading up to this moment help to set the scene and are fascinating. Toward the end of the second set, the band launched into "Mike's Song," which did not pass into "I Am Hydrogen" but rather into the inchoate debut version of "Simple." "Simple," in turn, led back into "Mike's," but the ensuing jam was a bit more restrained than usual as the band drifted to a seemingly hesitant stop. At this point Andrea Baker stepped on stage and strolled up to Trey's microphone. Without uttering another word she reared back and warbled three minutes of an opera aria ("O Mio Bambino Caro"). Then she swiftly stopped, bowed, and departed to the enthusiastic if bewildered applause of the audience. While she moved offstage, Brad Sands and a few other crew members walked past and started pelting phans with boxes of macaroni and cheese.

A few hundred boxes later, without any prompting from Phish, people started shaking the Flintstones pasta containers like maracas. The band remained silent until Page briefly tickled the opening piano riff to "Possum." Then Fishman stepped in and began drumming in time with the audience. He continued doing this for a minute or two until Mike counted out the song. However, before the band drove full tilt into "Possum," Trey offered up a musical wink to the brand of macaroni and cheese with a brief performance of the *Flintstones* theme. Then, after the band had completed the first verse of "Possum," Fishman stood up and repeatedly barked, "Shake your macaroni! Shake it! Shake it!" The audience gleefully complied. The band responded to these rhythms, jamming with their phans for a frenzied five minutes before returning to complete a smoking "Possum."

Mmmmm . . . Chocolate

Halloween is a time for dressing up and scaring your friends (which Phish did admirably on 10/31/95 with its *Thriller* teases). But most of all Halloween is a time for candy. Fortunately, Phish is in touch with this. As a result, when Halloween returned to the band's tour docket in 1994, Phish fashioned some appropriate chocolate treats that were handed to phans as they walked into Glens Falls Civic Center—chocolate coins embossed with the band's logo and the date and venue of the show. The band repeated this tasty offering at the 1995 Halloween show at Rosemont Horizon. Oh yeah, and if you want to hear Trey-Homer drool over chocolate, listen to the 12/1/95 show from Hershey, Pennsylvania.

Ping-Pong Balls

As the band members entered the giant kosher hot dog on New Year's Eve 1994 and sailed across the audience, they grabbed handfuls of Ping-Pong balls, proudly emblazoned with the Phish logo, and began throwing them at members of the crowd. The assault reached a fevered pitch as the hot dog hesitated just above the taper section. A wild melee ensued, with the tapers grabbing the balls and returning fire.

Rubber Chickens

Rubber chickens have served as the calling cards of the Dude of Life. On those increasingly rare circumstances in which he takes the stage with Phish, he often has tried to win some unconditional love with sensational free gifts: chickens. Many of these chickens have been signed by the band members and include messages and phrases that are often completed on other chickens. For example, one chicken said, "The dust bunnies in my house are so tough . . . the other night I went to bed with my Dustbuster on the nightstand next to me . . ." The second chicken read, ". . . and when I woke up there was a dust horse head in my bed."

Secret Language

As Phish returned for the second set on the first date of the 1992 spring tour at the Portsmouth Music Hall (3/6/92), Trey stopped the music after two songs to make an announcement. He revealed that the band had decided during the set break to clue the audience in on the band's secret language. Trey indicated that the band had developed musical signals that allowed them to talk with each other onstage. He then explained that he would let the audience in on the language as well so that they could participate. The idea was that the band would perform its signals, inducing a collective response from those in the know while confounding the people at the show who were not aware of the language.

In order to understand better the band's ability to confuse and amuse, it is necessary to explain the language. As Trey described it, each member of the band has a particular trill that he can perform on his instrument that allows everyone to know a signal is coming (everyone except Fish, that is—Trey explained that he isn't allowed to speak the language onstage because he talks too much the rest of the time). Once the initial call is made, Trey performs one of the five signals. The first (and most common) signal occurs when he plays the first few lines of the *Simpsons* theme song. The audience of course is supposed to respond with loud Homer Simpsonesque cries of "D'Oh!" Next is the "all fall down" signal. For this one Trey plays a series of descending notes on his guitar, which is supposed to trigger everyone in the audience to collapse to the floor (until Fish hits his high hat to call everyone back up). The third signal is produced when Trey plays a bit of the chorus to the Byrds' "Turn, Turn, Turn." In this case the audience is supposed to turn around to the rear of the hall and cheer as if the band were playing back there (this one's a real ego booster for Chris and Paul). The fourth of the original signals is a circus theme similar to the one played at the beginning of "Esther." This is the signal for everyone in the audience to sing a random note. Finally, there's the "asshole in the front row signal," which Trey triggers by strumming a few notes of "Me and My Arrow." This clues everyone in that he intends to point at someone. If you want to hear Trey's description of the language, listen to 3/6/92, 3/13/92, 3/20/92, 4/22/92 (West Coast debut), and 5/14/92. Also, the band later introduced another signal. Trey makes a few sharp sawing noises across his guitar, after which people are supposed to scream "Aww fuck!" as if their fingers had been sliced off.

Those of you who are astute tape collectors and listeners are no doubt aware that although 3/6/92 represents the first time that the band taught the secret language to phans, Phish had been using the language themselves for a few years to trigger changes in tempo and musical direction along with some weird effects (collective spasmodic laughter). These earlier signals are often easy to find because the musical phrase that announces a signal is to follow sounds like the *Charlie Chan* theme. For some instances of these early language appearances, pull out your tapes and listen to 6/23/89 ("Lizards," "Run Like an Antelope"), 9/16/90 ("Antelope"), 11/2/90 ("Possum"), 10/13/91 ("David Bowie"), and many, many more—from 1989 on in particular, listen carefully during "Antelope," "Possum," and "Bowie."

Silent Jam

The silent jam evolved out of the section of "Foam" that becomes quieter and quieter. Eventually, Trey began taking that segment all the way down to silence while at the same time continuing to manipulate his fingers along the guitar as if he were still playing. The other band members began contributing to this moment as well, by pretending to perform their instruments. But it's not quite accurate to say that they were pretending to perform—they actually were performing, miming the appropriate notes on their instruments for a jam that played silently in their heads (for instance listen to the 8/28/93 "Foam").

From this beginning the band has performed some truly monumental jams during other songs as well. For instance, at Knickerbocker Arena in Albany, New York, on 12/9/95 the band played a raging silent jam that really needed to be seen to be appreciated. In the middle of "You Enjoy Myself," the band brought the music to silence and then built the jam up again, only they did so without actually producing any sound from their instruments. This silent jam close cascaded upward over a thirty-second span, ultimately ending in an all-out screamer that doesn't quite make it onto tape. Phans who were there, particularly those close enough to really watch the band in action, were curdled by that raging silent jam.

Somewhat Less Secret Language

As Trey has explained, the intent of the secret language is to surprise those persons who come to a show and are unaware of the existence of the language. On New Year's Eve, 1992, nearly nine months after Trey explicitly introduced the language to phans, the band attempted a variation on the theme. As phans entered Boston's Matthews Arena, they were handed flyers that revealed the band's plan of action. The flyers explained that since the show would be broadcast on Boston's WBCN, the band had been "blessed with the opportunity to play with people's minds." In this instance the language was modified to visual clues so that a radio listener would have no idea why the audience was responding in such a curious, collective manner. The flyers instructed phans to look at the signs that Trey would hold and then respond accordingly, with reactions ranging from a foot stomp, one loud clap, a whistle, hysterical screams, yays and boos, finger snaps, cries of "Eggplant!" and finally the ever popular "lip-flop" (flopping one's lips with one finger while humming). And the results? . . . Find yourself a copy of the simulcast and listen particularly closely to "I Didn't Know," "Colonel Forbin's Ascent," and "Harpua."

Trading Places Jam

The trading places jam debuted at the Hampton Coliseum on 11/25/95 and was truly a sight to behold (if you have the tape, it's not so bad to hear either). The jam took place out of "Mike's Song." As the band drifted out of that song and into a groove, Page stood up and walked over to the drums. Fish in turn picked up Mike's bass, Mike moved to the guitar, and Trey played on the piano. They continued jamming in this fashion for a little while longer until the clockwise rotation began again. The jam concluded after the band had completed an entire rotation. The jam remains cohesive because, regardless of the proficiency of the individual band members on particular instruments, each of them continues to listen to the others (no small feat when one is not performing on one's usual instrument). An abbreviated trading places jam also took place at the Spectrum in Philadelphia on 12/15/95.

Trampolines

Trampolines are said to be good for the heart—supposedly they promote good circulation. If this is the case, Trey's and Mike's cardiologists must be proud. Ever since the trampolines first appeared in 1989, the two have perfected an orchestrated trampoline routine that they present while continuing to play their guitars. Most typically, Trey and Mike have taken to the tramps during "Mike's Song" and "You Enjoy Myself." However, a few other tunes have also served as springboards, such as "Walk Away."

An interesting evolution in the trampoline jam took place after Trey tore all the ligaments in his ankle at the Buffalo show on 4/10/94. While Trey could continue to play, he could no longer perform on the trampoline. Mike, ever a booster of good circulatory health, of course, was not about to stop. So, for the first tramp show after the mishap, at Snively Arena on 4/11/94, Trey announced, "Ladies and gentlemen, there's been a slight change in the program. The part of the trampoline jumper will not be performed by Trey tonight but will be performed by his understudy Brad— the guy who throws the balls out." Brad then took to the tramp carrying an inflatable guitar and attempted the routine. As the tour continued south, Trey brought audience volunteers on stage to perform in his place, and on one notable instance Dave Matthews stepped in (at the Virginia Horse Center on 4/20/94).

Some fine jokes have ensued as well. For instance, John Popper took the stage with Phish at Roseland Ballroom on 3/14/92 to join them in a trampoline jam. Sadly, he broke right through the tramp. A similar thing happened on 7/27/93 at the Classic Amphitheater as a wheelchair-bound Popper dropped down and crashed through a tramp (actually, it was a prop tramp and a prop Popper).

Photo credit: Stew Robertson

You also may wonder what happens to the trampolines when they become worn and lose their spring. On a few occasions the band has offered them to the audience. The last time this occurred from the stage was at the Portsmouth Music Hall on 12/7/91. On that night, just before the encores, Trey announced that Phish had returned from a long tour and their trampolines were a bit worn, so they had decided to give them away. Eager hands rushed forward and gripped the tramps, which found new owners peacefully after a few rounds of rock-paper-scissors. Eventually everything worked out for the best, with one proud owner performing his own tramp routine during "Golgi Apparatus."

5 phriends

Dave Abrahams

Dave Abrahams is the childhood friend of Trey who bears more than a passing resemblance to Rutherford the Brave. No, strike that—it is Rutherford who "looks too much like Dave." But Dave is not the only member of his family to appear in a Phish song. His mother is Guelah of "Papyrus" fame. His father, Elihu, is seen dancing on the bed in "Sample in a Jar."

Dave also has contributed directly to a few Phish songs, including "Glide," "Runaway Jim," "Slave to the Traffic Light," and, of course, "Dave's Energy Guide."

Aquarium Rescue Unit

The Aquarium Rescue Unit's (r)evolving lineups have featured some of the most talented musicians performing today. The ARU personnel have included Reverend Jeff Mosier, Matt Mundy, Jimmy Herring, Oteil Burbridge, Kofi Burbridge, Jeff Sipe (Apt. Q258), and, of course, Colonel Bruce Hampton, retired. The group's musical style reflects the band members' various influences from blue-grass to funk to jazz to southern rock.

Colonel Bruce provided the impetus for the group's formation. The initial lineup included Hampton, Mosier, Oteil, and Sipe—the latter two were discovered at separate wedding gigs. Herring came along in 1990, as did Mundy, to solidify the roster that remained in place for another four years. At that point the grind of constant touring finally wore down Mundy and later the Colonel himself, who retired once again to form a somewhat more sedentary outfit, the Fiji Mariners.

The two bands have collaborated on a number of occasions. For instance, listen to 5/5/93 at the Palace Theater, Albany, in which the second set closes with a jam out of "You Enjoy Myself" featuring the entire ARU lineup (ARU opened for Phish that evening). Also, Jimmy Herring appeared for the last three songs of the second set at the Roxy Theater in Atlanta on 2/19/93. The colonel joined Phish for "You Enjoy Myself" and "Who by Fire" in Atlanta at the Fox Theater on 4/23/94. The members of Phish have reciprocated as well—for instance, Fish played vacuum cleaner with ARU at Night-stage in Cambridge on 5/11/93. Mike joined ARU on bass at the Paradise Theater in Boston on 3/9/94. Page performed with the band at KD Churchills in Burlington on 3/21/93. Lastly, Trey per-formed with ARU at Club Metronome in Burlington on 3/11/94 in a show that also featured Dave Grippo, Michael Ray, and Leftover Salmon.

The colonel remains an inspiration to the members of Phish. Various band members often quote his musical philosophies. As noted in chapter 1, they often reiterate his notion that musicians should aspire to a state of vomiting, whereby music comes out of them without their cognizant control. Also, Fish often recites the colonel's quote that a musician should not be serious about himself but should be serious about his music. Additionally, as described in chapter 3, Fish paid tribute to his hero by bringing Hampton on stage at the Civic Coliseum in Knoxville in order to croon "Wind Beneath My Wings" to him.

Bad Hat

Bad Hat evolved out of Burlington mandolin player Jamie Mase-field's collaborations with other local musicians at the Last Elm Cafe, a nonprofit community-run coffeehouse. Two musicians who enjoyed performing with Masefield in this setting were Trey and Fish, both of whom had some passing familiarity with Masefield from their days at UVM. In early 1993 Stacey Starkweather (of Michael Ray and the Cosmic Krewe) joined the trio on bass, and a collaboration took tentative form. As if to underscore the provisional nature of this association, the group performed under the moniker of the Jazz Mandolin Project. By the fall of 1994 the group opted for a new name (and a new look) with the appropriate title of Bad Hat. In the period since then, the quartet has regrouped for a few performances (for example, at the Iron Horse Music Hall in Northampton on 9/10/94 and the debut of Carmel's Coffee House at UVM on 1/26/95).

A typical Bad Hat set list includes selections by Miles Davis ("So What," "Milestones in the Sunshine") followed by something by Charlie Parker ("Donna Lee"), a composition by Duke Ellington ("In a Sentimental Mood"), and one by Page McConnell ("Magilla"). Some original songs also are performed, two of which pay tribute to Trey's mentor Ernie Stires ("Ernie's Groove" and "Jazz for Ernie"). The band's sets are completed with some of Jamie's original compositions as well ("Contois" and "Nardis").

Karl Boyle

Karl Boyle joined the faculty of Goddard College in 1987 as a professor of music theory and composition. Here he developed friendships with the band members and also served as the faculty adviser for Page's Senior Study. He appears on one fairly common tape, adding his saxophone (but not his cymbal or his skyscraper) to "Take the A Train" at the Goddard College Springfest show on 5/14/88.

Photo credit: Daniel Owen

Shelly Culbertson

You know her as the lilting voice that provides you with all your necessary tour information on the Phish telephone hotline. Or you know her as the voice of reason and information on the Phish.net. Either way, you know her and appreciate her. Or at least you should.

Shelly began her affiliation with the band as a fervid phan. She was living on the West Coast when she first heard about the band while on-line. Shelly made an effort to see Phish when they finally made it out her way and she was impressed. In turn, she made frequent contributions to the emerging on-line Phish community, which evolved into a listserve and then a Usenet newsgroup. Meanwhile, Shelly befriended the band and its management, striving to make Phish's West Coast travels as comfortable and as stimulating as possible.

Following Phish's triumphant 1992 New Year's run, which reached its apogee at Matthews Arena on 12/31/92, Shelly's "voice" was conspicuously absent from the Phish.net for quite a while. However, her voice had merely been transplanted to the Dionysian

Productions office and onto the hotline message (where she made her debut announcing the spring 1993 tour). Despite her heavy workload in the Dionysian Productions office, Shelly continues to add information and insight (and the occasional obligatory reality check) to the Phish.net whenever possible.

Marc Daubert

Marc Daubert is a former member of Phish and another friend of Trey's from New Jersey. He appeared in Burlington in late 1984 to join the band on percussion. Indeed, he appeared at the band's first big gig, upstairs at Nectar's on 12/1/84, during which he joined Fish for a rhythm devils duet.

Although Marc's performing days in the band soon ended, his relationship with Phish continued. He contributed the lyrics to the song "The Curtain," and if you read the *Lawn Boy* liner notes, you'll also see that Tom Marshall's lyrics are printed by permission of Marc. Also, listen to a copy of 12/31/95 and during "Runaway Jim" you'll hear Trey's tribute to Marc and Dave.

The Dude of Life

The Dude of Life made his first appearance onstage with the band in 1984. Since then he has appeared with Phish on more than a dozen occasions. Typically, the Dude has emerged in costume, bearing props, to croon a song toward the end of the second set. For example, at the 1992 New Year's show at Matthews Arena in Boston, the Dude took the stage in a mask while pushing a lawn mower and tossing rubber chickens into the audience. Then he stepped up to the microphone, and Phish backed his off-kilter version of the Seals and Croft lite classic "Diamond Girl." More commonly, he has sauntered onstage to perform one of his own compositions, such as "Crimes of the Mind" (although on a few occasions he has joined Phish for multiple songs—three at Wetlands on 9/13/90, three at Amy's farm in Auburn, Maine, on 8/3/91, and four at the Ivory Tusk in Tuscaloosa, Alabama, on 11/8/91).

The Dude's actual name is Steve Pollak, and he is significant to

Phish fans for more than his occasional onstage appearances. He also is important for his prowess as a lyricist. Pollak first collaborated with Trey in high school when he joined his friend onstage in Space Antelope. Their friendship and musical collaboration continued beyond twelfth grade, and the Dude has contributed the lyrics to four Phish songs that the group commonly still performs. "Fluffhead," "Suzie Greenberg," "Dinner and a Movie," and "Slave to the Traffic Light" are all a product of Pollak's semifertile pen.

In 1991 the Dude of Life entered the studio and recorded eleven of his compositions. Phish supported him at these sessions, both arranging the music and backing him on all of the tracks. Although this recording was not released until 1994, most of these songs made their debuts at Phish shows in 1990 and 1991 during the Dude's three extended appearances (in particular, listen to the Tuscaloosa show, where a good portion of the audience leaves the club once the Dude comes on-

Photo credit: Jeff Davis

stage). The Dude's recording session is also of interest because Phish later appropriated some of the music that it contributed (for example, pull out "Crimes of the Mind" and listen to "Self" and then listen to "Chalkdust Torture").

More recently, the Dude has branched out on his own. In the spring of 1994 he mounted a minitour of the Northeast, returning to many of the clubs where Phish had once appeared. These shows were all the more noteworthy because Trey, Mike, and Page joined the Dude of Life Band, which featured Fish on drums, for some tunes at Paradise, Wetlands, and Nectar's. The Dude's band continues to perform club dates (without Fishman but with Dan Archer, who produced the Dude's album, and some former members of the band Shockra). While there have been no recent guest appearances by Phish with the Dude of Life Band, the Dude could yet emerge at any given Phish show.

Mimi Fishman

Marianne "Mimi" Fishman is the mother of Phish's drummer. She's a big fan of the band and can often be spied in one of the front rows, boogeying along with other phans. However, she has earned a place in this chapter because she can play a mean vacuum.

On occasion Fish credits his mother with developing his vacuum prowess. He claims that as a boy when he was very bad, he had to wash out his mouth with soap. But when he was very, very bad, he had to use the vacuum. You can believe that if you want, but if you've ever had a chance to speak with Mrs. Fishman at a show, I'm sure your opinion would change.

Photo credit: Tom Sabo

Although some feel that she lacks the full range and tone of her son, Mimi Fishman nonetheless can elicit a variety of notes from the instrument (hey, he practices more than she does). If you want to hear Mimi on vacuum, listen to 10/28/91, 11/23/92, or 4/23/93, among others.

Bela Fleck

Bela is the banjo player extraordinaire who began his career with the more traditional New Grass Revival and then left that group to form the Flecktones. Phish invited the 'Tones to open for them at Salt Air in Salt Lake City, Utah, on 8/21/93, and a relationship formed between the two bands. As you might expect, the Flecktones joined Phish that evening for much of the second set, which included particularly satisfying versions of "Llama," "David Bowie," and "Daniel." Bela later performed "Scent of a Mule" and "Lifeboy" with Phish on *Hoist*. At Vanderbilt University Memorial Gym on 10/18/94, he joined the band for those two songs and a few more during the second set. When Phish returned to his hometown of Nashville a year later, on 11/29/95 at the Municipal Auditorium, the band welcomed Bela onstage once again.

Branford Marsalis recently described a Phish moment that he shared with Bela. The two of them drove through Nashville listening to *A Live One* on the car's CD player. Branford and Bela ended up outside a Krispy Kreme donut shop with the car doors open, grooving to the sublime music of Phish (oh to be a cruller on that dashboard).

Warren Haynes

Warren Haynes, of course, is that man who revitalized the Allman Brothers Band. After his work in Dickey Betts's band, Warren joined the ABB when it reformed in 1989 to complement and challenge Dickey. Over the years he certainly has done his share both of complementing and challenging, which is why many people feel the ABB currently is reaching new peaks. Phish phans were treated to a hint of this on 12/11/95 at Portland, Maine's Cumberland County Civic Center. On that evening Haynes took the stage and joined Phish for both "Funky Bitch" and "While My Guitar Gently Weeps."

Giant Country Horns

The Giant Country Horns, or GCH for you acronymphiles, joined Phish for a fourteen-show tour during the summer of 1991. The initial version of the Giant Country Horns featured three members.

Dave "the Truth" Grippo played alto saxophone, Russell "the Killer" Remington played tenor saxophone, and Carl "Gears" Gerhard completed the trio on trumpet. The members of GCH wore white tuxedos and read from horn charts that the various members of the group had arranged along with Phish. The trio also was equipped with individual trampolines.

In 1994 Phish premiered its *Hoist* material at the Flynn Theater on April 4 with a new brawny, brassy six-member version of the Giant Country Horns. Grippo and Gerhard returned, along with Chris Peterman on tenor sax, Mike Gaillick on baritone sax, Don Glasgo on trombone, and Joseph Somerville Jr. on trumpet. That same lineup also appeared at the Beacon Theater a week later. On May 2 of that year a slightly different horn section joined Phish at the State Palace Theater in New Orleans. This group, which also featured members of Michael Ray and the Cosmic Krewe, appeared as the Cosmic Country Horns. Grippo and Gerhard returned, along with Michael Ray on trumpet, Jerome Therio on baritone sax, Rick Trolson on trombone, and Tony Tate on tenor sax. Next, as Phish traveled west in December 1994 recording shows for *A Live One*, the band assembled a GCH that included Gerhard, Grippo, and Ray, with James Harvey on trombone, and Peter Applebaum on tenor saxophone. Finally, to support its rendition of *Quadrophenia* on 10/31/95, Phish welcomed Grippo, Glasgo, Somerville, and Alan Parshley on French horn.

Jazz Mandolin Project

Jamie Masefield's initial collaboration with Jon, Trey, and Stacey took place under the name the Jazz Mandolin Project. However, when the foursome elected to call themselves Bad Hat, Jamie was left with an unused name. He also was left with quite a bit of time on his hands while half of Bad Hat performed with Phish. Content with his collaboration with Stacey Starkweather, the two musicians recruited a new drummer, Gabe Jarrett, to gig as a three-piece. This Jazz Mandolin Project performs some jazz standards along with Masefield's originals in an even looser, more exploratory manner than Bad Hat.

Chris Kuroda

Chris Kuroda, Phish's lighting director, began his career with the band due to a guitar lesson. In early 1989 Chris, who lived in Burlington, hoped to improve his skills on the instrument. So he approached the man that he felt to be the best guitarist in town, Trey Anastasio. Soon after Trey began giving lessons to Chris, the band decided that they were in a position to hire someone to carry their gear from gig to gig. Trey asked Chris if he would like to do this and he agreed. So Topher began traveling with the band, still primarily on weekend gigs in New England.

On one fateful day, Chris was standing back near the lightboard when the band's then-current lighting operator, also named Chris, had to run off to the men's room. He asked Chris to take over for him on "Famous Mockingbird" while he went off. Chris did, and thought nothing more of it until later, when he saw Trey tell the other Chris that for the first time he'd really gotten it right, perfectly capturing the mood of the band and contributing the right vibe to "Famous Mockingbird." Chris heard this, and just to set the record straight, he later called Trey aside and told him that he was the one who worked the light board during "Mockingbird." The next Thursday Chris received a call at home from Trey, telling him that the other Chris wouldn't be there for their gigs that weekend and asking him to fill in. A bit hesitant at first, Chris tossed his hat into the ring, and it's been there ever since.

Chris has no formal training, so he has been forced to learn the mechanics of each new lighting system that the band has added over the years. The results have been spectacular. Phish's light show is both subtle and nuanced while remaining playful and full of energy. The band members have credited Chris's work with creating a mood onstage that has influenced their own musical direction. If you're at a show and sitting in his vicinity some evening, take a few minutes and watch Chris call a show—it's quite a sight.

Two other Chris tidbits before we move on. First, a couple years back someone approached him and he accepted a job as Tito Puente's lighting director for a stadium tour in South America. Chris said he did the same light show that he'd always done, "Phish lighting," and the people really seemed to enjoy it. Second, an aggressive but clueless taper once asked Chris if he could patch into his board. A straight-faced Chris obliged.

Lamb's Bread

The reggae band Lamb's Bread were Burlington contemporaries of Phish. In the mid-1980s the two bands shared similar spirits, and they also shared bills on occasion. For instance, the two teamed up for a benefit for African Relief at Hunt's on 3/4/86. Lamb's Bread featured the Hackneys Brothers, Bobby and Dennis, along with Jeff Kennedy and Rick Steffen. The band performed a number of covers (including "Rawhide") along with some originals. One song that falls somewhere in between these two is "Fire Up the Ganja," a song reworked from "Fire on the Mountain." The reason this bit of arcane knowledge is so important to phans is that a tape circulated for a while that allegedly featured Phish performing at Nectar's. It wasn't until someone familiar with Lamb's Bread's live repertoire heard the tape that J-cards everywhere could be corrected.

Paul Languedoc

Paul began his association with Phish in 1984 when he was working as a guitar maker at Time Guitar and crafted one that Trey purchased. Paul also repaired guitars, which is how Trey came to spend some time with him. The two soon struck up a friendship, and in the fall of 1986 Phish asked him to provide sound at their shows. Paul didn't have much experience doing this, but he agreed to give it a try (10/15/86 was his debut). Initially his sound work with Phish was not a full-time job, but he did remain committed to the band. He even traveled with them out to Telluride in 1988, and his mechanical skills came in handy after some van mishaps. By the spring of 1989 Phish had become his full-time gig. Of course, Paul's work with Phish continues outside of shows. He has custom designed most of Trey's guitars and Mike's basses as well.

Marley

Photo credit: Bart Stephens

Marley is Trey's confidant, spiritual adviser, and musical inspiration. She's also his dog. Marley traveled with the band to gigs through 1992 (as Trey announced from the stage at the Portland Expo on 2/3/93, the opening date of the spring tour, "a sad bit of news . . . this tour Marley is not touring with us." As Fish added, "She's just too old and fat to go out on tour"). If you listen to some of Phish's early outdoor shows, you can hear Trey try to quiet a barking Marley (for instance, 8/21/87 and 8/29/87). Trey later introduced her to the crowd at Wilbur Field on 4/18/92. She also appeared onstage in the role of Harpua on 3/26/92. Trey wrote "Dog Log" with her in mind. In most versions of this song, Trey says, "This one's for you, Marley," in between verses. By the way, if you get the opportunity to stand really close to one of Trey's Languedoc guitars, move your eyes all the way up the neck. On the headstock you'll see a mother-of-pearl inlay of Marley as a puppy saying, "I'm the Mar Mar." (On Trey's backup guitar Marley appears as an adult, chasing a cat.)

Tom Marshall

Tom is the guy. The original family berserker himself, Tom grew up with Trey in New Jersey, where they formed a tight-knit band that included Dave Abrahams, Aaron Woolfe, Mike Christian, Roger Rutherford, and Marc Daubert.

It was Tom who helped to initiate the majesty that is Gamehendge. Tom cowrote the original version of "Wilson" along with Trey and Aaron Woolfe. Then, as Trey and Tom continued to

Photo credit: Bart Stephens

communicate through the mail while Trey was off in Burlington and Tom was at school in New Jersey, Tom sent Trey the original McGrupp poem. Over the years Tom and Trey's tandem songwriting skills have flourished, yielding many memorable results. Indeed, it is fair to say that if you were to name your three favorite Phish songs, Tom undoubtedly has had his hand in at least two of them.

Dave Matthews Band

The Dave Matthews Band is another group of talented musicians who share a mutual respect with the members of Phish. Fish, Mike, Page, and Trey first learned of the Virginia-based band through their southern phriends and made a few unsuccessful efforts to catch DMB on some evenings after their own gigs. Eventually, they were able to do so and came away impressed with the musicianship, affability, and other habits and hobbies of Carter Beauford, Stefan Lesard, Dave Matthews, Leroi Moore, and Boyd Tinsley. In turn, Phish has invited DMB to open for them on a number of occasions.

The net result of these bills has been a range of cooperative jams between the two bands. For instance, listen to 4/20/94, 4/21/94, or 6/17/95.

Dr. Jack McConnell

Dr. Jack McConnell helped to create a community medical clinic and has achieved some measure of notoriety for his commitment to the medical profession. However, to many phans he's simply known for his father-son piano boogie. Dr. Jack McConnell first joined his son onstage during a Phish show at the Grady Cole Center in Charlotte, North Carolina, on 7/28/93. He appeared for the encore, performed a boogie-woogie piano duel with Page, and then assumed lead vocal duties on "Won't You Come Home Bill Bailey." He has returned to appear with Phish by popular demand on a couple of occasions since then, most recently at the Coliseum in North Charleston, South Carolina, on 11/18/95.

Cameron McKenney

Cameron was only ten years old when he joined the band on saxophone during "Simple" on 11/28/94. He holds the record for the youngest performer ever to perform an instrument onstage with Phish, but he didn't set it in Bozeman. Listen to 3/14/93 or 4/19/92. For that matter, check out 5/14/88. Cameron's mother, Merry, is a longtime phriend of the band, and it would be accurate to say that Cameron is a phriend of the band, too, although unlike his mother he gets to jam a bit.

Marjorie Minkin

Marjorie Minkin is the artist who has created many of Phish's backdrops. If you listen to 12/31/91, you can hear the band discuss one of her creations. Her earliest designs for the band appeared on canvas. Some of her later works were produced on glass, which permitted Chris Kuroda to light them from various angles to produce a number of effects. Minkin also has designed one of Phish's T-shirts sold through Phish Dry Goods. It's quite possible that she's devoted so much time to working with the band because her name has been enshrined in song, via "Minkin," which appears on Phish's *White Tape* demo. Or it could be because she's Mike's mom.

Jeff Mosier

Reverend Jeff joined the initial Aquarium Rescue Unit roster when that band formed in 1989. He left the band soon after to pursue his vocation and to concentrate on his bluegrass picking. Phish invited him to join the band on the road for a week during the fall of 1994 to tutor them in bluegrass. Mosier proved an active and able teacher, taking the band through a number of traditional blue-grass songs (including "I'm Blue, I'm Lonesome" and "Long Journey Home"). Mosier provided lead vocals on the group's initial efforts while playing banjo as well. If you want to hear Reverend Jeff's lessons, find any tape between 11/16/94 and 11/20/94.

Ninja Custodian

While Phish ultimately removed the Minkin backdrops because the group felt they drew the audience's attention away from the band, the members of Ninja Custodian would freely admit that their own backdrop often drew the band's attention away from the audience. One of this group's claims to fame was its insect presentation, as Ninja Custodian would use an overhead projector to cast images of live bugs onto a screen over the band. Their bassist, Hamdi Akar, was a trained entomologist, and before each gig he would select appropriate insects to feature. At times his efforts were dramatic and at other times disastrous (such as the time the light from the projector grew too hot and fried the little entertainers).

Ninja Custodian began playing in Burlington around 1986. The band's influences ranged from rap to rock to punk. Mike Billington, drummer and covocalist in the band, grew up with John Paluska and Ben Hunter, introducing them to Phish. Before the Ninja boys made their westward move in 1991, the two bands maintained a close relationship. Ninja often opened for Phish, and the group even played at Fish's graduation party when he finally completed his degree at Goddard. Also, Phish performed the group's "Funky (Breakdown)" a few times in 1989. Finally, Phish presented a Ninja Custodian vocal jam when they traveled to California on 4/17/92, featuring the band members' names.

The Ninja boys appeared onstage with Phish a number of times as well. If you listen to the end of the second set on 5/28/89, that's Ninja Mike and Magoo (one of Ninja's guitarists). Over the years, when Fishman would take his solo spot onstage to perform with his trombone and later his vacuum, Ninja Mike occasionally felt the urge to rush the stage and start playing on drums before Trey could get a chance. On 10/22/89, at an all-ages show at The Front, Ninja Mike ran from the bar onto the stage, attempting to bounce on his head during the group's trampoline segment. As one might expect, he failed, plowing into Trey's guitar and amp. He ended up on the floor behind the Minkin backdrop as the room fell silent. "This is a sad day indeed," Fish called from the stage as Ninja Mike remained in hiding. Ninja Mike's last onstage appearance with the band took place at The Coach House in San Juan Capistrano, when he appeared during "Terrapin." Before leaving the stage at the close of the song, he raised Fish's dress, puckered up, and kissed the drummer's behind. Now that's friendship.

John Paluska

John Paluska is the cofounder of Dionysian Productions and the current manager of the band. J.P. has been with Phish in a managerial capacity since 1988. John first saw the band in Nectar's in 1988 while he was a junior at Amherst College and invited them down to perform at his cooperative house, The Zoo. The rest, as they say, is phishtory.

Jim Pollock

Jim Pollock is the artist who designs much of the Phish merchandise and for a period contributed the Grungy Dudes comic to the newsletter. The members of Phish met Jim at Goddard College, where his work appeared in such publications as the *Goddard Review*. As Phish increased in popularity and required the assistance of a graphic artist, Jim stepped into the fray. Some of his more popular images include the poster from the original Giant Country Horns tour in 1991, and the ever popular band caricature on the 1994 tour travel mug. Also, if you have some of your old newsletters lying around, you can pull out the winter 1991 issue, which contains a gallery of Jim's images, offered as a special tribute by the band.

John Popper

John Popper is a man of many attributes. He is the singer-songwriter–harmonica wizard who performs with Blues Traveler, he is the architect of the HORDE tour, and he is a veteran of episodic television (having appeared as Dan Connor's childhood buddy on the TV sitcom *Roseanne*). John's relationship with Phish touches on the first two aspects of his career. In 1989–90 Blues Traveler often appeared on twin bills with Phish as both bands sought to expand their audience support into new regions of the country. John appeared onstage with Phish at a number of these occasions (for instance, 11/8/90 in Madison, Wisconsin). At the Capitol Theater on 10/6/90, Phish debuted "Don't Get Me Wrong," a song that Trey and John cowrote. Phish also joined with Blues Traveler for the first week of the initial HORDE tour in July 1992.

Since this period Phish has invited John onstage a number of times with various entertaining results. For instance, on February 6, 1993, after John had broken his leg in a motorcycle accident, he was wheeled out onstage under a tarp that was then removed while he added his distinctive sound to "Buried Alive." The trampoline entry in chapter 4 recounts two occasions on which John joined Phish and broke their tramps (3/14/92 and 7/27/93). Most recently, he came onstage with Phish at Waterloo Village on June 23, 1995, in the middle of "Harpua" as Jimmy enjoyed "a rocking harmonica solo." Phans were treated to one as well.

Medeski, Martin, and Wood

John Medeski, Billy Martin, and Chris Wood perform a modern free-form jazz that integrates some traditional components and compositions with their own eclectic interests and influences. The trio performs with Medeski on organ, Martin on drums, and Wood on acoustic bass. No guitar. There's no need. Listen to these guys play Duke Ellington's "Chinoiserie" followed by their own "The Lover" and you'll understand.

Phish invited MMW to open for them at the State Palace Theater in New Orleans on 10/17/95. As that show approached, a number of phans who also were plugged into the MMW network noted that the trio had scheduled a gig four days earlier at Emo's in Austin, Texas. This was the same evening as Phish's first performance at the Austin Music Hall. Moreover, Emo's had scheduled the trio for a late show. Speculation as to the possibility of some sort of cross-mingling heightened, and no one was disappointed. Early in the evening, Medeski, Martin, and Wood joined Phish onstage for an extensive musical improvisation during "You Enjoy Myself." Then, after the Phish show, Trey sat in with MMW for two complete sets at Emo's. Medeski, Martin, and Wood also joined Phish onstage for a similar musical melee four days later at the State Palace Theater show.

Michael Ray and the Cosmic Krewe

Michael Ray performed with Kool and the Gang for ten years, and he appeared as Intergalactic Research Tone Scientist in the Sun Ra Arkestra. Eventually Ray set out on his own, producing music that fuses the elements of both these units. The result has been the Cosmic Krewe, which released its debut album in 1994. The Krewe includes, among others, Giant Country Horn members Dave Grippo, Don Glasgo, and Ray himself, along with Bad Hat bassist Stacey Starkweather. The members of Phish have appeared onstage with the Krewe on a few occasions, most typically Trey and Fishman (for instance, at Club Toast in Burlington on 3/8/94 and

2/10/95). The Krewe is well worth taking in with or without any Phishy additions, promising to provide an entertaining, absorbing evening of music.

Nectar Rorris

Nectar's the man. He's the owner of Nectar Rorris's restaurant, a Burlington staple since 1975 (give or take the 1983–84 period when Nectar briefly moved on to other ventures). Nectar is famous for three things: his gravy fries, his evenings of music without a cover charge, and his association with Phish. The band eventually settled in to a regular series of performances at Nectar's before it outgrew the space in 1989. In appreciation for his initial commitment, Phish dedicated their major-label release to him (that's his face in the orange). Nectar's continues to thrive with live music seven nights a week and never a cover.

Brad Sands

Brad is yet another person from the phan-made-good category. Persistence paid off for Brad, whose stretch of touring eventually landed him on the Phish road crew. Brad, whose current title is production assistant, is one of the more visible members of the crew since it is his job to bring the trampolines on and off the stage (he replaced Pete Schall in this duty). The band appreciates Brad's efforts and honored him with a birthday cake at the 10/31/94 show in Glens Falls. The band also has sung his praises with a sound check version of "Rollaway Brad."

Pete Schall

Pete Schall served as the band's monitor engineer. He stood to the side of Page, where he controlled the mix that the band members hear onstage. He also was the big ball distributor and the tramp guy before he pawned those jobs off on Brad Sands. And speaking of pawns, Pete also was the one who introduced the audience chess movers during the 1995 fall tour. Phish occasionally has sung Pete's praises as well, in particular with "Pete Schall" screeches during the "You Enjoy Myself" vocal jam (listen to 12/30/92). Pete retired from these duties in the spring of 1996 and moved on to other projects (the band paid tribute to him in the spring newsletter).

Amy Skelton

Amy's official title is "first phan." As legend has it, Amy was the first one to come out and see the band. (And as the band members sometimes state with amazement, she continued to come out to see them.) As Phish began to mount full-scale tours, Amy took to the road with them as their official merchandise vendor. Her title eventually escalated to merchandise representative. She also hosted the celebrated Amy's farm show on August 3, 1991. Finally, Amy's horse Maggie is being hoisted onto the cover of *Hoist*.

Space Antelope

As chapter 1 relates, Space Antelope was the first band in which Trey performed on guitar. He formed Space Antelope while attending the Taft School in Watertown, Connecticut. Space Antelope's most ambitious but least successful venture was an interpretation of Pink Floyd's "Dogs" before an unappreciative school assembly. Space Antelope broke up soon afterward, following one final gig at a Taft School dance. The group also featured the occasional vocals of the Dude of Life. And yes, it was in regard to this band that the Dude coined that famous phrase, imploring the listener to run like a Space Antelope out of control.

Ernie Stires

Ernie Stires is Trey's friend and mentor. Stires agreed to school Trey in composition when the University of Vermont music department wouldn't do so. Through his study with Ernie, Trey learned to appreciate the complex arrangements of the big bands, one source of

Ernie's passion. Many of Trey's more complex, scripted compositions are a direct result of his work with Ernie ("Foam," "Divided
Sky," and "Asse Festival," for instance). Similarly, Phish's horn tour
evolved out of Trey's lessons with Ernie. Trey had long desired to
employ the horn charts that he had composed for "Flat Fee," which
he wrote under Ernie's tutelage. Trey continues to pay homage to
his mentor through his Bad Hat compositions "Ernie's Groove" and
"Blues for Ernie."

Sugar Blue

Sugar Blue is a blues harmonica player who settled in Chicago. He
appeared onstage with Phish at the Aragon Ballroom on 4/10/93.
This was not Sugar Blue's first appearance with a rock band however, as he performed with the Rolling Stones in the late seventies
and occasionally took to the road with them. If you listen to the
second set of the 4/10/93 show prior to Sugar Blue's appearance,
Trey teases the Stones' "Miss You" during "Mike's Song," an appropriate selection because Sugar Blue played harmonica on that track
and a few others on the Stones' *Some Girls* album. At the Aragon
Ballroom he performed with Phish on three Chicago blues tunes:
"Funky Bitch," "Help Me," and "Hoochie Coochie Man."

Surrender to the Air

Surrender to the Air is the name of the improvisational jazz project
that Trey organized. He set things in motion by inviting Sun Ra
Arkestra veterans Marshall Allen, Damon Choice, and Michael
Ray to a recording session along with Kofi and Oteil Burbridge,
Fish, Bob Gullotti, James Harvey, John Medeski, and Marc Ri-
bot. The result captures some of the spirit of Sun Ra's work.
In order to celebrate the release of this album, the musicians
who appeared on *Surrender to the Air* coordinated their schedules
on April 1 and 2, 1996, to appear at New York's Academy nightclub
in Times Square.

Nancy Taube

Nancy is the enigmatic and often contentious figure who wrote both "I Didn't Know" and "Halley's Comet." Nancy also joined Phish onstage to help them interpret these songs at a number of shows in the mid-eighties (for instance, 5/14/88). The members of Phish met Nancy at Goddard College, where he attended school in the mid-eighties (that's right Nancy's a he—which is why the band modified the lyrics to "Rocky Raccoon" on 10/31/94). The band continues to invoke his name from the stage and quite literally sing his praises. (For example, listen to 10/1/89—the first "Reba" is dedicated to the spirit of Nancy, 8/3/91, and 3/27/93.)

Butch Trucks

Butch Trucks is one of the drummers in the Allman Brothers Band. He joined Phish on drums during "Possum" at the Auditorium in West Palm Beach, Florida on 11/16/95. This is the same show during which Jimmy Buffett appeared onstage to sing "Brown Eyed

Girl" for the band's encore. Butch's appearance with Phish is additionally important as it ultimately led to the appearance of Page McConnell with the Allman Brothers Band, sitting in for Greg Allman at the first of the ABB's record seventeen performances at the Beacon Theater on March 1, 1996.

As the story goes, Gregg had crashed his motorcycle a few days before the show, breaking a few ribs and rendering him in need of medical attention. As a result, when Gregg appeared at the premiere show of the Allman Brothers Band's Beacon run, he felt very much under the weather. His playing was subdued and he was unable to perform his share of vocal duties, handing them off to Warren Haynes. Early in the second set, Gregg's physical discomfort overtook him and he walked off. As the band members stepped backstage following their second set, they encountered Page and encouraged him to return with them for their encores (both Warren Haynes and Butch Trucks had played with Page and were quite aware of his capabilities). So Page filled in for Gregg on organ during "One Way Out," "Southbound," "True Gravity," and "Whipping Post."

Widespread Panic

When Phish started traveling south and building up their southern phan base, they were aided in their efforts by Widespread Panic. Phish returned the favor up north, allowing Widespread to open for them on a few dates. The two bands also shared the bill on the initial shows of the HORDE tour in 1992. In addition, Panic directly influenced some of Phish's personal habits, as the band notes from the stage during the Jaegermeister song on 5/6/90. Page later appeared on Panic's rereleased *Space Wrangler* album and added some organ to "Holden Oversoul." Trey and Page both joined Widespread onstage for two encores at the Roxy in Los Angeles on 11/11/93 while Phish was in the area recording *Hoist*.

6 phishing lures

his chapter presents brief reviews of a number of shows that are well worth adding to your tape collection. All of these tapes circulate among traders. The chapter concludes with a list of some additional shows that you may want to hear as well (although some of them may be a bit harder to find).

12/1/84 Nectar's, Burlington, VT

This is the earliest of the commonly circulated Phish tapes. It comes from the band's first gig upstairs at Nectar's. Two versions of this tape tend to circulate: a forty-five-minute version and a ninety-minute version. A forty-five-minute section of this show also often makes the rounds as 12/31/84. Both Jeff and Marc Daubert appear on this tape, so you can discern their contributions to this early incarnation of the band.

Many phans feel that the "Scarlet" into "Fire" into "Fire" that opens this tape is enough to recommend it, but although these interpretations and juxtapositions are clever, there's more interesting stuff to find on here. For instance, "Spanish Flea," with its accompanying band introductions, provides a bizarre treat that allows you additional historical insight as to who's playing. The Dude takes the stage for the first time in three years to belt out "Skippy (the Wondermouse)," featuring music that Phish will later add to "McGrupp." Early versions of both "Makisupa" and "Slave" also appear on this tape as does "Don't Want You No More," a Spencer Davis song that the Allman Brothers Band covered on their first album. Phans who enjoy percussion will want to check out the Rhythm Devils segment with Fish and Daubs. Finally, the tape closes with another rendition of a Grateful Dead song "Eyes of the World."

5/3/85 Last Day Party, University of Vermont, Burlington, VT

This tape features Page's first performance with Phish. It's worth listening to this one to compare it with the 12/1/84 tape in order to hear the contributions that Page makes right from the start—in particular listen to "Eyes" and "McGrupp." This show also features Jeff's lead vocals on an early run through "Whipping Post" (a duty that would later pass to Trey and ultimately to Fish). "McGrupp" remains in its larval stage before this song swallows "Skippy," with Trey reciting the words at the beginning. "Makisupa" is another interesting early version, with much elucidation on the proclivities and propensities of the narrator and the band members along with some additional lyrics about South Africa. Historically minded phans also will want to hear the band's take on "The Other One," which features some fine early exchanges between Mike and Fish.

10/17/85 Finbar's, Burlington, VT

Here's another interesting show that features both Page and Jeff. This tape includes a number of early versions of the songs that the

band still performs today, along with a few that have fallen by the wayside. In the former category, listen to an early "Mike's Song" (which Trey introduces as "Microdot"), a protean "Antelope" and a spoken "McGrupp." This tape also offers a version of "Dave's Energy Guide" (well worth hearing—particularly if you want to offer an educated opinion as to whether the band has revived this one in recent years or just played something that sounds close). Jeff chimes in here on lead vocals and some explanation of his song "Camel Walk." Plus, you won't want to miss the band's punk offerings "Revolution" and "Anarchy."

10/30/85 Hunt's, Burlington, VT

Here's another show from this same period that provides a glimpse at the band's early days. This performance is from New Music Night at Hunt's, and Trey indicates that he hopes to milk this type of showcase for all it's worth (he also thanks everyone who had come out to see the band at Goddard the previous week). Speaking of milk, this show is notable for the first appearance of "Harry Hood," followed by a quip about possible sponsorship from the dairy. This tape also allows you to hear Jeff's vocals on his song "Opossum," with a timely comment about *B.J. and the Bear* as well. Other songs worth hearing include the band's takes on "I Wish" and "Revival" as well as set closers "Prep School Hippie" and "Skippy" (with no Dude appearance).

4/1/86 Hunt's, Burlington, VT

This tape is another that captures the early days of Phish. The band alternated sets with The Jones on this night, which features two forty-five-minute Phish performances. Set one opens with a fun "Mighty Quinn," with Trey calling out to Jeff to take charge. Other highlights of this set include "Harry," "Dave's Energy Guide," and an entertaining "Icculus" that Trey introduces as written by Phish's favorite band, "Sneazeblood Eyeball." The short second set begins with a transition from the Grateful Dead's "Help on the Way" into "Slipknot" into "AC/DC Bag"! Phish staples circa 1986 complete this set: the still spoken "McGrupp," "Alumni Blues," "Letter to Jimmy Page," and "Mrs. Reagan." Jeff then makes a speech about International Lemming Day while Trey invites The Jones on stage for a "guitar army" that performs "Not Fade Away."

4/15/86 University of Vermont, Burlington, VT

Trey's dad is in attendance for this Earth Day concert. A mellow "AC/DC Bag" gets this one started. From here, the set list includes many early Phish favorites ("Mrs. Reagan," "Prep School Hippie," "Dog Log," "Anarchy," "Camel Walk," "Alumni"). This show also features some entertaining nonmusical moments, including the "Bob Dylan Band" introduction that surfaced time and again during this period. The transition between "Mighty Quinn" and "Slave" is also well worth hearing. Finally, this tape offers yet another chance to hear Jeff introduce "a song I wrote called 'Opossum' with that tune's original lyrics" (which tell the story of a truck driver and not Icculus).

10/31/86 Goddard College, Plainfield, VT

This tape opens with a jam while Trey asks, "Are you ready for us?" From here the first of Phish's annual Goddard College Halloween sets begins with "AC/DC Bag." Two fine instrumentals, the "Swing Low, Sweet Chariot" jam, and "Peaches En Regalia" follow. Other noteworthy moments on this tape include "Have Mercy," which is notable because you can hear Jah Roy start to sing from the audience and then move his way onto the stage. He eventually picks up a microphone while the band backs him. "Sanity" also makes an early appearance in this set, with its original slower pace. "Skin It Back" follows and moves into a mellow "Icculus," during which Trey reveals that "Icculus" was born in 1948 (?!).

12/6/86 The Ranch, Shelburne, VT

Here's another Phish performance from the intial era after Jeff's departure. (You can listen to a few tapes from both before and after he left the band to note some changes in song arrangements.) This is a fine show in an interesting venue. (Trey announces from the stage a couple of times that there is a can in the kitchen for contributing money.) Given the December date of this show, the transition from "Mike's" to "Little Drummer Boy" seems appropriate. Other moments you'll want to hear include the segues from "David Bowie" into "Clod" then back into "Bowie," an amusing "Dog Log," a fierce "Prep School Hippie" (soon before its departure), and another gripping "Icculus" narration. This tape also is worth hearing for Trey's earnest promise to honor a Barry Manilow request as the band romps through ZZ Top's "Tush."

3/6/87 Nectar's, Burlington, VT

This show is principally known for the band's (pre–a cappella) romp through "Freebird." "Romper Room" might be a more appropriate characterization of a slushy Ninja Mike's take on this song (with some half-hearted backing from the band). Aside from these moments, this is the earliest 1987 tape that circulates, and it also features an early "Funky Bitch," an independent "Mike's" (a few months before the addition of "Weekapaug"), and a fine "Sneaking Sally" with a vocal jam.

4/24/87 Billings Lounge, University of Vermont, Burlington, VT

Another Earth Day show. This set opens with "Golgi" (at a time that predates ticket stubs in anyone's hand). The ubiquitous "AC/ DC Bag" is next, with an increased tempo from versions of the song just a year earlier. "Possum" is next, with Mike now assuming lead vocal duties. An extended "Dave's Energy Guide" appears in this set, too. However, this show may be most noteworthy for the unaccompanied appearance of "I Am Hydrogen." This version trails on quite a bit longer than the later "Hydrogen's" sandwiched between "Mike's" and "Weekapaug," and it also drifts into "Bundle of Joy" before Phish moves into "Bowie."

8/21/87 Ian Maclean's Farm, Hebron, NY

I've been reminded time and again over the years that music was secondary (but certainly welcome) at all of Ian's gatherings, and fewer than fifty people were at these parties. Be that as it may, it's the music that remains with us, and with three sets on this day, there's plenty of it. The show opens with "Dog Log," enhanced by some appropriate barking by Marley and phriends. The ensuing three sets offer both plenty of banter (if that's your thing) and a number of noteworthy musical moments. In the former category you'll want to hear the "BBFCFM" introduction, for instance. Similarly, after "Clod" Trey asked those in attendance "Would you like to hear something normal or something else weird?" Someone requests " 'Mrs. Reagan.' " "That's too weird," Trey responds. " 'Lushington'?" someone asks. " That's weird," he responds, but the band doesn't play it. On the musical side, along with the aforementioned "Clod," you'll want to hear an early "Harpua" without narration but with "Bundle of Joy" in the middle, the back-to-back performances of both of Phish's "Fee's," a fine "Mike's" with the bonus opening verse, an extended "Makisupa" preceded by a "Stir It Up" jam and a reggae rap, as well as the appropriate "Light Up or Leave Me Alone." You also won't want to miss the "Hold Your Head Up" tease ("We'd like to do a song by Argent. . . . Fish doesn't think that's funny. . . .").

8/29/87 Shelburne, VT

This is the "Mar Mar" gig, which Phish played to thank a friend for taking care of Marley during the summer. As you might expect, Marley receives a bit of attention from the stage during the show (Trey jokingly introduces "Ya Mar" as a song they wrote about Marley and adds a lyric or two to that effect). Musical moments of note include Phish's take on "Mustang Sally," one of the band's final performances of "Lushington," a thick "Sneaking Sally" vocal jam, an early "Divided Sky" with an alternate ending, and two (count them, two) "Hold Your Head Up" teases in "Suzie." "Harpua" once again appears without narration but with "Bundle of Joy." This is also the show where Trey introduces his thesis theme as " The Man Who Stepped into a Pile of Yesterday (and Stopped in Israel on His Way There)."

3/11/88 Johnson State College, Johnson, VT

This show took place soon after the death of Andy Gibb, whom the band eulogizes with James Brown's "The Chicken." Tim Rogers comes onstage to add some harmonica to "Sneaking Sally" and "Curtis Lowe." The band's takes of Taj Mahal's "Corrine, Corrina" and its own "David Bowie" are well worth hearing (as is Trey's reaction when Fish loses his drumsticks). The band also performs "Harpua" with the standard early story without the extended exploits of Jimmy and ending with saliva dropping from Harpua's mouth. Finally, during the beginning of "Antelope" Trey sets out the various nicknames for Fish.

3/12/88 Nectar's, Burlington, VT

As Phish's interpretation of Mingus's "Jump Monk" ends, storytime at Nectar's begins. This is the band's first live performance of the Gamehendge saga and it is well worth hearing. Phish introduces the tale with "McGrupp," and Trey's narration begins as Page's keys trail out of that song. This is the only live Gamehendge in which Trey reveals that Tela is a spy. It is also the sole live version of the song cycle that concludes with "Possum." During the course of this tale, an appreciative audience reveals its familiarity with the great and knowledgeable Icculus. Find a copy of this tape and introduce yourself to Colonel Forbin, "The Man Who Stepped into Yesterday."

5/14/88 Springfest, Goddard College, Plainfield, VT

Both this show and the next day at the Vermont Farm Festival make the rounds. If forced to choose, I'd go with this show (which is a bit shorter than 5/15/88) for the overall musical and comic experience (and for the guest stars). Of course, some of the guests are a bit reluctant—listen to the band try to coax Bobby Brown onto the stage during "Fire." Nancy is a bit more willing to take the stage as he performs with Phish on the two songs that he authored, "I Didn't Know" and "Halley's." Bobby does eventually take the stage by the way, joining the band for "Jesus Left Chicago" along with Cameron McKenney (!?!). Finally, while waiting for Karl Boyle to join them for "A Train," Phish performs a brief selection from Fish's "favorite band . . . Argent" (that's right: "Hold Your Head Up").

5/25/88 Nectar's, Burlington, VT

This show is a fine mid-1988 Nectar's three-set affair (just a few months before the move up the street to The Front). This one incorporates the many diverse elements of the Phish experience— a raging vocal jam (during "Sneaking Sally"), explosive jamming (in "Whipping Post"), some well placed hints and teases for those paying attention (a *Flintstones* quote in "BBFCFM"), and some entertaining dialogue ("Harpua," a "light man's choice" on this evening, tells

Photo credit: Bart Stephens

the story of "a poster nutbag named Cat."). Also for the historically minded, "The Curtain" contains an extended take on the riff that becomes the backbone of "Rift," "Fluffhead" finally subsumes "Clod," and Jah Roy adds some vocals to "Ya Mar."

6/20/88 Nectar's, Burlington, VT

Here's my second recommendation of a commonly trafficked tape that paints a sonic picture of a Nectar's show just before the band made the move to The Front. This tape has an added element as the band talks to a phriend of theirs who will receive a copy of this tape, who is out west fighting fires after jumping out of airplanes (as the story goes). "Slave" opens the show, which is a good indication of the fun to follow. Listen to Trey's tweaks of the "Fluffhead" words, Mike's efforts during "YEM," and Page's work during the jazz standards. Also, the Jah Roy appearance during "Ya Mar" is many phans' favorite of the Jamaican's collaborations with the band (and it includes forays through a number of Bob Marley classics).

7/23/88 Pete Danforth's House, Underhill, VT

This tape is one of the most common from this time period (it is often identified as Pete's Phabulous Phish Phest on the J-cards). This three-set affair offers numerous musical treats, including a horn-sweetened "Slave," a "YEM" vocal jam based on "wash me, don't drive me" that segues into "Contact" (and an extra–lounge lizardy version at that), a funky "Weekapaug" with some vocal interplay, "No Dogs Allowed," and some fine percussion on "Possum." Both Pete Danforth and Cameron McKenney make stage appearances. Finally, if you enjoy Phishy stage banter, listen to the comments before and after "Walk Away" as well as Fish during "Terrapin" (which he performs with his trombone—the vacuum is still a few months away, but he makes a fascinating discovery with that trombone).

8/3/88, 8/6/88 The Roma, Telluride, CO

These are the two circulating tapes from Phish's initial visit to Telluride. Listen to the audience chatter between songs; it's clear that this is a very small room. It's also clear that by this point during their visit, the band knows most of the people in the room—many of whom they identify by name. The earlier tape includes some extensive narration after "Sloth," which Trey introduces as from the band's musical *The Man Who Stepped into Yesterday*, which is appearing on Broadway. Trey then laments that they should have performed the musical in order (but, alas, this doesn't happen) before the band moves into "Icculus." Also, two versions of "The Curtain" are offered: "with or without." The second tape includes a choice move from "Cities" into "Dave's" and back into "Cities" as well as eminently listenable versions of "A Train," "Satin Doll," and "Sanity," along with the onstage presentation of a "Baked in Telluride" T-shirt.

9/24/88 Humphries House, Amherst, MA

Humphries House, perhaps better known as The Zoo, was John Paluska's cooperative home when he lived at Amherst. The band dedicates "YEM" to JP, stating that "the reason we played this gig is because we knew John could get in without ID." The show offers a number of aural pleasures—for instance, listen to the quotes and teases in both "Divided Sky" and "AC/DC Bag," the transition from "YEM" to "Wilson" and then to "Peaches," the ending to "Curtain" and "Sparks." Most copies of this show are additionally noteworthy as the stage mike picks up some of the band's conversations between songs.

11/3/88 Molly's,
Boston, MA

Ben Hunter arranged this gig, which was Phish's Boston area debut. A number of Burlington phans made the trip south, and the band thanks both Ben and the Burlington contingent from the stage a few times. A fierce "Whipping Post" (with Trey on vocals) provides one of this show's musical high points, particularly as the song segues into "Dave's Energy Guide" for a short while before it concludes. The transition from "Fluffhead" to "Possum" is also worth hearing, along with Lightin' Hopkins's "Shaggy Dog," and an early, slowed-down "Foam." "I Didn't Know" includes the somewhat common introduction of Fish as "Vermont's second greatest trombonist-drummer, Moses Brown, Moses Heaps, and Moses Dewitt." "Harpua" is described as "a story, and as with all good stories, this story begins with an oompah-pah." All in all, an entertaining evening (which is why the band returned to Molly's a month later and the Paradise a month after that, as the momentum began to build. . . .).

2/6/89, 2/7/89 The Front,
Burlington, VT

These two nights showcase the state of the band's development as they moved away from Nectar's to the larger room during this period. The first night has fine moments, in particular, the first set cooks when the band moves from "La Grange" to "YEM" to Miles Davis's "All Blues" to "Sanity" to "A Train." The "Icculus" to "Whipping Post" tandem also raises a few hackles. The second night features Fish adding some trombone to "McGrupp," Mike's fine take on "Contact," and be sure to listen to "Makisupa" to get a handle on its lyrics during this period. "Bike" and "Whipping Post" are also noteworthy as Fish ("Moses Yastrzemski") begins to exhibit his newly found vacuum prowess.

4/30/89 Nightstage, Cambridge, MA

Put on this tape and before Phish begins its set, you can hear a rare band introduction provided by Ben "Junta" Hunter himself. As you'll hear, Ben's not the only one there. Trey's grandparents are in attendance as well, "at their first rock-and-roll concert." Listen further and you'll discover that the members of Phish are in reality traveling minstrels from Gamehendge. As the band moves from "McGrupp" through "Lizards," "Divided Sky," and "Wilson," Trey sketches the Gamehendge story, including the role of the Rhombus. Truth be told, Trey's grandparents may have ended up with a skewed perception of what a rock concert is really like—give this tape a listen and decide.

5/28/89 Ian Maclean's House, Hebron, NY

This tape has been the source of conjecture for some time—although most phans enjoy the performances, they debate the date on the tape. At some point late in the second set, Trey notes that it's snowing and says, "Merry Christmas," but if you listen to the intonation in his voice, you can hear that it's a joke. In all likelihood the snow comes from the ashes leaving the fire where Ian and friends had roasted a pig. As for the show itself, first off, if you're a sucker for Phishy stage banter, you have to get this tape. (It's worth it

Photo credit: Rich Luzzi

for the introductions of Fish and "Possum" as well as the great beer-run debate.) If you're a sucker for special guest stars stirring up the mix a little, you have to get this tape (with the magnificent duo of Mike and Magoo from Ninja Custodian). If you're a sucker for occasionally sloppy but undeniably fun versions of Phish songs, then get this tape ("YEM," "Mike's," and "Sanity" come to mind). If you're a sucker for—ohhh forget it. Just get the damn tape.

8/12/89 Burlington Boat House, Burlington, VT

Did you ever fantasize that Phish might play at your graduation? Your bar mitzvah? Your wedding? Well, find this tape and you can live vicariously through Steve and Beth. The set (reception) opens with the Allman Brothers' "Blue Sky," the couple's first song. Phish then moves back and forth through various tunes to get the contingents up and dancing ("Suzie," "Ya Mar," "Rocky Top," "Night and Day"). At the groom's request, the band then performs "YEM," with the appropriate wedding trampoline solos. Finally, no nuptials would be complete without a special tribute from the band, which Phish provides with a touching "Icculus" during which Fish plays trombone.

10/1/89 The Front, Burlington, VT

This tape chronicles another development in the history of the band: the beginning of the all-ages shows at The Front (which further expanded the scope of Phish's live audiences). Trey mentions this fact from the stage. Phish commemorated this particular night with some song debuts—"Reba," with the extra instrumental section, was dedicated to the spirit of Nancy. "Highway to Hell" also made its first appearance, without any dedications. Other moments to hear include "If I Only Had a Brain" and "YEM" (for contrasting reasons, but listen). Finally, if you've noted some musical similarities between "McGrupp" and "Golgi," then you should find this show because the two sounds are juxtaposed for all the world to hear.

10/20/89 The Front, Burlington, VT

If you're a phan of the Giant Country Horns, this tape's for you. In fact, much of this show's second set features two-thirds of the initial version of the GCH, Russ Remington and Dave Grippo (which is none too surprising, as they were in the studio with Phish at this time contributing horns to "Split Open and Melt"). "Harpua" is without narration, but "Reba" contains extra bag-it-and-tag-its. Also, the "Antelope" is an interesting one, with both "Old Macdonald" and *Benny Hill* theme quotes, along with repeated Marco Esquandolases and a respectable jam. Also, for you *Gus the Christmas Dog* phans, the second set opens with "No Dogs Allowed." Beyond this, get this show to hear Phish perform with the horns: "I Didn't Know" with Fish, then "The Truth" taking solos, "Split Open and Melt" (started again by Trey due to a missed light cue), the brassy *Odd Couple* intro to "Harry," "Swing Low, Sweet Chariot," and "Slave." Also the debut of the soon-to-disappear "I'm in a Hole."

10/26/89 Wetlands Preserve, New York, NY

Phish at Wetlands—the city kids were very happy with the band's few appearances here. This show's a keeper (and its not too hard to find). The first set includes a fine "Mike's Groove," but most of the musical highlights occur in the second set, which opens with a jam that sounds quite reminiscent of "Good Morning Little Schoolgirl." From here it's on to "Dinner and a Movie" in a set that incorporates some of the instrumental segments of "Fluffhead" as segues between songs. Listen to transitions from "Dinner" to "AC/DC Bag" and later from "Sloth" to "Possum." "PMITE" follows "Possum" in all its multidimensional splendor (that's right, not "PYITE"—listen to the tape). From here it's "I'm in a Hole" followed by a dramatic reading of a poem by Fish ("Gull Swerves," sweetened with some handiwork from Page) . Trey then introduces the story behind "No Dogs Allowed" along with the coauthor of the song— his mom, Diane Anastasio. Finally, the set closes with David Bowie's "Major Tom" providing the introduction and inspiration to Phish's "David Bowie."

2/25/90 8 × 10 Club, Baltimore, MD

This show may be slightly harder to come by than some of the others listed here, but if you can get hold of it, you should do so. For starters, most versions of this show come with a bonus sound check. So before the band breaks into "Foam," you can hear Phish perform an Allman Brothers jam (based on "Revival") and run through "Donna Lee." Then, as an extra bonus, before the first note Trey dedicates the band's version of "Foam" to Nectar's gravy fries. As for the music, this show features fine takes on "Funky Bitch," "Reba" (with a *Jeopardy* introduction), and "Makisupa." However, this one is worth seeking out for two other musical moments. First, listen to the music before the band breaks into "Bowie" . . . isn't that . . . why, yes, it is, the "Tweezer" theme, two months before it officially crystallizes into a song. Soon after, you can hear the very first live performance of "Rift." Although the words are pretty much the same (a few extras at the end), the music is quite different, and a bit clunky as the words don't quite fit (this is pre–"Curtain" integration). As an added bonus, you should seek out this show if you're a stage banter phan. There's plenty to choose from—including the band's comments before "Rift" and Trey's introductions of Fish before "MSO."

3/28/90 Beta Intramural Hockey Party, Denison University, Granville, OH

On their way out to Colorado, Phish performed their inaugural gig in the state of Ohio for an intramural hockey team at Denison

University. This show is noteworthy for many debuts and early versions of songs, including: "Tweezer" (" Tweezer So Cold"), "Runaway Jim" (with the initial extra verse), "Sweet Adeline" (Fish explains "that was the first public appearance of that song"), "Rift" (one of the final versions with the original music), and "Cavern" (with all its original lyrics, some of which Trey forgets during this slow, ragged take on the song). Of course Trey dedicates most every song to the Beta Intramural Hockey Team ("I love you guys like brothers . . . what a season, what a season. I'll never forget the 1990 intramural hockey season"). Other noteworthy tunes include "A Train," "Jesus Left Chicago" and "Mike's Groove" (beginning with Trey's introduction of "Gacht's Song" and building to a rapid-fire "Weekapaug" climax).

4/5/90 J. J. McCabes, Boulder, CO

This tape represents yet another milestone in the band's career, their first return trip to Colorado following the Telluride gigs in 1988. In anticipation, Trey announces that Phish has worked up some new songs: "Cavern," "Tweezer," and "Uncle Pen." "Cavern" and "Tweezer" (introduced as "Tweezer So Cold") are both well worth hearing to give you an idea of their evolutions (some say the "Cavern" is worth it for "Penile Erector" alone). This show has other features as well: Page plays clavinet on a few numbers (borrowed from the Samples' Al Laughlin), Trey repeatedly quotes the *Bonanza* theme (listen for it in "Ya Mar" and "Bowie," among others). You also get a guest doctor on "Jesus Loves Chicago," a brand-new vacuum, and a moving "If I Only Had a Brain." Try it, you'll like it.

4/18/90 Herman's Hideaway, Denver, CO

This show starts off in a satisfying manner with Mike thumping into his groove. Other noteworthy musical moments include "A

Train," "Funky Bitch," and "Bowie" (with a "Lawn Boy" quote). A noteworthy nonmusical moment occurs as the band attempts to find a date for lighting director Chris Kuroda. ("Hot lights from a hot guy . . . sexy light show . . . we just want to show you how sexy lights can be. Let's have a little light solo.") The debut of "Jaegermeister" falls somewhere between these categories ("Jaegermeister me all night long!").

9/13/90 Wetlands Preserve, New York, NY

On this night the band returned to live performance after a three-month break, so there are plenty of new songs and frisky onstage moments to appease almost everyone (there are few standout mind-numbing jams, but listen to the transitions from "AC/DC Bag" to "A Train" with "Buried Alive" to "Sparks" to "Reba"). The tunes that received their initial onstage treatments on this night include "Tube," "Buried Alive," "Magilla," and "Stash." One debut that never made it any further is Fish's take on "Minute by Minute." Also, the show features an early "Landlady," which Trey dedicates "to the spirit of Carlos" (little did he know). Finally, the second set closes with a triad of Dude tunes notable for the "Chalkdust" riff in "I Don't Care about Anyone but Myself" and the "Done Me Wrong" vocal jam.

11/2/90 Glen Miller Ballroom, Boulder, CO

The first words you hear on this tape are ones of great sadness—Phish has disbanded. Fortunately, however, a piscine phoenix has risen from the oceanic ashes: "Ladies and gentlemen, I give you Phish 2000." This Phish 2000, which sounds remarkably like the Phish that you know and love, has quite a bit to offer you as well, of particular note: an entertaining "Esther," a swell first-set closing sequence that moves from "Asse Festival" to "Possum" to "Buried Alive" and back to "Possum" with some signals thrown in, and a

"YEM" tailored for lovers of basketball and mothers. Finally, as a final fitting tribute to their predecessors, Phish 2000 teases a number of Phish classics before "David Bowie." Find this tape and make a game of it: How many Phish songs can you distinctly identify before "Bowie" begins?

11/4/90 Fort Ram Nightclub, Fort Collins, CO

This show does have a number of moments that draw phans back to it. For instance, the venue must have had a disco ball or a disco feel to it because the band makes a few musical and vocal references to that fact (listen closely to "Weekapaug" for a choice seventies selection or two, along with the introduction to "Contact"). Many also enjoy the "Manteca" very much (apparently Sir Duke was a Woody Woodpecker fan). Beyond this, there's a "Tube" (always nice to have on a tape), a funky "Suzie," and a dense "YEM" (listen to Mike's bass solo and the vocal jam in particular). Finally, a number of phans identify the "Harry" on this tape as one of their all-time favorites.

12/28/90 The Marquee, New York, NY

This show is many phans' favorite of this year's three-show New Year's run (the first of the Northeast New Year's runs, although 12/30/90 was an off date). The first set is a solid representation of the band during this period ("Forbin" into "Mockingbird" with min-imal story, a funkier but less exploratory "Mike's Groove"). As an added bonus for you Tom Marshall boosters, the lyricist, gadfly, and ne'er-do-well was in the audience that night, and Trey acknowl-edges his contributions from the stage after "Horn." The second set combines performance, humor, and guest star: a "Possum" ode to Christmas past, a fine transition from "Coil" to "Tweezer" (and a "Manteca"-enhanced "Tweezer" at that), a debut Fish foray through the Syd Barrett songbook ("No Good Trying"), an extended John

Popper appearance (check out the vocal jam at the end of "Don't Get Me Wrong"), and a well-received sneeze (listen, for it).

2/7/91 Pickle Barrel Pub, Killington, VT

Here's an interesting show from a curious venue that represents Phish in the spring of 1991. This one has spring's two debuts, "Chalkdust" and "Guelah" along with "Destiny Unbound," which the band first performed in the fall. For rarities, you have the famous abandoned "Lizards," where Trey flubs the lyrics so mercilessly that he has to bail. If it's comedy you like, listen to Fish explain what it means to be Zero Man or listen to Trey tease him about the composition of "My Sweet One." Finally, if you're just a phan of playing, the "Tweezer" that emerges from "Stash" is worth hearing (and particularly representative of this period), as is the "YEM," which is a keeper (you Looney Tunes fans won't want to miss the vocal jam).

3/17/91 Wheeler Opera House, Aspen, CO

This one's a story show. If you want to hear the band kick back in a nice venue with plenty of their friends present and having a good, loose time, check this out one. This show has some musical moments worth hearing ("Mike's Groove," "Bowie," "La Grange"), but you want to hear the stories. A Telluride contingent is present on this evening, and the band makes repeated references to its first visit there in 1988. In fact, the band is so happy to see the Telluride group that they solicit a request from one of them and perform "Slave" late in the second set. "Slave," however, is preceded by Fish's story of his adventures with a bear. The song is followed by Trey's story about the mysterious disappearance of the drummer before one of the Telluride shows in 1988, resulting in the three other members' performing "Jazz Odyssey" (a fine *Spinal Tap* reference). Of course, before the encore, Henrietta tries to set the record straight. It's well worth hearing (with a bonus "HYHU" while Fish sets up his high hat taboot).

4/11/91 The Cave, Carleton College, Northfield, MN

This is the one that started it all. Yes, indeed, this is the tape to get if you want to hear . . . the prison joke. It's not such a funny joke, and it's certainly in poor taste (both of which Fish pretty much admits as the rest of the band goads him into telling it; he also explains the origins of the joke and ties it into their touring). Nonetheless, if you've been wondering what it is that people have been calling for ever since, here you go. Is the prison joke enough to make this a recommended show? Some would say yes. But fear not, there are a number of musical moments that will reward you if you seek out this tape. For instance, another interesting "Tweezer," circa spring 1991, with extra vocals (Fish calls the song "A hell of an excuse to jam"), a solid "YEM" with a poignant vocal message for canines, a colorful, exploratory "Reba," a great transition between "Landlady" and "Destiny," and finally a bonus vocal jam of sorts when the band emerges onstage for its encore.

7/11/91 Battery Park, Burlington, VT

This free show was presented through the Burlington Arts Council as part of the two-hundredth-anniversary celebration of the city. It's also the debut performance of the Giant Country Horns. The show opens with "Oh Kee Pah" into the most enduring legacy of the horns—their take on "Suzie." Once you've heard "Suzie" with horns, you'll never hear it quite the same way again. This show also features "Flat Fee," finally reunited with the horns that Trey had charted for it six years earlier. All of these songs take on a new meaning and authority with the addition of the horns, but "Landlady," "Lizards," "Dinner and a Movie," "Cavern," and *Avenu Malkenu* are particularly well served. This show also features the debut of a

Photo credit: Kurt Zinnack

new song worked out for the tour—Henrietta the Lizard Queen's run through "Touch Me" along with the Edgar Winter rave-up "Frankenstein."

7/21/91 Arrowhead Ranch, Parksville, NY

Another celebrated venue that is no longer with us (although there is talk of reviving it now and again). Phish performed here on two consecutive nights during the summer of 1991, and this is the second of the shows (it is the more common tape, and most feel it is the better show). Carl Gerhard's mother is in attendance this night, and if you want to enhance your collection with the show where his dad shows up, find yourself a copy of 7/15/91 at the Academy in New York City. Both sets of this one showcase what the horns can add to Phish. Listen to the beginning of "Divided Sky" with Trey's long sustain, subsequently juxtaposed with the explosive darts of the horns. Other songs that are well served on this

Photo Credit: Kurt Zinnack

particular evening include "Tweezer," "AC/DC Bag," "Contact," "Mike's," and "Lawn Boy" (Page sounds considerably less like a lounge singer and more like a jazz vocal stylist). The one element that is missing from this night is the lack of jazz instrumentals (which is all the more reason to add yet another horn show to your collection). Still, you do get a washboard bonus for the encores, along with a very special invitation from the band to attend Amy's farm in two weeks.

8/3/91 Amy Skelton's Farm, Auburn, ME

Phish had spread the word about this free gig at the farm of "phirst phan" Amy Skelton in the few weeks prior to the show (listen, for instance, to Trey's announcement from the stage on 7/21/91). The resulting three sets of music on a sunny Saturday offered plenty of good vibes (after the first set Trey tells phans, "We're gonna take a break. Go wild because nobody's gonna stop you here." At the end of the show he says, "Have a good time tonight, we're gonna be out there partying with you"). However, some phans feel that the band's performance itself is solid but not searing. The show opens with some mutual introductions from Trey and Amy, followed by a long, rambling monologue by Fish about a political action group, which Trey mercifully cuts off ("We usually don't let him talk"), as the band begins "Wilson." The three sets that follow include entertaining versions of "Divided Sky," "YEM" (with an I Love Lucy quote and a rodent vocal jam), "Stash" (Trey holds a note that rivals his sustain on 8/17/92), "Possum," and three songs with the "Dude of Life" (Sofi Dillof appears for "Bitchin' Again").

10/13/91 North Shore Surf Club, Olympia, WA

This is often billed as the second complete Gamehendge show. That isn't quite right; "Lizards" is missing. Also, unlike the four others that circulate, this one does not have a cohesive narrative with a linear flow. Instead, the band plays "Wilson," then Trey narrates a bit, then Phish returns for "Forbin" into "Mockingbird" after two other songs and fills in the gaps. This is fine if you really enjoy the Gamehendge songs, but if you want to be swept into the narrative flow of the tale, I recommend any of the others before this one. This show does feature a dandy first-set closing "Mike's Groove" along with a charging "Llama," a sultry "Jesus Left Chicago," and a tease-y, spacy "Bowie" (with a high hat solo taboot).

10/31/91 Armstrong Hall, Colorado Springs, CO

This show is renowned for two elements—the costume contest and the debut of "The Wait." The costume contest starts out the second set, with its coveted first prize being a year on the band's guest list. All of the contestants are required to bounce on the tramps for a bit, and the losers are told to stage dive. After the contest the band starts "Fee," and Trey has some difficulty . . . so begins the "Wait" saga. Phish performs a riff from "It's Ice" (which had debuted just the month before), and the members all say "wait" in unison. They continue doing this for a few minutes before each song through the end of the set. At various points the audience members collectively yell "No!" at the off beat. By the end of the set the band varies things as well, replacing their "wait" chant with a vocal jam of similar phrases: "hold on," "time out," etc. If that's not enough for you, this show also features fine versions of "Brother," "YEM" (with a pizza vocal jam), and "Bowie," with an additional random "bucket of lard" chant or two.

12/6/91 Middlebury College, Middlebury, VT

Another tough call. The next night has plenty of moments, with a fine "Harpua" (as Harpua's owner returns after being away for three months), a fine "Forbin" into "Mockingbird," and the trampoline giveaway, among other moments. Still, this show is more entertaining overall. Part of the reason is that most copies of the show include the sound check. Listen to the band's displeasure with their soundchecked performance of "Memories" (after the second time the band agrees that it's improved a bit, which now raises it "all the way up to the level of sucked," according to Trey). "Dog Log" is next which ends with Trey inquiring about the band's long-departed rhythm guitarist: "Where's Holdsworth gone, where's Holdsworth gone? . . . Jesus." A blues jam, "Shaggy Dog," and "Makisupa" follow. The actual show contains a number of festive holiday moments (Trey's solo in "Lawn Boy") and nonholiday moments as well: "Magilla" drifts into one of Woody Allen's jazz favorites, Fish taking another stab at fretless guitar in "Whipping Post," a listener-friendly "Tela" and "YEM"—featuring signals and random alligator call. This one also includes the short-awaited return of . . . "The Wait" (without the "It's Ice" music).

3/13/92 Campus Club, Providence, RI

This show is renowned for its "Antelope" into "BBFCFM" into "Antelope" combo. If you pick up this show for that reason alone, you'll be satisfied. The "Big Black Furry Antelope" is preceded by a "Follow the Yellow Brick Road" tease and an "Up and Away (in My Beautiful Balloon)" quote. From here it's on through a full-tilt "Antelope," which extends, but before reaching its climactic final chorus, the song veers off into a scorching "BBFCFM" (which also contains an interesting variation, as Mike says "oh why," then "Hawaii," which the band members repeat in turn before blasting through "Big Black Furry" and into "Antelope," which reaches a crescendo that Trey tops with a concluding language signal). Speaking of signals, Trey offers up the second session of language lessons in the second set, which he encourages everyone to put on a tape to tell their friends. The show also offers, among other moments, some fine bagpipe action by Henrietta.

3/20/92 Broome County Forum, Binghamton, NY

Apparently the band ate well before this show (or so Trey claims from the stage). At any rate, they certainly ate something because they're in a mood on this evening. The first set offers the new "Rift" and "Maze," which the band had introduced two weeks earlier, along with some fine versions of some old favorites, in particular, a steaming "Antelope" with Fish on trombone. The second set opens with a "Roundabout" tease that yields to a screaming "Mike's." A litany of nicknames for Mr. Gordon are pronounced during this song and the subsequent "Sanity." Later, the band performs the "Cold as Ice" introduction, which has replaced "Hold Your Head Up" as the Henrietta theme this spring (the Campus Club show has it as well). After Fish takes center stage, Trey leads the crowd in a "prison joke" chant, but Fish doesn't cave. He does offer a fine bagpipe-abetted "Terrapin," however, after which Trey tells the audience, "Maybe Pete Schall will tell the prison joke. . . ." Obviously in the mood to talk, Trey then inquires, "You guys know the language?" and walks through it once more. Following this, Mike introduces "a song about brutal death," and a stomping "Possum" closes the set.

4/18/92 Wilbur Field, Stanford University, Palo Alto, CA

Phans love this week. The run of shows from 4/16 to 4/22 are all hailed for the band's spirited performances. Great sound boards exist of all these shows—get as many as you can. The Wilbur Field Show was a free outdoor affair with some interesting sidelights—a "Marley" introduction and repeated "squirt-gun breaks" during the second set. Musically speaking, this one is renowned for its fine "Manteca" and a "Manteca" reprise, a "Possum" with a segment that sounds suspiciously like the Grateful Dead's "Mind Left Body" jam to many phans, an enthusiastic "Bathtub Gin," a well-paced "Antelope" with "Frere Jacques" contained within, and finally a gorgeous "Harry Hood" with the "Linus and Lucy" theme that many phans hail as their all-time favorite. Two other noteworthy moments—first, during *Avenu Malkenu*, Trey indicates that "Mike 'Cactus' Gordon will now play a happy Passover bass solo." Second, the "Cold as Ice" introduction goes on a bit long and fulfills its intention of irritating Fish, who mutters "Okay, okay, I think we get it. . . . I apologize for that." No apologies necessary for this show, though.

4/21/92 Redwood Acres Fairgrounds, Eureka, CA

This show contains a number of stellar versions of Phish originals, along with an interesting cover. The majestic setting no doubt contributed to a magnificent show with enjoyable renditions of "SOAM," "Possum," "Tweezer," and "Mike's Groove." The "Forbin" into "Mockingbird" is a keeper as well, as a Houseboat and a Hang Glider carry the audience away. The show also reveals the little-known fact that both "Hydrogen" and "Weigh" were written by former Boston Red Sox left fielder and first baseman Carl Yastrzemski. (On a similar baseball note, on 8/26/89 Trey reveals that "Slave" and "Avenu" were written by Pete Rose.) Finally, this tape features Mike's a cappella "Catapult" followed by his vacuum cleaner debut during Fish's take on "Lively Up Yourself." A vocal jam follows and leads into "Sanity."

5/2/92 Cabaret Metro, Chicago, IL

A fine sampling from the band's pass through the Midwest on their way back home. Aquarium Rescue Unit opened this show—no doubt goosing Phish to higher level. Things start off right, as "Runaway Jim" trails off to Gamehendge with an extended "Forbin" batting second. The narration carries the audience up in the air and off to that land where Trey introduces the deity of Gamehendge and the Helping Friendly Book in proper fashion with a screeching "Icculus" ("We showed the book to Colonel Bruce Hampton and the Aquarium Rescue Unit. They used to be a feeble bluegrass band until they read the book"). This drifts into a soaring musical accompaniment to "Famous Mockingbird." This show took place shortly after the LAPD police officers were acquitted of beating Rodney King, which leads to some modified lyrics in an appropriately enraged "Stash." The "Bowie" contains some signals as well as demonstrations of the band and crew football theme songs. The "YEM" vocal jam is interesting as are the plaintive squeaks during "Sleeping Monkey."

6/19/92–6/24/92 Germany

These four shows took place during a five-day run from Hamburg to Nuremberg (the band's three other European dates are a bit harder to find). All of these shows took place as opening acts for the Violent Femmes, with forty-five-to-fifty-minute sets from the band. These tapes are recommended for their historical (and comic) value. From Trey's initial remarks at the first show it's clear that the band is somewhat uncomfortable with the situation. "Good evening," he opens. "We're Special Guests from the United States" (the handbills and the marquee read "Violent Femmes plus Special Guests (from the United States)." On a few other occasions the band makes it clear that it is not made up of former members of the band Marillion (one of whose name is Fish). Beyond this, on the 6/20 tape listen to Fish inquire if anyone knows Syd Barrett and introduce his vacuum cleaner. The band loosens up a bit more before the next show, which includes a vacuum solo in "BBFCFM." That same night the set-closing "Golgi" includes the German word for "ticket stub" in one of its verses. Finally, in the 6/24 show, which features fine performances of "Runaway Jim" and "Llama," Trey repeatedly introduces two audience members, Jurgen and Rudy, from the stage and finally "reveals" that Fish is busting his butt for the two of them (the band later acknowledged them in the liner notes to *A Live One*). The shows concludes on this night with Trey's explanation that Phish is from Burlington, not Seattle. In all fairness, if you want to hear the one show that the members of Phish did think was respectable, check out their ninety-minute European set at the Roskilde Festival in Denmark.

7/25/92 Stowe Performing Arts Center, Stowe, VT

Phish performed this single set while opening for Santana. This tape is worth hearing because Carlos honors the group and delights local phans with a guest appearance. He emerges during "You Enjoy Myself" along with two members of his band, Raul Rekow on congas and Karl Perazzo on timbales. "YEM" takes off, featuring some playful dual guitar work as well as an extended percussion session. "Llama" follows, with Trey and Carlos mirroring each other and dueling back and forth. The set doesn't end here, however, as Trey announces that they're allowed to perform one more song, a screaming "Funky Bitch."

8/17/92 The Coach House, San Juan Capistrano, CA

This was the only night during the Santana tour that Phish had an opportunity to perform two sets by themselves, and they made the most of it. Ninja Custodian opened in the last of the tandems between these two bands. This show is worth hearing for the note Trey holds in "Mike's" and the fact that Ninja Mike lifts Fish's dress after "Terrapin" and kisses him on the butt. Although the latter point doesn't translate too well on tape, you can still savor the former. You can also enjoy the jam between the two, with Ninja Mike on drums and Fish singing. Other moments of note in this show: a "Camel Walk" intro to "Wilson," the a cappella intro to

Photo credit: Richard Waltein

"Suzie," the *Flintstones* theme before and during "A Train," and a complete "Somewhere Over the Rainbow."

11/19/92 Ross Arena, St. Michael's College, Colchester, VT

Apparently, the band was feeling sentimental as it opened its fall tour at St. Michael's. Trey quotes "Those Were the Days," the theme to *All in the Family*, during "Divided Sky," "Antelope," and "Weekapaug." Perhaps his mood is enhanced in this regard by the addition of Gordon Stone, who performs on pedal steel guitar on a number of tunes. This show has its share of debuts, too: "Axilla" (not called "Axilla (I)," as there was no thought of an "Axilla II" as yet), "Fast Enough for You," "Lengthwise" (with a more reggae-inflected tone than the later versions), and Mike's take on the man in black, Mr. Johnny Cash, with "I Walk the Line." Another debut that night is the Big Ball Jam, which the band performs and then explains toward the end of the second set. One other first is Trey's use of the megaphone during "Fee." Also, listen for "The Price of Love" in "Weekapaug."

11/28/92 Capitol Theater, Port Chester, NY

Another sad one—the final show at Port Chester's Capitol Theater. The band makes the best of it, though, beginning with an early pun after Mike experiences problems with his bass during "My Sweet One." If you're not a big fan of puns (and most of the people in Port Chester that night were not), then there are plenty of musical moments to satisfy you, with "Mike's Song" (Is that "Walk This Way" in there?) and "Tweezer" (Is that "Alumni Blues" in there?) of particular note. Many phans also enjoy the "Harpua," which, like the "Forbin" narration from the night before, takes place in Fish's brain and features the Spin Doctors' "Jimmy Olsen's Blues." "Honey Love" contains both some atypical drum flourishes from Trey and a veeeeerrrry looooooong vacuum solo from Fish. Oh yeah, and Trey dances with his grandma during "Contact"—you can't see this, but you can hear Mike's reaction (he gets a bit distracted and has some problems with the lyrics).

2/20/93 Roxy Theater, Atlanta, GA

All of the shows from this three-night stand in Atlanta are enjoyable, but the second set from this evening remains many phans' all-time favorite. All of the songs that Phish performs during the set contain innovative, entertaining moments (for instance, the speed-metal in "Wilson" or the ad-libbed lyrics to "Glide"). "Tweezer" is particularly interesting. The band adds a rap section before moving into "Walk Away" and then back into "Tweezer." "Mike's Groove" is a jam-packed phun phest. This version is exceptional from the opening notes, when Fish encourages Mike to sing his song. Mike's vocals are followed by a medley of Phish songs, including "Wilson," "Fluffhead," "Tweezer," "Stash," "Lizards," and "My Mind's Got a Mind of Its Own." After the first notes of "Hydrogen," Phish also performs the Vibration of Life and "Kung." "Weekapaug" drifts into "Have Mercy" before the band completes the "Groove." "Terrapin," "Harry Hood," and "Sleeping Monkey" induce smiles as well.

3/14/93 Western State College Gym, Gunnison, CO

This show is another phan phavorite. It begins in fine fashion with Page still making the most of his new baby grand on "Loving Cup." The first set has a few other notable moments—in particular, "Foam," "Guela," and "Stash." Cameron McKenney appears as well, adding the "Indian War Dance" and some "bag it, tag its" to "Reba." The second however, is the real keeper here. This one opens with—boom!—"Halley's Comet," the triumphant return of the song after a four-year absence. A tension-laden "Bowie" and the rare "Curtis Lowe" are followed by a lengthy showcase "YEM" that teases and quotes a number of songs, including "Owner of a Lonely Heart," "Low Rider," "Spooky" (with vocals). The vocal jam is another paean to seventies rock, with "We Are the Champions" and "Welcome to the Machine" phrases. There's more fun to be had with this one, too, as in keeping with this spirit, Fish debuts his new Pink Floyd cover, "Great Gig in the Sky." The "Squirming Coil" that ends the show gives Page an opportunity to showcase his new acquisition for the good people of Colorado.

3/22/93 Crest Theater, Sacramento, CA

This show is noteworthy because it represents the third complete Gamehendge narration (actually the second, because 10/13/91 is not complete). The first set has its moments—"Weigh" is enjoyable, as is "Llama," but it's the second set that you want. The action begins during "It's Ice," which gradually dissolves into "Lizards." At this point Trey compliments the audience on its attentiveness and carries everyone down through the ice and into Gamehendge. Before Trey brings Colonel Forbin into the story, he narrates a bit of the history of Gamehendge , explaining the arrival of Wilson and his enslavement of the Lizards. From here you discover Colonel Forbin out walking with McGrupp as he finds the passage to the other land. The traditional story follows, with a few light moments. (Trey apologizes for the pause after "Wilson" because he is "looking at this guy down here.") Otherwise, Trey offers the standard revised version of the story, without the death of Tela. By the way, her song provides one of the set's musical highlights, along with "AC/DC Bag." The song cycle ends as the Shepherd sings "McGrupp." Trey then promises more Gamehendge saga to come, featuring the later years of the war-torn land. The band then rewards the audience for their patience and responsiveness with the "Mike's Groove" that ends this lengthy set.

5/8/93 University of New Hampshire Fieldhouse, Durham, NH

Three months of touring came to an end on this evening. The show begins a bit slowly, but by the fifth song the band starts mixing things up a bit, taking "Stash" into the nether regions and inserting "Kung" before returning to "Stash." A subsequent notable moment is "Satin Doll"s ("A Love Song to the Crew.") Things really get cooking in the second set. If you're the kind of phan who enjoys a tasty musical sandwich, this set provides two of them. "David Bowie" into "Have Mercy" into "David Bowie" opens the set (with "Jessica" in there as well). And it'll fill you up, too, if you don't leave room. Both "Horse" into "Silent" and "It's Ice" are satisfying, but for true hearty fare, how about the "Squirming Coil," with a flavorful full Phish jam after Page's solo? A bit of BBJ. Then more tasty eats: "Mike's" into "Crossroads" into "Mike's," which continues through "Hydrogen" and "Weekapaug," yielding the a cappella "Amazing Grace" and then a set-closing, spine-tingling "Amazing Grace" jam. It'll give you chills (even if initially Fish does speed the thing up a little too quickly for some tastes). Oh yeah, and a well-cooked "AC/DC Bag" for dessert.

8/2/93 Ritz Theater, Tampa, FL

Years from now, when the biorhythmic readouts and astrological charts are properly tabulated, we'll find out why August 1993 was such a remarkable period for the band. Until then, all we can do is listen to the music and shake our heads in merriment and wonder. This first set includes a wonderfully abrasive "Brother"—the first in more than a year and then a noteworthy set-ending sequence that moves from "Bathtub Gin" through "Makisupa" into "My Mind's Got a Mind of Its Own." "Dog Log" follows (for Paul) along with a fine set-closing "La Grange." Phish doesn't ease up in the second set either—2001 charges into an intense "Mike's," which builds and builds until heavy vocalist Joe Rooney takes the stage to scream along with the band. This jam carries into "Sparks," which segues into "Curtis Lowe." Phish returns for the "Weekapaug" out of "Coil."

Bike comes next as Fish shows off his brand new 1953 Electrolux Floor Sweeper ("This baby's got power. No more of this wimpy shit . . . Don't try this at home, you'll bleed"). The set closes with an unrestrained "Antelope" that somehow ends up in a "Makisupa" reprise before galloping home with the conclusion to "Antelope." "Sleeping Monkey" encore, too.

Photo credit: Rich Luzzi

8/9/93 The Concert Hall, Toronto

Plop either set of this show into your deck and enjoy. This one is two, two, two treats in one. The "Chalkdust" that opens the show takes a few atypical turns, at one point cascading out into "Who Knows," and offers a few hints of what is to come. The segue from "Fee" to "Split Open and Melt" is brief but intriguing, as is the move from "Split" to "Glide." Listen carefully for signals and quotes in "Glide" as well as "Divided Sky." The "Coil" 's a keeper, too. The second set opens with an extended, active musical sequence that carries the listener from "Dinner and a Movie" into "Tweezer" (with a hint of "Down with Disease?"), into "Tela" into "My Friend My Friend." The "You Enjoy Myself" contains many interesting elements including a "Smoke on the Water" tease, two lines of lyrics from the "Speed Racer" theme and a "Psycho Killer" vocal jam. Then after Phish makes fine "Contact" "The Dude" emerges to reveal his "Crimes of the Mind."

8/20/93 Red Rocks Amphitheater, Morrison, CO

Majestic venue, majestic show. When Trey screams, "This is Red Rocks! This is the edge!" on the 7/25/88 "Sanity" later pressed onto *Junta*, the band could not have anticipated that one day they would headline at this venue (then again, maybe they could have—remember that "Sanity" is from the band's good-bye gig before heading out to Telluride). At any rate, there they were, playing for the good people of Colorado who had supported them over the years. The atmosphere elected to celebrate as well, as the rain clouds cleared just before show time and the band took the stage for a celebratory "Divided Sky." With the cheers still echoing across the rocks, Phish showed that they wanted to make this one really special with the distinctive oompah-pah of "Harpua." This story takes on a particular Red Rocks flavor with the powers of the Red Rocks iguana (listen to this one for the tale's dramatic ending). There's more to this set as well—the reworked "Wedge" (particularly appropriate for Red Rocks—a geological divide reached via the highway) and a slamming "Antelope." The second set opens with the familiar sounds of 2001 dissolving into the freshly revived "Slave." And after the band brings that tune to a screaming conclusion, the familiar notes of "SOAM" begin. You want more? How about a fine midset "Coil"? A zippy "Chalkdust?" Or a funky "YEM" that drifts into "Purple Rain" with Mimi Fishman on vacuum? Or a "Mango Song"–"Freebird" encore?

12/30/93 Cumberland County Civic Center, Portland, ME

This is another epic show that routinely makes it onto phans' top ten lists. Two intense sets of Phish at a creative height. The band came right out and let everyone know what was in store with a show-opening "Bowie" that incorporates Aerosmith's "Dream On" among other themes and textures. Next, an uncommon pass through the elliptical mind that is Mike Gordon with "Weigh." The equally uncommon "Curtain" evolves into a sweet "Sample." "Paul and Silas" gallop by next, and then Trey carries us up and away to Gamehendge with "Colonel Forbin." After a decent pass through "Rift" and a squawking "Bathtub Gin," the set closes with an a cappella phan fave, "Freebird." And then the band turns it up a notch in a masterful performance that spans the entire second set, with segues from song to song. 2001 leads into a welcome "Mike's" (listen to this jam for a few hints of things to come), which moves into "The Horse," a moving Silent jam, and then into a kicking "PYITE." The band doesn't stop, however, as an outro jam leads into a solid "McGrupp," which in turn carries into a high-energy "Weekapaug," which drifts into "Purple Rain." A quick pause to catch a breath, and then "Slave." To quote Marv Albert, "Yessssss."

12/31/93 Worcester Centrum, Worcester, MA

Phish's first arena New Year's show offers a number of musical highlights and one enduring mystery (were they really hoisted to the ceiling in wet suits and dropped into the clam at midnight?). The festivities begin with "Peaches," a tribute to the late Frank Zappa, which the band continues to quote from throughout the evening (in "It's Ice," "Possum," and "Suzie" among others). This show also offers pleasing versions of "Tweezers," "Poor Heart," "Split Open and Melt," and a stunning "Harry Hood." Also listen for a "Roundabout" tease before "Ginseng Sullivan," a Banana Splits quote in "Tweezer," a guest appearance by Tom Marshall during "Antelope" ("to perform the first lyrics he ever wrote for a Phish song") and an extended "Down with Disease" jam at midnight, four months before the release of "Hoist," as Phish provides Mike with some footage for his video.

4/4/94 Flynn Theater, Burlington, VT
4/15/94 Beacon Theater, New York, NY

These two shows feature the return of the Giant Country Horns, now six players strong. Phish debuted many of the *Hoist* songs at the Flynn, and the horns assisted on "Julius" and "Wolfman's Brother." Other highlights include the show-opening a cappella "Back in My Old Home Town" introduction to "Divided Sky," "Reba," "I Wanna Be Like You," "Split Open and Melt" (with horns), the "Harry Hood"–"Cavern" encores (the latter features the original "Brothel Wife" lyrics), and Trey's occasional updates from the NCAA basketball final being played that evening. The Beacon show, which culminated a three-night run, offers some appealing first-set moments, including "Harry Hood," a "Wilson"-"Chalkdust" combo, and "Down with Disease." Early in the second set, after completing the first verse of "Suzie," Trey announces, "Ladies and gentlemen, straight from Gamehendge, the Giant Country Horns!" Highlights of this appearance include "Suzie," "Landlady," "Magilla," and one verse of "Alumni Blues."

5/7/94 The Bomb Factory, Dallas, TX

The first set is solid, but it's the second set you want, the second set you *need*. This set is often billed, and bears itself out as, a sixty-three-minute "Tweezer." It is a precursor to the "Tweezer" that appears on *A Live One* (11/2/94), but it is much more playful. During the course of this "Tweezer" the band moves back and forth through moments of exploration into snippets of songs and then back into "Tweezer." Listen carefully to the teases and transitions as Phish drifts into a blues jam, a tribute to the band GWAR (which was playing next door), "Sparks," "Makisupa," "Sweet Emotion," and the Breeders' "Cannonball." The "Hold Your Head Up" also is noteworthy because it features a prolonged jam. Sound boards of this show circulate, so do yourself a favor and find one.

5/27/94 Warfield Theater, San Francisco, CA

This show placed an exclamation point on the band's three-show run at the Warfield. The show opens with some audience participation during "Wilson," but nothing like the Beacon version. Indeed, most of the audience participation during this set comes from extensive clapping following "Bowie" and "PYITE" into "Harry." In the second set, fine versions of "Reba" and "Julius" precede the stripped-down acoustic takes on "Nellie Cane" and "My Mind's Got a Mind of Its Own" which are augmented by the guest fiddle of Morgan Fichter. And then things really get good. Listen carefully as "Mike's" begins, drifts outward and then stutters a bit before moving into the premiere version of the still-evolving "Simple." This work in progress passes back into "Mike's" for a ferocious extensive jam, which then spirals to a close as Andrea Baker of the San Francisco Opera Company takes the stage to interject an unmiked opera aria. As she walks off, the crew distributes boxes of macaroni and cheese to the audience to induce a bit more participation, which occurs throughout the ensuing "Possum" (which includes a *Flintstones* tease—and numerous cries from Fish of "Shake your macaroni! Shake it!"). The action continues during the "Fire" encore.

6/17/94 Eagle Auditorium, Milwaukee, WI

The surrealistic events of the day manifested themselves on stage during this notable show. This was the day of the O.J. Simpson low-speed chase. After a well-played first set (in particular, "SOAM," "Bathtub Gin," and "Cavern"), the band emerged to perform 2001 with an erratic chorus of "Run, O.J., Run" that returns throughout the set. O.J. runs through "Poor Heart," "Mike's," and "Simple" ("we've got O.J. in the band"). All of these songs are charged up with an extra burst of energy as is the "Weekapaug" and the "Harpua," which incorporates "Kung" and "Simple" while Jimmy listens to Jimi ("Voodoo Child"). Fine "Frankenstein," too.

6/26/94 Municipal Auditorium, Charleston, WV

Find this tape and pop the first set into your tape deck. The striking of a cymbal and then . . . wait, this can't be right, something must be cut—"Kung" to open? That's right, "Kung" to open, with "Llama" to follow, and then . . . Gamehendge, and a fine one at that. Trey explains that this is the band's first gig in West Virginia, excepting a brief performance on Mountain Stage. So, by way of introduction they decide to share a story. The band (particularly Page) backs Trey's narration, which adds to the overall effect and impact of this run-through. The set concludes with the Gamehendge coda, "McGrupp," and a "Divided Sky" with some Rhombus narration. Then, for the second set, in order to give the good people of West Virginia a true taste of Phish, circa 1994, the band performs the entire *Hoist* album in order, including the "I'm Serious" rap in "Axilla" and culminating with the "SOAM" jam and *"Yerushalim Shel Zahav"* out of "Demand." The encores include the debut of "Old Home Place," the return of "Tube," and "Fire."

7/8/94 Great Woods, Mansfield, MA

Another one that caught people by surprise. Phans were still buzzing about the Charleston Gamehendge two weeks later as "Llama" opened the show and collapsed into "N_2O." Then Trey announces, "There's a fifty-two-year-old man sitting in a dentist's chair . . . ," and off we go once again. Like the 6/26 show, this Gamehendge features the instrumental backing to Trey's story. Unlike that show or any other Gamehendge, this one contains an additional element—the fervid screams of fifteen thousand phans. As each new character is introduced, the crowd raises a collective cheer. The narration itself is a bit unfocused but at times quite hilarious (listen to the description of the rebels' efforts before "Wilson"). The set ends with the same "McGrupp"–"Divided Sky" combo as Charleston, but the "Divided Sky" has more inventive improv after the written out section. No second-set *Hoist* here, but rather an intense celebratory amalgam of all the band's material, featuring an epic "Stash" (that made it onto *A Live One*), an unexpected move from "Reba" to the haunting "*Yerushalim Shel Zahav*," and a "YEM" that swallows "Frankenstein."

10/29/94 Memorial Auditorium, Spartanburg, SC

This show immediately preceded the Glens Falls Halloween extravaganza, so a number of phans entered this one with low expectations—which were promptly exceeded. The first set offers an interesting grouping of songs that charges on home with a concluding romp: from "SOAM" through the rare "Buffalo Bill," then "Makisupa" into "Rift." The second set contains a number of surprising segues, as "Down with Disease" leads into "TMWSIY" into "*Avenu*" into "TMWSIY," which itself carries into a punchy "Sparks" and into "Uncle Pen." "YEM" is explosive and "Antelope" into "Sleeping Monkey" into "Antelope" is another treat. And the encore? Uhhh, "Harold Hood."

10/31/94 Glens Falls Civic Center, Glens Falls, NY

Phish presented its first Halloween Costume at this an epic show that lasted until 3:30 in the morning. The opening set includes stellar versions of "Simple," "Divided Sky" and "Harpua" (which features a story about Halloween 99 years in the past, the "Vibration of Death," and a "War Pigs" quote). The second set opens with a musical tease or two until Ed Sullivan announces, "Ladies and gentlemen, the Beatles!" as Phish storms into "Back in the USSR" and the *White Album*. The band performs the album in near-entirety (no "Birthday" or "Good Night"), with Page singing the mellow McCartney tunes and Trey providing vocals on most others. All in all the Costume yields some faithful interpretations ("Dear Prudence," "Julia," "Cry Baby Cry"), some Phishy variations ("Don't Pass Me By," "While My Guitar Gently Weeps"), and some lyric modifications (listen carefully to "Glass Onion," "Honey Pie," and "Rocky Raccoon"). The results are exhausting yet glorious (and there's still a set yet to come). The band doesn't skimp on set three either, with notable versions of "Bowie," "Antelope," and "Slave," followed by the costume contest and "Squirming Coil," as Page ends this momentous evening (morning) with a solo serenade.

11/16/94 Hill Auditorium, Ann Arbor, MI, 11/19/94 Parking Lot, Indiana University, Bloomington, IN

You definitely want to hear at least one of the shows during Jeff Mosier's traveling bluegrass clinic from 11/16 to 11/20. The first show and the parking lot jam are two fine examples of the band during this period with Mosier. The Hill Auditorium show features Jeff Mosier appearances in both sets as well as a number of fine moments without the banjo. "Reba," "Stash," the jam from "Mike's" to "Simple" (which sounds a bit "Tweezer"-esque) and "Chalkdust" (which appears on *A Live One*) all make for a solid show. This one's also worth getting, though, to hear Reverend Jeff with the band on "Pig in a Pen," "Tennessee Waltz," Bill Monroe's "Bluegrass Break-down," "Swing Low, Sweet Chariot," "I'm Blue, I'm Lonesome," and "Long Journey Home." Reverend Mosier's bluegrass tutorial did not end onstage, however. He joined the band for bluegrass jams on the tour bus after most of his shows with Phish. The postshow jam on 11/19/94 was recorded by one intrepid phan. This extended bluegrass performance includes many of the songs that the group had played onstage, along with "Mountain Dew," "Midnight Moon-light," and "Will the Circle Be Unbroken." It's a bonus acoustic set and one that you'll want to hear.

11/30/94 Evergreen College Recreation Center, Olympia, WA

This show features two strong sets. The first opens with a stomping "Frankenstein" and closes with the end product of Reverend Jeff's lessons ("I'm Blue, and I'm Lonesome," "Long Journey Home"), with an enjoyable "Forbin"-"Mockingbird" (including the Vibration of Life as the audience holds onto a line of sound) and "Down with Disease" in between. The second set is nearly seamless; the band's really thinking on its feet as an extended run of songs segue into one another. The action begins with "Halley's," which carries into "Antelope," which dissolves into "My Sweet One" and then back into "Antelope." This song segues into another Mosier legacy, "Fixin' to Die," which drifts into a sprightly "Ya Mar," which carries into a dense "Mike's," which yields "Catapult" before finally finishing with "McGrupp."

5/16/95 Lowell Memorial Auditorium, Lowell, MA

When Phish announced that it would play a Voters for Choice benefit after a five-and-a-half-month break, no one knew what to expect. Luckily, Gloria Steinem took the stage and explained everything. Phans would hear "the most new music you've never heard before . . . for as Emma Goldman said, 'If there's no dancing, it's not my revolution.' " With that, Phish took the stage and launched into a traditional gospel song, "Don't You Wanna Go." From here the band moved through a number of new songs—"Ha Ha Ha," "Spock's Brain," and "Strange Design"—before appeasing some phans with a version of "Reba" that some still rank as among their all-time favorites. Following "Theme from the Bottom," Fish introduces the names of the previous songs (although "Strange Design" is called "Ahhhh Page Sing"). This culminates with an audience vote for the title of "Spock's Brain." After Fish's run through "Lonesome Cowboy Bill," the new "Glide II" segues into a decent "YEM." Mike's Brian Eno cover, "I'll Come Running," serves as a fine encore, followed by a hint of the much-anticipated "Gloria" as Ms. Steinem returned to the stage for some waves, hugs, and a shuffle or two.

6/16/95 Walnut Creek Amphitheater, Raleigh, NC

The summer of '95 featured a number of explosive and exploratory second sets. Perhaps this is because the sun went down, Chris Kuroda was allowed to work, and his creations affected those of the band. This first set has its moments—the "Halley's" into "Down with Disease" opener in particular. Beyond that, the "Cry Baby Cry" is a treat, and listen to Fish before "Dog Faced Boy." The second set, however, sets this one apart. The "Runaway Jim" is a mammoth product of exploration and collaboration. The transition to "Free" is satisfying in its own right (although the summer's best transition into "Free" takes place at Saratoga ten days later, from "Down with Disease"). This set has more, too, as after an a cappella interlude with "Carolina," the band breaks into "YEM," with a special appearance by Boyd Tinsley on fiddle. Listen to his contributions as he plays off the various band members—intense stuff (and if you're a DMB fan, check out the "Three Little Birds" encore the next night with Dave and Leroi).

6/22/95 Finger Lakes Performing Arts Center, Canandaigua, NY

Was this the worst Phish show ever? Or at least the worst two-set affair? A number of phans thought so by the middle of the second set. It's the second set that earns this show whatever distinction you may deem appropriate. The set list reads " Theme"—"Tweezer"— "Tweezer" reprise. That's all there is. Of course, there's plenty of music contained within those two (maybe three) songs, including some "My Generation" vocals. Your opinion of this set will depend on how much you enjoy listening to the band members showcase their improvisational skills and drills to find "heys" and fill "hey holes" with few recognizable melodies. Some phans point to this show as the zenith of their Phish experience—others think it sucks. Give a listen and form an opinion.

10/14/95 Austin Music Hall, Austin, TX

Medeski, Martin, and Wood were in town this night to perform, and a number of phans crossed their fingers, hoping for some cross-pollination (they'd get it on both counts). But first, "Kung" proves enjoyable as a stand-alone, as do "Free," "Tela," and the "Stash" into "Catapult" combo. The second-set opening "Reba" is pleasant, but you want to hear the "YEM" that comes third. During this song the members of MMW join Phish onstage. Over the course of a long, involved jam, both John Medeski and Page play keyboards, Fish plays vacuum and trombone, Billy Martin plays his drums, Chris Wood plays a one-string bass, Trey moves from guitar to his drum kit, Mike plays bass and later horn, and a member of the MMW crew joins both bands onstage to add a bit of trumpet. It's as chaotic as you might think but well worth parsing through to hear the various combinations and the interplay. You'll be too drained at the end of this one to devote much attention to the rest of the set, but the "Scent" duel should keep you smiling.

10/31/95 Rosemont Horizon, Chicago, IL

Once again the pressure was on and the band didn't gag. The evening starts in high style with a special Halloween "Icculus" in-

Photo credit: Jay Crystal

cantation, and the set also includes a soaring "Free," the long-awaited return of "Guyute" (slightly tweaked after an eleven-month absence), and a frightful "Harpua" (after Mike shares a horrifying raccoon dream, Jimmy plays the album that Phish is performing for its Halloween Costume and it's . . . *Thriller!*). The second set begins with the aural clutter that introduces "I Am the Sea" and then the "Giant Country Horns"

(richly enhanced by Alan Parshley on french horn) steps in for "Real Me," as The Who's *Quadrophenia* begins in earnest (*Quadrophenia* had placed second in the phan vote, just behind Frank Zappa's *Joe's Garage*). Page supplies most of the lead vocals throughout the set, during which the band masterfully produces the dense layerings and textures of the album. Standout moments include a scorching "5:15," a costumed guest crew vocalist on "Bell Boy," and Fish's earnest efforts to drag the set-closing "Love Reign O'er Me" into his vocal range. Once again, the third set is a keeper as well, opening with a forty-two-minute "YEM" (more than one phan thought that this song would comprise the entire set, as if the band were to say, "Here's one set during which we'll perform a double album by the Who; here's another when we'll perform one of our songs"), followed by the appropriate "Jesus Left Chicago" with help from Dave Grippo, "Day in the Life," and a brassy "Suzie." The encore features an acoustic "My Generation" (?!?) performed with Fish on a toy drum kit followed by the systematic destruction of Trey's acoustic guitar and Fish's drums. Good night, Chicago!

11/16/95 Auditorium, West Palm Beach, FL

This show has a number of interesting moments that make it well worth seeking out. The audience had laid down its king during the chess game the night before, so a new game started. Perhaps emboldened by the previous night's victory, the band offers a number of auditory delights—in particular the set-closing trio of "Timber," "Guyute," and "Funky Bitch." The second set contains a decent "Bowie," and a "Harry" with some interesting textures, but it really reaches its peak with the set-closing "Possum" as Butch Trucks from the Allman Brothers Band steps in on drums while Fish plays trombone and Trey's percussion kit during an all-out romp through the song. They say you can really see the stars in West Palm, though, and when the band returns for their encore, they have Jimmy Buffet in tow to lend his vocals to the band's debut take on "Brown Eyed Girl."

12/1/95 Hershey Park Arena, Hershey, PA

The first set starts off auspiciously with a nice move from "Buried Alive" to "Down with Disease." "Wolfman's" contains some interesting moments, including a Trey mistake that he covers to comic effect ("I liked that line so much I'm gonna sing it again"). However, it is the "Forbin" narration that is particularly enjoyable, as it integrates Trey's reading from the Tao of Physics, along with the

Rhombus and, of course, chocolate. The second set is no slouch either, as "Halley's" carries into "Mike's," which passes into a funky "Weekapaug" (apparently there is no "Hydrogen" in the land of chocolate). The "Mango Song" pleases as does Fish's Elvis impersonation on "Suspicious Minds." "Bowie" closes the set with "Catapult" and Homer Simpson "mmm . . . chocolate" references to sweeten this one a bit.

12/11/95 Cumberland County Civic Center, Portland, ME

Phish has performed a number of memorable shows in Maine over the past few years, and this one is no exception. The first set features the great "Dog Log" experiment. Trey announces that the band intends to make an album featuring fifteen different versions of the sound check standby, "Dog Log." He asks the audience to be quiet (as if it were a sound check) and then to boo on cue. The phans comply after being treated to a shortened version of the song. Then, after "Llama" Trey announces that he'd like another take, this one with obnoxious shrieking. A different, lounge lizard take on the song follows (reminiscent of "Lawn Boy"). As a reward for the phans' help, Trey announces that Phish will perform a rare one, and the band breaks into "Tube." The fun doesn't end here, however. The second set moves from an opening "Curtain" through an effects-laden "Bowie," into a sparkling "Mango." Still, the real excitement occurs following Fish's downward-spiraling "Elvis" bit as Warren Haynes takes the stage. The Government Muler drives the band through "Funky Bitch." He returns for the encore to trade licks with Trey once again on a screaming run through "While My Guitar Gently Weeps."

12/29/95 Worcester Centrum, Worcester, MA

A few phans are partial to the next night, but by most accounts this was the best of the three pre–New Year's Eve shows. The first set has its moments ("NICU" and "Stash" in particular) but it's the second set that left phans smiling. A "Makisupa" opener certainly didn't cause anyone's mouth to turn downward. The "Cars Trucks and Buses" that follows is enjoyable and gave some northeastern phans a first look at the Paging pleasure (the band had eased up on this one by the time they'd come east in December). Then the fun really begins. As you listen to "Bathtub Gin" traveling in the Phishy nether regions, focus especially on how the band finds themselves in the "Real Me" chorus—and then, not being ones to let such a moment pass, they bring it around and launch into this song full force. Then they drive this one home as they return to "Bathtub" after completing "Real Me" (which many feel was performed with a ferocity far exceeding the Halloween appearance of the song). A lengthy "McGrupp" and ripsnorting "BBFCFM" follow. Then Jim Stinnette, Mike's former bass teacher, takes the stage to jam with his pupil and remains onstage as the band kicks into "La Grange," By the way, the "Golgi" that closes the two-show Worcester run is the first "Golgi" encore since the summer.

12/31/95 Madison Square Garden, New York, NY

This show has quickly emerged as a phan phavorite, featuring an intriguing set-list and some inspired performances to culminate a New Year's run without a single song repeat. The show opens in atypical, welcome fashion with a "Punch You in the Eye," "Sloth" tandem. The first set also includes pleasing versions of "Reba" and "Maze" as well as Tom Marshall's third annual New Year's Eve appearance (during "Colonel Forbin" Trey reveals that Phish spends its hours offstage in the Gamehendge time laboratory with the Helping Friendly Book's recipe for time. Then to emphasize this point he calls on the audience to imagine what would happen if time had stopped in the middle of 1994 with the same song heard over and over on the radio . . . as Tom steps onstage to sing the first verse of Collective Soul's "Shine"). The second set opens with Page in peak form during "Drowned," which leads through an exploratory jam that features a "Fire on the Mountain" tease and into an exhilarating, joyful "Lizards." Other fine moments include an extended "Runaway Jim" (with a lyrical nod to "Dave Daubs" and Trey moving over to his drum kit), which justaposes nicely with "Strange Design," and a set-closing "Mike's" that ends with Trey alone onstage working his effects pedals. The mad scientists emerge for a third set to transform Fish's "Father Time" into baby New Year and to transform "Auld Lang Syne" into a funky "Weekapaug" and then into a lilting "Sea and Sand." The remainder of the set satisfies as well with "You Enjoy Myself," the rare "Sanity," and the appropriate "Frankenstein." For the encore Johnny B. Fishman drives "Johnny B. Goode" into the new year.

6/6/96 Joyous lake, Woodstock, NY

Phish performed this club gig billed as "the Third Ball" in order to thank the people of Woodstock for their hospitality while the band completed its work in the studio. Phish showcased two of these new offerings late in the second set: the earnest, tentatively titled "Waste," which ends abruptly ("thank you that song has no ending, we hope you liked it"), and the driving "Character Zero" ("a world debut"). Other notable musical moments include the show-opening "Split," "Scent" (with a "Sunshine of Your Love" quote and some fine vocals by Mike), "Stash," and "Bowie" (with a brief "Alumni" tease).

Bubbling Under

3/4/85, 11/23/85, 5/11/87, 8/1/87, 9/12/87, 6/18/88, 7/25/88, 9/12/88, 11/11/88, 12/2/88, 3/3/89, 3/30/89, 4/20/89, 5/20/89, 5/26/89, 6/30/89, 9/9/89, 1/28/90, 3/3/90, 3/9/90, 3/28/90, 5/4/90, 5/6/90, 5/19/90, 6/16/90, 9/22/90, 11/17/90, 12/31/90, 3/9/91, 3/29/91, 4/15/91, 5/3/91, 5/4/91, 5/12/91, 7/26/91, 9/28/91, 10/28/91, 11/7/91, 11/8/91, 11/20/91, 3/6/92, 3/14/92, 4/17/92, 4/19/92, 4/22/92, 5/14/92, 11/23/92, 12/7/92, 12/29/92, 12/30/92, 2/3/93, 2/6/93, 2/12/93, 2/19/93, 3/2/93, 3/28/93, 4/10/93, 4/21/93,

4/29/93, 5/5/93, 5/6/93, 7/15/93, 7/22/93, 7/24/93, 8/6/93, 8/7/93, 8/13/93, 8/14/93, 8/21/93, 8/25/93, 8/28/93, 4/9/94, 4/20/94, 4/21/94, 4/23/94, 5/2/94, 5/4/94, 5/28/94, 5/29/94, 6/11/94, 6/16/94, 6/18/94, 6/22/94, 6/24/94, 6/30/94, 7/2/94, 7/5/94, 7/13/94, 7/16/94, 10/8/94, 10/14/94, 10/21/94, 11/2/94, 11/17/94, 11/22/94, 11/26/94, 11/28/94, 12/1/94, 12/3/94, 12/29/94, 6/10/95, 6/14/95, 6/17/95, 6/28/95, 7/3/95, 10/7/95, 10/21/95, 10/29/95, 11/25/95, 11/30/95, 12/9/95, 12/30/95, 4/26/96.

7 bagged and tagged

his chapter presents a representative sampling of Phish setlists. The lists from 1984 to 1993 collect a limited number of shows, while the lists after that time are far more inclusive.

Abbreviations"

"ATR"—"All Things Reconsidered"
"BATR"—"Bouncing Around the Room"
"BBFCFM"—"Big Black Furry Creatures from Mars"
BBJ—big ball jam
"DWD"—"Down with Disease"
"FEFY"—"Fast Enough for You"
"GTBT"—"Good Times, Bad Times"
"Guitar"—"While My Guitar Gently Weeps"
"MSO"—"My Sweet One"
"PYITE"—"Punch You in the Eye"
"SOAM"—"Split Open and Melt"
"TMWSIY"—"The Man Who Stepped into Yesterday"
"YEM"—"You Enjoy Myself"

Sat. 12/1/84
Nectar's, Burlington, VT

"Scarlet"—"Fire"—"Fire on the
Mountain"—"Makisupa"—"Slave"—
"Spanish Flea"—"Don't Want You No
More"—"Cities"—"Skippy"*—"Fluffhead"*
E: "Eyes"

*with Dude of Life on vocals

Thu. 10/17/85
Finbar's, Burlington, VT

"Alumni"—"Letter to Jimmy Page"—
"Alumni"—"Mike's"—"Dave's Energy
Guide"—"Revolution"—"Anarchy"—
"Camel Walk"—"Antelope"—"McGrupp"

Wed. 10/30/85
Hunt's, Burlington, VT

"Harry"—"Dog Log"—"Possum"—
"Slave"—"Sneaking Sally"—"I Wish"—
"Revival"—"Alumni"—"Letter to Jimmy
Page"—"Alumni"—"Prep School
Hippie"—"Skippy"

Tues. 4/1/86
Hunt's, Burlington, VT

1: "Mighty Quinn"—"Have Mercy"—
"Harry"—"Icculus"—"YEM"
2: "Help"—"Slip"—"AC/DC Bag"—
"McGrupp"—"Alumni"—"Letter to Jimmy
Page"—"Alumni"—"Dear Mrs. Reagan"
E: "Not Fade Away"*

*with The Jones

Tues. 4/15/86
University of Vermont, Burlington, VT

"AC/DC Bag"—"Dear Mrs. Reagan"—
"Prep School Hippie"—"Mighty
Quinn"—"Slave"—"Makisupa"—"Have
Mercy"—"Dog Log"—"Possum"—
"YEM"—"Anarchy"—"Camel Walk"—

"Alumni"—"Letter to Jimmy Page"—
"Alumni"

Fri. 10/31/86
Sculpture Room, Goddard College, Plainfield, VT

"AC/DC Bag"—"Swing Low, Sweet
Chariot"—"Peaches"—"Bowie"—"Have
Mercy"*—"Harry"—"Sanity"—"Skin It
Back"—"Icculus"—"Alumni"—"Letter to
Jimmy Page"—"Alumni"

*with Jah Roy

Sat. 12/6/86
The Ranch, Shelburne, VT

"Mike's"—"Whipping Post"—"She Caught
the Katy"—"AC/DC Bag"—"Bowie"—
"Clod"—"Bowie"—"YEM"—"Dog Log"—
"Tush"—"Sneaking Sally"—"Prep School
Hippie"—"Icculus"—"McGrupp"—
"GTBT"—"Skin It Back"—"Cities"

Fri. 4/24/87
Billings Lounge, University of Vermont, Burlington, VT

"Golgi"—"AC/DC Bag"—"Possum"—
"Fluffhead"—"YEM"—"Dave's Energy
Guide"—"Alumni"—"Letter to Jimmy
Page"—"Alumni"—"Hydrogen"—
"Bowie"—"Dear Mrs. Reagan"—"Slave"

Wed. 4/29/87
Nectar's, Burlington, VT

1: "She Caught the Katy"—"Alumni"—
"Letter to Jimmy Page"—"Alumni"—
"Golgi"—"Swing Low, Sweet Chariot"—
"Fire"—"Skin It Back"—"Cities"
2: "Lushington"—"Dog Log"—"Melt the
Guns"—"Dave's Energy Guide"—"A
Train"—"Halley's"—"Mighty Quinn"
3: "AC/DC Bag"—"Peaches"—
"Fluffhead"—"GTBT"—"Anarchy"—

"Makisupa"—"Antelope"—"Boogie on
Reggae Woman"—"Timber"—"Slave"—
"Sparks"—"McGrupp"—"Curtis Loew"—
"Let the Good Times Roll"—"Hydrogen"

Fri. 8/21/87
Ian's Farm, Hebron, NY

1: "Dog Log"—"Peaches"—"Divided
Sky"—"Funky Bitch" —"Harry"—"Clod"—
"Curtain"—"Light Up or Leave Me
Alone"—"Shaggy Dog"—"Wilson"—
"Camel Walk"
2: "Mike's"—"Harpua"—"Bundle of Joy"—
"Harpua"—"Golgi"—"Sparks"—"Flat
Fee"—"Fee"—"Skin It Back"—"Low
Rider"—"Oh Kee Pa"—"Sloth"
3: "BBFCFM"—"McGrupp"—
"Makisupa"—"Bowie"—"Sanity"—"Swing
Low, Sweet Chariot"

Sat. 8/29/87
Shelburne, VT

1: "Alumni"—"Letter to Jimmy Page"—
"Alumni"—"Curtis Loew"—"Sneaking
Sally"—"Makisupa"—"BBFCFM"—"Flat
Fee"—"Lushington"—"Suzie"—"Mustang
Sally"—"Ya Mar"—"TMWSIY"—"Avenu"—
"TMWSIY"
2: "Clod"—"Slave"—"Swing Low, Sweet
Chariot"—"Curtain"—"McGrupp"—
"Possum"—"Harry"—"Timber"—"AC/DC
Bag"—"Divided Sky"—"Harpua"—"Bundle
of Joy"—"Harpua"

Fri. 3/11/88
Johnson State College,
Johnson, VT

1: "The Chicken"—"Funky Bitch" —
"Sneaking Sally"—"A Train"—"YEM"—
"Wilson"—"Golgi"—"Slave"—"Flat Fee"—
"Corrine, Corrina"—"Lizards"—"Bowie"
2: "Fluffhead"—"Dinner and a Movie" —

"Harry"—"Curtis Loew"—"Harpua"—"AC/
DC Bag"—"Alumni"—"Letter to Jimmy
Page"—"Alumni"—"Antelope"

Sat. 3/12/88
Nectar's, Burlington, VT

1: "Jump Monk"—"McGrupp"—
"Lizards"—"Tela"—"Wilson"—"AC/DC
Bag"—"Col. Forbin"—"Mockingbird"—
"Sloth"—"Possum"—"Antelope"

Sat. 5/14/88
Springfest, Goddard College,
Plainfield, VT

"Fire"—"I Didn't Know"*—"Halley's"*—
"Light Up or Leave Me Alone"—
"YEM"—"Lizards"—"BBFCFM"—"Jesus
Left Chicago"**—"Fluffhead"—
"Alumni"—"Letter to Jimmy Page"—
"Alumni"—"A Train"***

*with Nancy Taube

**with Bobby Brown

***with Karl Boyle

Wed. 5/25/88
Nectar's, Burlington, VT

1: "Curtain"—"Rocky Top"—"Funky
Bitch" —"Alumni"—"Letter to Jimmy
Page"—"Alumni"—"Peaches"—"Golgi"—
"Sneaking Sally"—"Suzie"—"Fire"
2: "Jesus Left Chicago"—"Fluffhead"—
"Whipping Post"
3: "Sloth"—"I Didn't Know"—"Ya Mar"—
"Halley's"—"La Grange"—"Fee"—"I Know
a Little"—"BBFCFM"—"Corrine,
Corrina"—"Harpua"—"Antelope"

Sat. 7/23/88
Pete Danforth's House,
Underhill, VT

1: "Col. Forbin"—"Mockingbird"—
"Mike's"—"Hydrogen"—"Weekapaug" —

"Lizards"—"On Your Way Down"—"AC/
DC Bag"—"Possum"—"Walk Away"—
"Bold as Love"—"No Dogs Allowed"
2: "Sloth"—"Fire"*—"Curtain"—
"Terrapin"—"Antelope"—"Satin Doll"*—
"Blue Bossa"*—"La Grange"—"Alumni"—
"Letter to Jimmy Paige"—"Alumni"—
"Peaches"
3: "YEM"—"Contact"—"Harry"—"Dinner
and a Movie" —"Slave"*—"Curtis
Loew"—"GTBT"

*with Pete Danforth

Sat. 9/24/88
Humphries House, Amherst
College, Amherst, MA

1: "Golgi"—"On Your Way Down"—
"Alumni"—"Letter to Jimmy Page"—
"Alumni"—"YEM"—"Wilson"—
"Peaches"—"La Grange"—"A Train"—
"Divided Sky"—"Bold as Love"
2: "Bowie"—"Lizards"—"Walk Away"—
"Possum"—"Fee"—"Sparks"—"Whipping
Post"
3: "GTBT"—"Fluffhead"—"Curtain"—
"AC/DC Bag"

Thu. 11/3/88
Molly's, Boston, MA

1: "Fire"—"Golgi"—"Fluffhead"—
"Possum"—"Fee"—"Alumni Blues"—"Letter
to Jimmy Page"—"Alumni"—"GTBT"—
"Time Loves a Hero"—"Walk Away"—
"Lizards"—"Shaggy Dog"—"Foam"
2: "Whipping Post"—"Contact"—"Bold as
Love"—"A Train"—"Antelope"—"Suzie"—
"I Didn't Know"—"BBFCFM"—
"Harpua"—"Bowie"

Mon 2/6/89
The Front, Burlington, VT

1: "Suzie"—"Curtain"—"Wilson"—
"Peaches"—"Fee"—"La Grange"—
"YEM"—"All Blues"—"Sanity"—"A
Train"—"Golgi"—"Divided Sky"—"On
Your Way Down"—"I Didn't Know"
2: "GTBT"—"Walk Away"—"Harry"—
"BBFCFM"—"Curtis Loew"—"Icculus"—
"Whipping Post"—"Corrine, Corrina"
E: "Bowie"

Sun. 4/30/89
Nightstage, Cambridge, MA

"I Didn't Know"—"YEM"—"McGrupp"—
"Lizards"—"Divided Sky"—"Wilson"—
"Peaches"—"Antelope"—"Terrapin"
E: "Possum"

Sun. 5/28/89
Ian's Farm, Hebron, NY

1: "Divided Sky"—"Antelope"—"Col.
Forbin"—"Mockingbird"—"Fee"—
"Slave"—"Esther"—"Suzie"—"YEM"
2: "Fire"—"Mike's"—"Hydrogen"—
"Weekapaug" —"Bathtub Gin"—
"Sanity"—"Ride Captain Ride"—
"Peaches"—"A Train"—"Possum"—
"Contact"

Sun. 8/12/89
Burlington Boat House,
Burlington, VT

"Blue Sky"—"Suzie"—"AC/DC Bag"—"Ya
Mar"—"Rocky Top"—"On Your Way
Down"—"Night and Day"—"I Didn't
Know"—"YEM"—"Possum"—"Icculus"—
"Antelope"

Fri. 10/20/89
The Front, Burlington, VT
1: "Harpua"—"Bundle of Joy"—"Col.
Forbin"—"Mockingbird"—"YEM"—"Oh
Kee Pa"—"Reba"—"Divided Sky"—
"Golgi"—"Antelope"
2: "No Dogs Allowed"—"Walk Away"—
"Dinner and a Movie" —"I Didn't
Know"*—"AC/DC Bag"*—"Donna
Lee"*—"SOAM"*—"Harry"*—"Swing
Low, Sweet Chariot"*—"I'm In A Hole"*
E: "La Grange"*—"Slave"*
*with Russ Remington and Dave Grippo

Tues. 10/31/89
Goddard College, Plainfield, VT
1: "Oh Kee Pa"—"Suzie"—"AC/DC
Bag"—"Divided Sky"—"Fee"—"Walk
Away"—"Bathtub Gin"—"Possum"
2: "YEM"—"Bowie"—"Wilson"—"Reba"—
"Col. Forbin"—"Mockingbird"—
"Alumni"—"Letter to Jimmy Page"—
"Alumni"—"Lizards"—"Highway to Hell"
E: "Contact"—"Antelope"

Sun. 2/25/90
8 × 10 Club, Baltimore, MD
1: "Foam"—"MSO"—"Col. Forbin"—
"Mockingbird"—"Funky Bitch" —"Coil"—
"BATR"—"Bowie"—"Satin Doll"—
"Rift"*—"Possum"
2: "Reba"—"McGrupp"—"Makisupa"—
"Lizards"—"Fluffhead"—"BBFCFM"
*first time played

Fri. 3/28/90
Denison University, Granville, OH
1: "Possum"—"Ya Mar"—"Fee"—"Walk
Away"—"Tweezer"—"Uncle Pen"—"Oh
Kee Pa"—"Suzie"—"A Train"—"Runaway
Jim"—"YEM"—"GTBT"
2: "Carolina"—"Sweet Adeline"—

"Whipping Post"—"Funky Bitch"—
"Mike's"—"Hydrogen"—"Weekapaug"—
"Jesus Left Chicago"—"Lizards"—
"SOAM"—"Contact"—"La Grange"—
"Rift"—"Cavern"—"Highway to Hell"

Thu. 4/5/90
J. J. McCabes, Boulder, CO
1: "Possum"—"Ya Mar"—"Bowie"—
"Carolina"—"Oh Kee Pa"—"Suzie"—
"YEM"—"Lizards"—"Fire"
2: "Reba"—"Uncle Pen"—"Jesus Left
Chicago"*—"AC/DC Bag"—"Donna
Lee"—"Tweezer"—"Fee"—"Cavern"—
"Mike's"—"Hydrogen"—"Weekapaug" —
"If I Only Had a Brain"—"Contact"
E: "Golgi"
*with Dan Mosely

Wed. 4/18/90
Herman's Hideaway, Denver, CO
1: "Mike's"—"Hydrogen"—"Weekapaug"
—"Uncle Pen"—"Curtain"—"Foam"—
"YEM"—"MSO"—"A Train"—"Possum"
2: "La Grange"—"Fee"—"Sloth"—"Funky
Bitch"—"Reba"—"Walk Away"—"Oh Kee
Pa"—"Bold as Love"—"Lawn Boy"—
"Jaegermeister"—"Bowie"

Thu. 9/13/90
Wetlands Preserve,
New York, NY
1: "Landlady"—"Divided Sky"—"Foam"—
"Tube"*—"Asse Festival"*—"Antelope"—
"Minute by Minute"*—"Buried Alive"*—
"Paul and Silas"*—"BATR"—"Possum"
2: "Mike's"—"Hydrogen"—"Weekapaug"
—"Magilla"*—"Stash"*—"Going Down
Slow"*—"Oh Kee Pa"—"AC/DC Bag"—
"A Train"—"Sparks"—"Reba"—"Self"*—
"Dahlia"*—"Revolution's Over"*
*first time played
∧with the Dude of Life

Fri. 11/2/90
Glen Miller Ballroom, Boulder, CO
1: "Golgi"—"Landlady"—"BATR"—
"Divided Sky"—"Sloth"—"Mike's"—
"Hydrogen"—"Weekapaug" —"Esther"—
"Cavern"—"Asse Festival"—"Possum"
2: "Suzie"—"Col. Forbin"—
"Mockingbird"—"MSO"—"Foam"—
"YEM"—"Lizards"—"I Didn't Know"—
"Bowie"
E: "Lawn Boy"—"La Grange"

Sun. 11/4/90
Fort Ram Nightclub, Fort Collins, CO
1: "Carolina"—"AC/DC Bag"—
"Curtain"—"BATR"—"Tube"—"Harry"—
"Funky Bitch" —"Asse Festival"—
"MSO"—"Bowie"
2: "Golgi"—"Rocky Top"—"Llama"—
"Mike's"—"Hydrogen"—"Weekapaug"—
"Manteca"—"Runaway Jim"—"Oh Kee
Pa"—"Suzie"—"Jesus Left Chicago"—
"YEM"
E: "Contact"—"Highway to Hell"

Fri. 12/28/90
The Marquee, New York, NY
1: "Runaway Jim"—"Foam"—"Horn"—
"Reba"—"Llama"—"Col. Forbin"—
"Mockingbird"—"Mike's"—"Hydrogen"—
"Weekapaug" —"Golgi"
2: "Landlady"—"Possum"—"Coil"—
"Tweezer"—"Manteca"—"Oh Kee Pa"—
"MSO"—"Divided Sky"—"No Good
Trying"*—"Don't Get Me Wrong"*—
"Funky Bitch"*
E: "BATR"—"Highway to Hell"
*with John Popper

Thu. 2/7/91 Pickle Barrel Pub, Killington, VT
1: "Runaway Jim"—"Foam"—"MSO"—
"Landlady"—"Mango Song"—"SOAM"—
"BATR"—"Possum"—"Coil"—"Golgi"
2: "Chalkdust"—"Stash"—"Tweezer"—
"Guelah"—"Cavern"—"Love You"—
"Lizards"—"Sloth"—"Destiny Unbound"—
"YEM"
E: "AC/DC Bag"

Sun. 3/17/91
Wheeler Opera House, Aspen, CO
1: "Carolina"—"BATR"—"Landlady"—
"Mike's"—"Hydrogen"—"Weekapaug"—
"Foam"—"Fluffhead"—"Uncle Pen"—
"Stash"—"Lizards"—"Bowie"
2: "Runaway Jim"—"Esther"—"MSO"—
"Coil"—"Tweezer"—"Fee"—"Slave"—
"Chalkdust"
E: "Lawn Boy"—"La Grange"

Thu. 4/11/91
The Cave, Carleton College, Northfield, MN
1: "Runaway Jim"—"Cavern"—"Paul and
Silas"—"Tweezer"—"Magilla"—"Dinner
and a Movie" —"BATR"—"Foam"—
"Carolina"—"YEM"—"Coil"—"Chalkdust"
2: "MSO"—"Reba"—"Llama"—
"TMWSIY"—"Avenu"—"TMWSIY"—
"Lizards"—"SOAM"—"Lawn Boy"—
"Landlady"—"Destiny Unbound"—
"Mike's"—"Hydrogen"—"Weekapaug"
E: "Fee"—"Possum"

Thu. 7/11/91
Battery Park, Burlington, VT, with the Giant Country Horns
1: "Oh Kee Pa"—"Suzie"—"Divided
Sky"—"Flat Fee"—"MSO"—"Stash"—
"Lizards"—"Landlady"

2: "Dinner and a Movie"—"Cavern"—
"TMWSIY"—"*Avenu*"—"TMWSIY"—
"Mike's"—"Hydrogen"—"Weekapaug"—
"Touch Me"*—"Frankenstein"
E: "Contact"—"BBFCFM"
*first time played

Sun. 7/21/91
Arrowhead Ranch, Parksville, NY,
with the Giant Country Horns
1: "Cavern"—"Divided Sky"—"Guelah"—
"Poor Heart"—"SOAM"—"Lizards"—
"Landlady"—"BATR"—"Mike's"—
"Hydrogen"—"Weekapaug"
2: "Tweezer"—" "I Didn't Know"—
"Runaway Jim"—"Lawn Boy"—"Sloth"—
"Esther"—"AC/DC Bag"—"Contact"—
"Tweezer" rep.
E: "Gumbo"—"Touch Me"—"Fee"—
"Suzie"

Sat. 8/3/91
Amy Skelton's Farm, Auburn, ME
1: "Wilson"—"Foam"—"Runaway Jim"—
"Guelah"—"Llama"—"Fee"—"Coil"—"Poor
Heart"—"Sloth"—"Divided Sky"—"Golgi"
2: "Curtain"—"Reba"—"Chalkdust"—
"BATR"—"Tweezer"—"Esther"—
"Cavern"—"I Didn't Know"—"YEM"—
"Rocky Top"
3: "Stash"—"Ya Mar"—"Fluffhead"—
"Lawn Boy"—"MSO"—"Lizards"—"Buried
Alive"—"Possum"
E: "Magilla"—"Self"*—"Bitching
Again"*^—"Crimes of the Mind"*—
"Harry"
*with the Dude of Life
^with Sofi Dillof

Sun. 10/13/91
North Shore Surf Club,
Olympia, WA
1: "Runaway Jim"—"Wilson"—"Reba"—
"Landlady"—"Col. Forbin"—
"Mockingbird"—"Tela"—"AC/DC Bag"—
"Sloth"—"McGrupp"—"Mike's"—
"Hydrogen"—"Weekapaug"
2: "Llama"—"Bathtub Gin"—"Coil"—"It's
Ice"—"MSO"—"Jesus Left Chicago"—
"BATR"—"Love You"—"Bowie"
E: "Eliza"—"Uncle Pen"—"Carolina"

Thu. 10/31/91
Armstrong Hall, Colorado
Springs, CO
1: "Memories"—"Brother"—"Ya Mar"—
"Sloth"—"Chalkdust"—"Sparkle"—
"Foam"—"Bathtub Gin"—"Paul and
Silas"—"YEM"—"Runaway Jim"
2: "Landlady"—"Llama"—"Fee"—
"MSO"—"Bowie"—"Horn"—"Dinner and
a Movie"—"Tube"—"I Didn't Know"—
"Harry"
E: "Glide"—"Rocky Top"

Fri. 12/6/91
Middlebury College,
Middlebury, VT
1: "Memories"—"Foam"—"Reba"—"Uncle
Pen"—"Coil"—"Magilla"—"Landlady"—
"Guelah"—"I Didn't Know"
2: "It's Ice"—"Eliza"—"Sparkle"—
"YEM"—"Horn"—"Divided Sky"—
"Tela"—"Llama"—"Whipping Post"—
"Possum"
E: "Lawn Boy"—"Rocky Top"

Tues. 12/31/91
Worcester Memorial Auditorium,
Worcester, MA

1: "Possum"—"Foam"—"Sparkle"—
"Stash"—"Lizards"—"Guelah"—"Divided
Sky"—"Esther"—"Llama"—"Golgi"

2: "Brother"—"BATR"—"Buried Alive"—
"Auld Lang Syne"—"Runaway Jim"—
"Landlady"—"Reba"—"Cavern"—
"MSO"—"Antelope"

3: "Wilson"—"Coil"—"Tweezer"—
"McGrupp"—"Mike's"—"Hydrogen"—
"Weekapaug"

E: "Lawn Boy"—"Rocky Top"—"Tweezer"
rep.

Fri. 3/13/92
Campus Club, Providence, RI

1: "Curtain"—"SOAM"—"Poor Heart"—
"Guelah"—"Maze"—"Dinner and a
Movie"—"Divided Sky"—"Mound"—
"Fluffhead"—"Antelope"—"BBFCFM"—
"Antelope"

2: "Wilson"—"Brother"—"Horse"—
"Silent"—"Landlady"—"Lizards"—"My
Mind's"—"Sloth"—"Rift"—"Love You"—
"Possum"

E: "Contact"—"Fire"

Fri. 3/20/92
Broome County Forum,
Binghamton, NY

1: "Wilson"—"Reba"—"Brother"—
"Glide"—"Rift"—"Fluffhead"—"Maze"—
"Lizards"—"Mound"—"Antelope"

2: "Mike's"—"Hydrogen"—"Weekapaug"
—"Sanity"—"Sloth"—"Mango Song"—
"Cavern"—"Uncle Pen"—"Harry"—
"Terrapin"—"Possum"

E: "Lawn Boy"—"Fire"

Sun. 4/18/92
Wilbur Field, Stanford University,
Palo Alto, CA

1: "Wilson"—"Divided Sky"—"Guelah"—
"Poor Heart"—"SOAM"—"Esther"—
"Possum"—"It's Ice"—"Sparkle"—"ATR"—
"Antelope"

2: "Glide"—"Oh Kee Pa"—"Suzie"—
"Rift"—"Manteca"—"Bathtub Gin"—
"Manteca"—"Lizards"—"Mound"—
"Llama"—"TMWSIY"—*Avenu*—
"TMWSIY"—"Dinner and a Movie"—
"Harry"—"Love You"—"Rocky Top"

E: "Contact"—"BBFCFM"

Tues. 4/21/92
Redwood Acres Fairgrounds,
Eureka, CA

1: "Suzie"—"Uncle Pen"—"SOAM"—
"Rift"—"Guelah"—"Possum"—"It's Ice"—
"Eliza"—"NICU"—"BATR"—"Bowie"

2: "Dinner and a Movie"—"Col.
Forbin"—"Mockingbird"—"Tweezer"—
"Tela"—"Mike's"—"Hydrogen"—
"Weekapaug"—"Weigh"—"Catapult"—
"Lively Up Yourself"—"Sanity"—"Maze"

E: "Memories"—"Sweet Adeline"—
"Cavern"

Sat. 5/2/92
Cabaret Metro, Chicago, IL

1: "Runaway Jim"—"Col. Forbin"—
"Icculus"—"Mockingbird"—"Sparkle"—
"Reba"—"Maze"—"BATR"—"Stash"—
"Coil"—"Llama"

2: "Glide"—"Bowie"—"Tela"—"Foam"—
"YEM"—"Chalkdust"—" Cracklin'
Rosie"—"Cavern"

E: "Sleeping Monkey"—"BBFCFM"

Fri. 6/19/92
Stadtpark, Hamburg, Germany
"Landlady"—"Suzie"—"Stash"—"Coil"—
"Sparkle"—"Cavern"—"YEM"

Sat. 6/20/92
Waldbuhn, Nordheim, Germany
"Buried Alive"—"BATR"—"Foam"—
"Runaway Jim"—"It's Ice"—"Horn"—"Love
You"—"Llama"

Tues. 6/23/92
Philipshalle, Düsseldorf, Germany
"Chalkdust"—"Reba"—"Maze"—"Sweet
Adeline"—"Uncle Pen"—"BBFCFM"—"If I
Only Had a Brain"—"Golgi"

Wed. 6/24/92
Resi, Nuremberg, Germany
"Runaway Jim"—"Llama"—"Sweet
Adeline"—"Uncle Pen"—"Guelah"—"I
Didn't Know"—"Sparkle"—"Cavern"—
"Rocky Top"

Sat. 7/25/92
**Stowe Performing Arts Center,
Stowe, VT (opening for Carlos
Santana)**
"Runaway Jim"—"Foam"—"Sparkle"—
"Stash"—"Rift"—"YEM"*—"Llama"*—
"Funky Bitch" *

*with Carlos Santana, Raul Rekow, Karl Perazzo

Mon. 8/17/92
**The Coach House, San Juan
Capistrano, CA**
1: "Buried Alive"—"Poor Heart"—
"Landlady"—"Reba"—"Rift"—"Wilson"—
"ATR"—"Foam"—"My Friend"—"BATR"—
"Bowie"
2: "Suzie"—"It's Ice"—"Tweezer"—
"Esther"—"Mike's"—"Hydrogen"—

"Weekapaug"—"Horn"—"Terrapin"—"A
Train"—"Somewhere Over the
Rainbow"—"Cavern"
E: "Coil"

Thu. 11/19/92
**Ross Arena, St. Michael's College,
Colchester, VT**
1: "Maze"—"Fee"—"Foam"—"Glide"—
"SOAM"—"Mound"—"Divided Sky"—
"Esther"—"Axilla"*—"Horse"—"Silent"—
"Antelope"
2: "Mike's"—"Hydrogen"—"Weekapaug"
—"BATR"—"It's Ice"—"I Walk the
Line"*—"Tweezer"—BBJ*—"Poor
Heart"∧—"FEFY"*∧—"Llama"∧—
"Lengthwise"*—"Cavern"
E: "Bold as Love"

*first time played

∧with Gordon Stone

Sat. 11/28/92
Capitol Theater, Port Chester, NY
1: "MSO"—"Foam"—"Stash"—"Esther"—
"Chalkdust"—"Sparkle"—"FEFY"—
"Mike's"—"Hydrogen"—"Weekapaug"
2: "Suzie"—"Paul and Silas"—
"Tweezer"—"TMWSIY"—"Avenu"—
"Maze"—"TMWSIY"—"BATR"—"Coil"—
"Love You"—"Harpua"—"Golgi"
E: "Contact"—"Tweezer" rep.

Thu. 12/31/92
Matthews Arena, Boston, MA
1: "Buried Alive"—"Poor Heart"—
"Maze"—"BATR"—"Rift"—"Wilson"—
"Divided Sky"—"Cavern"—"Foam"—"I
Didn't Know"—"Antelope"
2: "Runaway Jim"—"It's Ice"—"Sparkle"—
"Col. Forbin"—"Mockingbird"—"MSO"—
BBJ—"Stash"—"Glide"—"GTBT"
3: "Mike's"—"Auld Lang Syne"—

"Weekapaug"—"Harpua"—"Kung"—
"Harpua"—"Coil"—"Diamond Girl"*—
"Llama"
E: "Carolina"—"Fire"
*with the Dude of Life

Sat. 2/20/93
Roxy Theater, Atlanta, GA

1: "Golgi"—"Foam"—"Sloth"—"Possum"—
"Weigh"—"ATR"—"Divided Sky"—
"Horse"—"Silent"—"Fluffhead"—"Cavern"
2: "Wilson"—"Reba"—"Tweezer"—"Walk
Away"—"Tweezer"—"Glide"—"Mike's"—
"Kung"—"Hydrogen"—"Weekapaug"—
"Have Mercy"—"Weekapaug"—
"FEFY"—BBJ—"Terrapin"—"Harry"—
"Tweezer" rep.
E: "Sleeping Monkey"

Sun. 3/14/93
Western State College Gym,
Gunnison, CO

1: "Loving Cup"—"Foam"—"Guelah"—
"Sparkle"—"Stash"—"Paul and Silas"—
"Sample"—"Reba"—"PYITE"—"Runaway
Jim"
2: "Halley's"—" "David "Bowie"—"Curtis
Loew"—"YEM"—"Lifeboy"—"Rift"—
BBJ—"Great Gig in the Sky"*—"Coil"
E: "Memories"—"Sweet Adeline"—"Golgi"
*first time played

Mon. 3/22/93
Crest Theater, Sacramento, CA

1: "Chalkdust"—"Guelah"—"Uncle
Pen"—"Stash"—"BATR"—"Rift"—
"Weigh"—"Reba"—"Sparkle"—"Bowie"
2: "Golgi"—"It's Ice"—"Lizards"—"Tela"—
"Wilson"—"AC/DC Bag"—"Col.
Forbin"—"Mockingbird"—"Sloth"—

"McGrupp"—"Mike's"—"Hydrogen"—
"Weekapaug"
E: "Amazing Grace"—"Fire"

Sat. 5/8/93
University of New Hampshire
Fieldhouse, Durham, NH

1: "Chalkdust"—"Guelah"—"Rift"—
"Mound"—"Stash"—"Kung"—"Stash"—
"Glide"—"My Friend"—"Reba"—"Satin
Doll"—"Cavern"
2: "Bowie"—"Have Mercy"—"Bowie"—
"Horse"—"Silent"—"It's Ice"—"Coil"—
BBJ—"Mike's"—"Crossroads"—"Mike's"—
"Hydrogen"—"Weekapaug"—"Amazing
Grace"
E: "AC/DC Bag"

Mon. 8/2/93
Ritz Theater, Tampa, FL

1: "Chalkdust"—"Guelah"—"Poor
Heart"—"Brother"—"Oh Kee Pa"—
"Suzie"—"ATR"—"Bathtub Gin"—
"Makisupa"—"My Mind's"—"Dog Log"—
"La Grange"
2: 2001—"Mike's"—"Sparks"—"Curtis
Loew"—"Rift"—"Coil"—"Weekapaug"—
"Bike"—"Antelope"—"Makisupa"—
"Antelope"
E: "Sleeping Monkey"—"Amazing Grace"

Sat. 8/7/93
Darien Lakes Performing Arts
Center, Darien Center, NY

1: "Llama"—"BATR"—"Poor Heart"—
"Stash"—"Makisupa"—"Reba"—"Maze"—
"Col. Forbin"—"Mockingbird"—"Cavern"
2: 2001—"Mike's"—"Sparks"—"Kung"—
"Mike's"—"TMWSIY"—"Avenu"—
"TMWSIY"—"Sloth"—"Sparkle"—"My

Friend"—"McGrupp"—"Purple Rain"—
"Antelope"
E: "Carolina"—"La Grange"

Fri. 8/20/93
Red Rocks Amphitheater, Morrison, CO

1: "Divided Sky"—"Harpua"—"Poor
Heart"—"Maze"—"BATR"—"It's Ice"—
"Wedge"—"Ginseng Sullivan"—"Rift"—
"Antelope"
2: 2001—"Slave"—"SOAM"—"Coil"—
"My Friend"—"Chalkdust"—"YEM"—
"Purple Rain"—"Cavern"
E: "Mango Song"—"Freebird"

Thu. 12/30/93
Cumberland County Civic Center, Portland, ME

1: "Bowie"—"Weigh"—"Curtain"—
"Sample"—"Paul and Silas"—"Col.
Forbin"—"Mockingbird"—"Rift"—"Bathtub
Gin"—"Freebird"
2: 2001—"Mike's"—"Horse"—"Silent"—
"PYITE"—"McGrupp"—"Weekapaug"—
"Purple Rain"—"Slave"
E: "Rocky Top"—"GTBT"

Fri. 12/31/93
Worcester Centrum, Worcester, MA

1: "Llama"—"Guelah"—"Stash"—"Ginseng
Sullivan"—"Reba"—"Peaches"—"I Didn't
Know"—"Antelope"*
2: "Tweezer"—"Halley's"—"Poor
Heart"—"It's Ice"—"Fee"—"Possum"—
"Lawn Boy"—"YEM"
3: "Auld Lang Syne"—"DWD" jam—
"SOAM"—"Lizards"—"Sparkle"—
"Suzie"—"Cracklin' Rosie"—"Harry"—
"Tweezer" rep.

E: "Golgi"—"Amazing Grace"
*with Tom Marshall

Mon. 4/4/94
Flynn Theater, Burlington, VT

1: "Divided Sky"—"Sample"—"Scent"*—
"Maze"—"Fee"—"Reba"—"Horn"—"It's
Ice"—"Possum"
2: "DWD"*—"If I Could"*—"Buried
Alive"∧—"Landlady"∧—"Julius"*∧—
"Magilla"∧—"SOAM"∧—"Wolfman's"*∧—
"I Wanna Be Like You"*∧—"Oh Kee
Pa"∧—"Suzie"∧
E: "Harry Hood"—"Cavern"∧
*first time played
∧with the Giant Country Horns

Tues. 4/5/94
Metropolis, Montreal, Quebec, Canada

1: "Runaway Jim"—"Foam"—"Fluffhead"—
"Glide"—"Julius"—"BATR"—"Rift"—"AC/
DC Bag"
2: "Peaches"—"Ya Mar"—"Tweezer"—"If
I Could"—"YEM"—"I Wanna Be Like
You"—"Chalkdust"—"Amazing Grace"
E: "Nellie Cane"—"Golgi"

Wed. 4/6/94
Concert Hall, Toronto, Ontario, Canada

1: "Llama"—"Guelah"—"Poor Heart"—
"Stash"—"Lizards"—"Sample"—"Scent"—
"Fee"—"Antelope"
2: "Curtain"—"DWD"—"Wolfman's"—
"Sparkle"—"Mike's"—"Lifeboy"—
"Weekapaug"—"Coil"—"Cavern"
E: "Ginseng Sullivan"—"Nellie Cane"—
"Sweet Adeline"

Fri. 4/8/94
Pennsylvania State University
Recreation Hall,
University Park, PA
1: "Maze"—"Glide"—"Foam"—"I Didn't
Know"*—"PYITE"—"Horse"—"Silent"—
"DWD"—"If I Could"—"Lawn Boy"—
"Llama"
2: "SOAM"—"McGrupp"—"It's Ice"—
"Sparkle"—"Harry"—"BATR"—BBJ—
"Bowie"—"Suzie"
E: "Contact"—"BBFCFM"
*with Mimi Fishman on cymbals

Sat. 4/9/94
Broome County Arena,
Binghamton, NY
1: "Magilla"—"Wilson"—"Rift"—"Bathtub
Gin"—"Nellie Cane"—"Julius"—"Fee"—
"ATR"—"Stash"—"Coil"
2: "Sample"—"Reba"—"Peaches"—BBJ—
"Demand"*—"Mike's"—"Hydrogen"—
"Weekapaug"—"Tela"—"Slave"—"Cavern"
E: "Amazing Grace"—"Highway to Hell"

Sun. 4/10/94
Alumni Arena, Amherst, NY
1: "Runaway Jim"—"It's Ice"—"Sparkle"—
"SOAM"—"Esther"—"Chalkdust"—"I
Didn't Know"—"Scent"—"DWD"
2: "My Friend"—"Ya Mar"—"Antelope"—
"Fluffhead"—"Ginseng Sullivan"—"I
Wanna Be Like You"—"Harry"
E: "BATR"—"Golgi"

Mon. 4/11/94
Snively Arena, University of New
Hampshire, Durham, NH
1: "Caravan"—"Poor Heart"—"Foam"—
"FEFY"—"Magilla"—"Julius"—"Glide"—
"Divided Sky"—"Cavern"
2: 2001—"Maze"—"Col. Forbin"—

"Mockingbird"—"Uncle Pen"—
"Sample"—BBJ—"YEM"—"Amazing
Grace"—"Oh Kee Pa"—"Suzie"
E: "Possum"

Wed. 4/13/94 Beacon Theater,
New York, NY
1: "Buried Alive"—"Poor Heart"—
"Stash"—"Lizards"—"Julius"—"Ginseng
Sullivan"—"Divided Sky"—"Golgi"
2: "Faht"—"Curtain"—"Sample"—
"Reba"—BBJ—"Fee"—"A Train"—
"Bowie"—"Purple Rain"—"AC/DC Bag"
E: "Sweet Adeline"—"GTBT"

Thu. 4/14/94
Beacon Theater, New York, NY
1: "Runaway Jim"—"Foam"—"Sparkle"—
"DWD"—"Glide"—"Rift"—"Demand"—
"SOAM"—"Coil"
2: 2001—"Antelope"—"Horse"—
"Silent"—"Scent"—"YEM"—"Nellie
Cane"—"Dog Faced Boy"*—"Slave"
E: "Rocky Top"
*first time played

Fri. 4/15/94
Beacon Theater, New York, NY
1: "Llama"—"Guelah"—"Paul and Silas"—
"Harry"—"Wilson"—"Chalkdust"—
"BATR"—"It's Ice"—"DWD
2: "Maze"—"If I Could"—"Oh Kee Pa"—
"Suzie"*—"Landlady"*—"Julius"*—
"Wolfman's"*—"Alumni"*—"I Wanna Be
Like You"—"Cavern"*
E: "Magilla"*—"Amazing Grace"
*first time played

Sat. 4/16/94
Mullins Center, Amherst, MA
1: "Runaway Jim"—"Fee"—"Axilla II"*—
"Rift"—"Stash"—"Fluffhead"—"Nellie
Cane"—"Antelope"
2: "Sample"—"Poor Heart"—"Tweezer"—
"Lizards"—"Julius"—"BATR"—"YEM"—
"Coil"—"Tweezer" rep.
E: "Fire"

*first time played

Sun. 4/17/94
Patriot Center, Fairfax, VA
1: "Loving Cup"—"Foam"—"I Didn't
Know"—"Divided Sky"—"Mound"—
"DWD"—"If I Could"—"MSO"—"Cavern"
2: "Bowie"—"Wolfman's"—"Uncle Pen"—
"Sloth"—"Reba"—BBJ—"Maze"—
"Contact"—"Golgi"
E: "Cracklin' Rosie"—"Bold as Love"

Mon. 4/18/94
Bob Carpenter Center,
Newark, DE
1: "Chalkdust"—"Glide"—"Poor Heart"—
"Julius"—"My Friend"—"Rift"—"SOAM"—
"Dog Faced Boy"—"Oh Kee Pa"—
"AC/DC Bag"
2: 2001—"Sample"—"Sparkle"—"Bathtub
Gin"—BBJ—"Ya Mar"—"Mike's"—
"TMWSIY"—"Avenu"—"TMWSIY"—
"DWD"—"I Wanna Be Like You"—
"Cavern"
E: "GTBT"

Wed. 4/20/94
Virginia Horse Center,
Lexington, VA
1: "Runaway Jim"—"It's Ice"—"Julius"—
"BATR"—"Axilla II"—"Stash"—"Suzie"

2: "Poor Heart"—"Antelope"—"Paul and
Silas"—"Sample"—BBJ—"Harry"—"Fee"—
"YEM"—"Somewhere Over the Rainbow"*
E: "Highway to Hell"

*with Dave Matthews Band

Thu. 4/21/94
Lawrence Joel Coliseum, Winston-Salem, NC
1: "Chalkdust"—"Sparkle"—"Foam"—
"Glide"—"SOAM"—"Lizards"—"DWD"—
"If I Could"—"Cavern"
2: 2001—"Maze"—"Fluffhead"—
"Mike's"—"Hydrogen"—"Weekapaug"—
"Scent"—BBJ—"Possum"—"Amazing
Grace"
E: "Jam"*—"Watchtower"*

*with Dave Matthews Band

Fri. 4/22/94
Township Auditorium,
Columbia, SC
1: "Llama"—"Horn"—"Uncle Pen"—
"PYITE"—"Sample"—"ATR"—"Nellie
Cane"—"Divided Sky"—"Horse"—
"Silent"—"Bowie"
2: "Suzie"—"Julius"—"Reba"—
"Tweezer"—"Lifeboy"—"Runaway Jim"—"I
Wanna Be Like You"—"Coil"
E: "McConnell Piano Duet"*—"Won't
You Come Home Bill Bailey"*

*with Dr. Jack McConnell

Sat. 4/23/94
Fox Theater, Atlanta, GA
1: "Funky Bitch" "—"Rift"—"Fee"—
"Peaches"—"Poor Heart"—"Stash"—
"Esther"—"DWD"—"Caravan"*—"Hi-Heel
Sneakers"*

2: "Wilson"—"Antelope"—"Mound"—
"Sample"—"Sparkle"—"Ginseng
Sullivan"—"Harry"—"YEM"—"Keyboard
Jam"∧†—"Who by Fire"∧†—"Golgi"
E: "Freebird"

*with Merle Saunders

∧†with Colonel Bruce Hampton

Sun. 4/24/94
Grady Cole Center, Charlotte, NC
1: "My Friend"—"Ya Mar"—"Axilla II"—
"Maze"—"Bathtub Gin"—"Dog Faced
Boy"—"Paul and Silas"—"It's Ice"—"Slave"
2: "Demand"—"Bowie"—"Mango"—
"Julius"—"Col. Forbin"—"Mockingbird"—
"Chalkdust"—"Contact"—"GTBT"
E: "Sweet Adeline"

Mon. 4/25/94
Civic Auditorium, Knoxville, TN
1: "Landlady"—"Runaway Jim"—"Fee"—
"Foam"—"DWD"—"Ginseng Sullivan"—
"Dog Faced Boy"—"Tela"—"Poor
Heart"—"SOAM"
2: "Curtain"—"Sample"—"My Mind's"—
"Antelope"—"Mound"—"Coil"—"Divided
Sky"—"BATR"—BBJ—"BBFCFM"
E: "Amazing Grace"—"Bold as Love"

Thu. 4/28/94
Sun Fest, West Palm Beach, FL
"Runaway Jim"—"Foam"—"Sample"—
"Rift"—"DWD"—"BATR"—"It's Ice"—
"Antelope"—"Coil"—"Julius"—"GTBT"
E: "Golgi"

Fri. 4/29/94
Boatyard Village, Clearwater, FL
1: "Halley's"—"YEM"—"FEFY"—"Scent"—
"Sloth"—"Divided Sky"—"I Didn't

Know"—"Dog Faced Boy"—"SOAM"—
"Sanity"—"My Mind's"—"Llama"
2: "Suzie"—"Maze"—"If I Could"—
"Reba"—"Fee"—"Uncle Pen"—"Mike's"—
"Hydrogen"—"Weekapaug"—"I Wanna Be
Like You"—"Cavern"
E: "Fire"

Sat. 4/30/94
The Edge, Orlando, FL
1: "Chalkdust"—"Mound"—"Stash"—
"Poor Heart"—"Sample"—"PYITE"—
"Rift"—"Ginseng Sullivan"—"Sweet
Adeline"
2: "Wilson"—"Bowie"—"Wolfman's"—
"Peaches"—"Harry"—"Axilla II"—
"McGrupp"—"Possum"—"Purple Rain"—
"BBFCFM"
E: "Sleeping Monkey"—"Highway to
Hell"

Mon. 5/2/94
Five Points South Music Hall,
Birmingham, AL
1: "Great Gig in the Sky"—"SOAM"—
"BATR"—"DWD"—"It's Ice"—"Glide"—
"Divided Sky"—"Suzie"—"Foam"—
"Sample"
2: "Runaway Jim"—"Mound"—"Reba"—
"Golgi"—"Lizards"—"Julius"—" "Lawn
Boy"—"Mike's"
E: "Cavern"

Tues. 5/3/94
The Veranda at Starwood
Amphitheater, Antioch, TN
1: "Rift"—"Guelah"—"Maze"—"Sparkle"—
"Stash"—"Coil"—"Scent"—"Sample"—
"Sweet Adeline"
2: "Bowie"—"If I Could"*—"Fluffhead"—

"DWD"—"Harpua"—"Chalkdust"—"I
Wanna Be Like You"—"Slave"
E: "Nellie Cane"—"Fire"
*with Alison Krauss

Wed. 5/4/94
State Palace Theater, New Orleans, LA
1: "Runaway Jim"—"Foam"—"Sample"—
"It's Ice"—"Sparkle"—"Axilla II"—
"Tweezer"—"Lifeboy"—"Rift"—"Tweezer"
rep.
2: "Antelope"—"BATR"—"YEM"*—
"Landlady"*—"Julius"*—"Wolfman's"*—
"Magilla"*—"Suzie"*
E: "Caravan"*
*with the Cosmic Country Horns

Fri. 5/6/94
The Tower, Houston, TX
1: "DWD"—"Oh Kee Pa"—"AC/DC
Bag"—"Poor Heart"—"My Friend"—"Ya
Mar"—"Stash"—"Esther"—"Chalkdust"
2: "Maze"—"Golgi"—"Uncle Pen"—
"Sample"—"Reba"—"Axilla II"—"Julius"—
"Bike"—"Bowie"
E: "Ginseng Sullivan"—"Freebird"

Sat. 5/7/94
The Bomb Factory, Dallas, TX
1: "Llama"—"Horn"—"Divided Sky"—
"Mound"—"Fee"—"Scent"—"SOAM"—"If
I Could"—"Suzie"
2: "Loving Cup"—"Sparkle"—
"Tweezer"—"Sparks"—jam—"Makisupa"—
jam—"Sweet Emotion"—jam—"Walk
Away"—jam—"Cannonball"—jam—
"Purple Rain"—"Hold Your Head Up"
jam—"Tweezer" rep.
E: "Amazing Grace"

Sun. 5/8/94
The Backyard, Austin, TX
1: "Runaway Jim"—"Foam"—"Axilla II"—
"Rift"—"DWD"—"BATR"—"Stash"—"Coil"
2: 2001—"Antelope"—"It's Ice"—"Fee"—
"Julius"—"Cavern"—"YEM"—"Halley's"—
"GTBT"
E: "Sweet Adeline"—"Golgi"

Tues. 5/10/94
Paolo Soleri Amphitheater, Santa Fe, NM
1: "Buried Alive"—"Poor Heart"—
"Sample"—"Divided Sky"—"Axilla II"—
"It's Ice"—"SOAM"—"If I Could"—
"Cavern"
2: "Maze"—"Wilson"—"Julius"—"Reba"—
"Scent"—"Harry"—"Ginseng Sullivan"—
"Dog Faced Boy"—"Nellie Cane"—
"Bowie"
E: "Coil"

Thu. 5/12/94
Buena Vista Theater, Tucson, AZ
1: "Catapult"—"Rift"—"DWD"—"Fee"—
"Maze"—"Axilla II"—"Foam"—"Bathtub
Gin"—"Lizards"—"Sample"
2: 2001—"Antelope"—"Horse"—
"Silent"—"Uncle Pen"—"Fluffhead"—
"Lifeboy"—"Possum"—"Love You"—
"Contact"—"BBFCFM"
E: "Amazing Grace"—"Rocky Top"

Fri. 5/13/94
Hayden Square, Tempe, AZ
1: "Runaway Jim"—"It's Ice"—"Julius"—
"Mound"—"Stash"—"If I Could"—"My
Friend"—"Slave"—"Suzie"
2: "Chalkdust"—"BATR"—"SOAM"—
"McGrupp"—"Peaches"—"Scent"—
"YEM"—"Purple Rain"—"GTBT"
E: "Freebird"

Sat. 5/14/94
Montezuma Hall, San Diego, CA
1: "Llama"—"Wilson"—"DWD"—"Fee"—
"Reba"—"Sample"—"MSO"—"Ginseng
Sullivan"—"Bowie"
2: "Curtain"—"Mike's"—"Hydrogen"—
"Weekapaug"—"TMWSIY"—"*Avenu*"—
"TMWSIY"—"PYITE"—"FEFY"—
"Lizards"—"Cavern"
E: "Bold as Love"

Mon. 5/16/94
Wiltern Auditorium,
Los Angeles, CA
1: "Buried Alive"—"Poor Heart"—
"Sample"—"Divided"—"Axilla II"—
"Rift"—"DWD"—"BATR"—"Stash"—
"Sweet Adeline"
2: 2001—"Antelope"—"Sparkle"—"It's
Ice"—"Julius"—"YEM"—"BBFCFM"—
"Amazing Grace"—"BBFCFM"
E: "Fee"—"Rocky Top"

Tues. 5/17/94
Arlington Theater,
Santa Barbara, CA
1: "Suzie"—"Maze"—"Mound"—"If I
Could"—"Scent"—"Ginseng Sullivan"—
"Dog Faced Boy"—"SOAM"—"Coil"
2: "Runaway Jim"—"Glide"—"Tweezer"—
"Lifeboy"—"Uncle Pen"—BBJ—
"Sample"—"Love You"—"Slave"
E: "Highway to Hell"

Thu. 5/19/94
Hult Center, Eugene, OR
1: "Halley's"—"Llama"—"My Friend"—
"Poor Heart"—"Stash"—"Horse"—
"Silent"—"DWD"—"Mango"—"Cavern"
2: "Sample"—"Sparkle"—"Mike's"—
"Hydrogen"—"Weekapaug"—"Lizards"—

"Julius"—BBJ—"Harry"—"Golgi"
E: "Ginseng Sullivan"—"Nellie Cane"—
"Sweet Adeline"—"Fire"

Fri. 5/20/94
Evergreen College Recreation
Center, Olympia, WA
1: "Fee"—"Maze"—"If I Could"—"It's
Ice"—"Bathtub Gin"—"FEFY"—"Scent"—
"Dog Faced Boy"—"Carolina"—"AC/DC
Bag"
2: 2001—"Antelope"—"Weigh"—"Axilla
II"—"Wolfman's"—"Rift"—"YEM"
E: "Chalkdust"

Sat. 5/21/94
Moore Theater, Seattle, WA
1: "Runaway Jim"—"Foam"—"Guelah"—
"DWD"—"Mound"—"Stash"—"Coil"—
"Tela"—"Llama"
2: "Dinner and a Movie"—"Sample"—
"Bowie"—"Contact"—BBJ—"Julius"—
"Bike"—"Harry Hood"—"Amazing Grace"
E: "Bold as Love"

Sun. 5/22/94
Vogue Theater, Vancouver, BC,
Canada
1: "Demand"—"Sloth"—"Divided Sky"—
"Glide"—"SOAM"—"Fluffhead"—
"MSO"—"Ginseng Sullivan"—"Dog Faced
Boy"—"Axilla II"
2: "DWD"—"BATR"—"It's Ice"—
"McGrupp"—"Tweezer"—"Lifeboy"—
"Rift"—"Slave"—"Tweezer" rep.
E: "Sleeping Monkey"

Mon. 5/23/94 Civic Auditorium,
Portland, OR
1: "Chalkdust"—"Sample"—"Foam"—
"Fee"—"Maze"—"Horse"—"Silent"—

"Julius"—"Reba"—"Cavern"
2: "Wilson"—"Antelope"—"If I Could"—
"Sparkle"—"PYITE"—"YEM"—"Possum"
E: "Ginseng Sullivan"—"Amazing
Grace"—"Highway to Hell"

Wed. 5/25/94
Warfield Theater,
San Francisco, CA

1: "Curtain"—"Sample"—"Uncle Pen"—
"Stash"—"Col. Forbin"—"Mockingbird"—
"Axilla II"—"Scent"—"MSO"—"Sweet
Adeline"—"Chalkdust"
2: "Rift"—"Tweezer"—"Lifeboy"—
"Maze"—"Contact"—BBJ—"Julius"—
"Purple Rain"—"Coil"
E: "Sleeping Monkey"—"Tweezer" rep.

Thu. 5/26/94
Warfield Theater,
San Francisco, CA

1: "Buried Alive"—"Poor Heart"—
"Cavern"—"Demand"—"SOAM"—
"Sparkle"—"It's Ice"—"Catapult"—
"Divided Sky"—"Sample"
2: 2001—"Antelope"—"Fluffhead"—
"DWD"—"Mound"—"Ginseng Sullivan"—
"Dog Faced Boy"—"YEM"—"Amazing
Grace"
E: "GTBT"

Fri. 5/27/94
Warfield Theater,
San Francisco, CA

1: "Wilson"—"Runaway Jim"—"Foam"—
"BATR"—"Bowie"—"If I Could"—
"PYITE"—"Harry"—"Golgi"
2: "Suzie"—"Peaches"—"My Friend"—
"Reba"—"Lizards"—"Julius"—"Nellie
Cane"*—"My Mind's"*—"Mike's"—

"Simple"†—"Mike's"—"Opera Aria"‡—
"Possum"
E: "Fire"
*with Morgan Fitcher
†first time played
‡performed by Andrea Baker

Sat. 5/28/94
Laguna Seca Daze, Monterey, CA

1: "Rift"—"Sample"—"Foam"—"BATR"—
"Stash"—"Horse"—"Silent"—"Sloth"—
"Maze"—"Cavern"
2: "Axilla II"—"It's Ice"—"Tweezer"—
"Lifeboy"—"Reba"—"Fee"—"Llama"—
"YEM"*—bass jam*
E: "Poor Heart"
*with Les Claypool

Sun. 5/29/94
Laguna Seca Daze, Monterey, CA

1: "Divided Sky"—"Guelah"—"Halley's"—
"DWD"—"Sparkle"—"Julius"—"I Didn't
Know"—"Bowie"
2: "Nellie Cane"—"SOAM"—"Esther"—
"Chalkdust"—"McGrupp"—"Oh Kee
Pa"—"Suzie"—"Antelope"—"Freebird"
E1: "Wilson"—"Golgi"—"Rocky Top"
E2: Trey-is-away jam—"Harry"—"GTBT"

Thu. 6/9/94
Triad Amphitheater, Salt Lake
City, UT

1: "Llama"—"Guelah"—"Rift"—"DWD"—
"It's Ice"—"If I Could"—"Maze"—"Fee"—
"Suzie"
2: "SOAM"—"Glide"—"Julius"—
"Halley's"—"Scent"—"Ginseng Sullivan"—
"Mike's"—"Hydrogen"—"Weekapaug"—
"Golgi"
E: "Highway to Hell"

Fri. 6/10/94
Red Rocks Amphitheater,
Morrison, CO
1: "Runaway Jim"—"Foam"—"Sample"—
"Nellie Cane"—"Demand"—"Bowie"—
"Lizards"—"Cavern"—"Julius"
2: "Axilla II"—"Curtain"—"Tweezer"—
"Lifeboy"—"Sparkle"—"Possum"—"I
Wanna Be Like You"—"Harry"—
"Tweezer" rep.
E: "Sleeping Monkey"—"Rocky Top"

Sat. 6/11/94
Red Rocks Amphitheater,
Morrison, CO
1: "Wilson"—"Chalkdust"—"YEM"—
"Rift"—"DWD"—"It's Ice"—"Tela"—
"Stash"
2: 2001—"Antelope"—"Fluffhead"—
"Scent"—"SOAM"—"Coil"—"Maze"—
"Contact"—"Frankenstein"
E: "Suzie"

Mon. 6/13/94
Memorial Hall, Kansas City, MO
1: "Buried Alive"—"Poor Heart"—
"Sample"—"Divided Sky"—"Wolfman's"—
"Dinner and a Movie"—"Stash"—
"Ginseng Sullivan"—"Julius"
2: "Mike's"—"Hydrogen"—"Weekapaug"
—"Esther"—"Cavern"—"Reba"—"Jesus
Left Chicago"—"Scent"—BBJ—
"Terrapin"—"Slave"
E: "Golgi"

Tues. 6/14/94
Des Moines Civic Center, Des
Moines, IA
1: "Llama"—"Guelah"—"Sweet Adeline"—
"Guelah"—"Rift"—"DWD"—"Fee"—"My
Friend"—"Uncle Pen"—"I Didn't

Know"—"MSO"—"I Didn't Know"—
"SOAM"
2: "Frankenstein"—"Demand"—"Bowie"—
"If I Could"—"It's Ice"—"Sparkle"—
"YEM"—"Bike"—"Possum"
E: "Sample"

Thu. 6/16/94
State Theater, Minneapolis, MN
1: "BATR"—"Julius"—"Fee"—"Maze"—
"Gumbo"—"Curtain"—"Dog Faced Boy"—
"Stash"—"Coil"
2: "Suzie"—"Antelope"—"Col. Forbin"—
"Kung"—"Mockingbird"—BBJ—"DWD"—
"Contact"—"BBFCFM"—"Purple Rain"—
"Golgi"
E: "Ginseng Sullivan"—"Amazing
Grace"—"GTBT"

Fri. 6/17/94
Eagle Ballroom, Milwaukee, WI
1: "Runaway Jim"—"Foam"—"Glide"—
"SOAM"—"If I Could"—"PYITE"—
"Bathtub Gin"—"Scent"—"Cavern"
2: 2001—"Sample"—"Poor Heart"—
"Mike's"—"Simple"—"Mike's"—"Simple"—
"Hydrogen"—"Weekapaug"—"Harpua"—
"Kung"—"Harpua"—"Simple"—
"Harpua"—"Sparkle"—BBJ—"Julius"—
"Frankenstein"
E: "Sleeping Monkey"—"Rocky Top"

Sat. 6/18/94
University of Illinois at Chicago
Pavilion, Chicago, IL
1: "Wilson"—"Rift"—"AC/DC Bag"—
"Maze"—"Mango"—"DWD"—"It's Ice"—
"Dog Faced Boy"—"Divided Sky"—
"Sample"
2: "Peaches"—"Bowie"—"Horn"—

"McGrupp"—"Tweezer"—"Lifeboy"—
"YEM"—"Chalkdust"
E: "BATR"—"Tweezer" rep.

Sun. 6/19/94
State Theater, Kalamazoo, MI
1: "Suzie"—"Julius"—"Lizards"—"Axilla
II"—"Curtain"—"FEFY"—"Scent"—
"Stash"—"Golgi"
2: "Faht"—"Antelope"—"If I Could"—
"Reba"—"Makisupa"—"Coil"—"MSO"—
"Highway to Hell"
E: "Freebird"

Tues. 6/21/94
Cincinnati Music Hall, Cincinnati, OH
1: "Runaway Jim"—"Mound"—"Sample"—
"It's Ice"—"Horse" {fire alarm}
2: "Fire"—"Poor Heart"—"DWD"—"My
Friend"—"SOAM"—"Esther"—
"Chalkdust"—"BBFCFM"—"Ginseng
Sullivan"—"BBFCFM"—"Dog Faced
Boy"—"Sweet Adeline"—"Julius"—
"Sparkle"—"Harry"—"Suzie"
E: "Amazing Grace"

Wed. 6/22/94
Veterans Memorial Auditorium, Columbus, OH
1: "Llama"—"Guelah"—"Rift"—
"Gumbo"—"Maze"—"If I Could"—
"Scent"—"Stash"—"Golgi"
2: 2001—"Mike's"—"Simple"—
"Catapult"—"Simple"—"Icculus"—
"Simple"—"Hydrogen"—"Weekapaug"—
"TMWSIY"—"Avenu"—"TMWSIY"—
"Fluffhead"—"MSO"—BBJ—"Jesus Left
Chicago"—"Sample"
E: "Carolina"—"Cavern"

Thu. 6/23/94
Phoenix Plaza Amphitheater, Pontiac, MI
1: "Buried Alive"—"Poor Heart"—
"SOAM"—"NICU"—"Foam"—"BATR"—
"DWD"—"Horse"—"Silent"—"PYITE"—
"Julius"
2: "Frankenstein"—"Bowie"—"Mango"—
"Axilla II"—"Uncle Pen"—"Tweezer"—
"Lifeboy"—"Slave"
E: "Sparkle"—"Tweezer"

Fri. 6/24/94
Murat Theater, Indianapolis, IN
1: "Divided Sky"—"Wilson"—"It's Ice"—
"Fee"—"Sloth"—"ATR"—"Paul and
Silas"—"Horn"—"Reba"—"Sweet
Adeline"—"Sample"
2: "Demand"—"Antelope"—"Halley's"—
"Curtain"—"McGrupp"—"Simple"—
"Sanity"—"Llama"—"Dog Faced Boy"—
"Poor Heart"—"Cavern"—"Carolina"—
"DWD"
E: "Rocky Top"

6/25/94
Nautica Stage, Cleveland, OH
1: "N$_2$0"—"Rift"—"Julius"—"NICU"—
"Stash"—"Mango"—"Sample"—"Scent"—
"Tela"—"Chalkdust"
2: "Suzie"—"Maze"—"Sparkle"—"Bathtub
Gin"—"Axilla II"—"YEM"—"Cracklin'
Rosie"—"Harry"—"Golgi"
E: "Highway to Hell"

Sun. 6/26/94
Charleston Municipal Auditorium, Charleston, WV
1: "Kung"—"Llama"—"Lizards"—"Tela"—
"Wilson"—"AC/DC Bag"—"Col.
Forbin"—"Mockingbird"—"Sloth"—
"McGrupp"—"Divided Sky"

2: "Julius"—"DWD"—"If I Could"—
"Axilla II"—"Lifeboy"—"Sample"—
"Wolfman's"—"Scent"—"Dog Faced
Boy"—"Demand"—"SOAM" jam—
"Yerushalim Shel Zahav"
E: "Old Home Place"*—"Amazing
Grace"—"Tube"—"Fire"
*first time played

Wed. 6/29/94
Walnut Creek Amphitheater,
Raleigh, NC

1: "Curtain"—"Sample"—"Reba"—
"Mound"—"Julius"—"Horse"—"Silent"—
"Catapult"—"Bowie"—"I Didn't Know"—
"Golgi"
2: "Landlady"—"Poor Heart"—
"Tweezer"—"It's Ice"—"Lifeboy"—
"Divided Sky"—"Suzie"—"Cavern"
E: "Ya Mar"—"Tweezer" rep.

Thu. 6/30/94
Classic Amphitheater,
Richmond, VA

1: "DWD"—"Gumbo"—"Rift"—
"Guelah"—"SOAM"—"Glide"—"Scent"—
"BATR"—"Frankenstein"
2: "Wilson"—"Maze"—"YEM"—
"Yerushalim Shel Zahav"—"YEM"—
"Sparkle"—"Axilla II"—"Harpua"—
"Antelope"—"Love You"—"Chalkdust"
E: "Sleeping Monkey"—"Poor Heart"

Fri. 7/1/94
Mann Music Center,
Philadelphia, PA

1: "Runaway Jim"—"Foam"—"Sample"—
"NICU"—"Stash"—"Mango"—"It's Ice"—
"Tela"—"Julius"—"Suzie"
2: "Bowie"—"If I Could"—"Fluffhead"—
"DWD"—"TMWSIY"—*"Avenu"*—

"TMWSIY"—"Possum"—"Terrapin"—
"Harry"—"Cavern"
E: "Rocky Top"

Sat. 7/2/94
Garden State Arts Center,
Holmdel, NJ

1: "Golgi"—"Divided Sky"—"Guelah"—
"FEFY"—"Scent"—"Tweezer"—
"Lifeboy"—"Sparkle"—"Tweezer" rep.
2: 2001—"Mike's"—"Simple"—"Mike's"—
"Yerushalim Shel Zahav"—"Hydrogen"—
"Weekapaug"—"McGrupp"—"Maze"—
"Sample"—"Slave"—"Highway to Hell"
E: "Rift"

Sun. 7/3/94
The Ball Park, Old Orchard
Beach, ME

1: "My Friend"—"Poor Heart"—
"DWD"—"Fee"—"NICU"—"Horn"—"Old
Home Place"—"Reba"—"Axilla II"—
"Bowie"
2: "SOAM"—"Lizards"—"BATR"—"It's
Ice"—"Horse"—"Silent"—"Julius"—
"Coil"—"Antelope"—"Suzie"
E: "Fire"

Tues. 7/5/94
Congress Center, Ottawa, Ontario,
Canada

1: "Rift"—"Sample"—"Curtain"—"Letter
to Jimmy Page"—"If I Could"—"Uncle
Pen"—"Stash"—"Esther"—"DWD"—
"Sweet Adeline"
2: 2001—"PYITE"—"Sparkle"—"Bathtub
Gin"—"Lifeboy"—"Cities"—"YEM"—
"Great Gig in the Sky"—"Ginseng
Sullivan"—"MSO"—"Amazing Grace"—
"Golgi"
E: "GTBT"

Wed. 7/6/94
Theater St.-Denis, Montreal,
Quebec, Canada
1: "Llama"—"Fluffhead"—"Julius"—
"BATR"—"Reba"—"Axilla II"—"My
Mind's"—"Carolina"—"Bowie"
2: "Landlady"—"Poor Heart"—
"Tweezer"—"Lawn Boy"—"Chalkdust"—
"BBFCFM"—"Sample"—"BBFCFM"—
"Harry"—"Tweezer" rep.
E: "Old Home Place"—"Nellie Cane"—
"Memories"—"Funky Bitch"

Thu. 7/8/94
Great Woods, Mansfield, MA
1: "Llama"—"N$_2$0"—"Lizards"—"Tela"—
"Wilson"—"AC/DC Bag"—"Col.
Forbin"—"Mockingbird"—"Sloth"—
"McGrupp"—"Divided Sky"
2: "Rift"—"Sample"—"Reba"—"Yerushalim
Shel Zahav"—"It's Ice"—"Stash"—"YEM"—
"Frankenstein"—"YEM"—"Julius"—"Golgi"
E: "Nellie Cane"—"Cavern"

Fri. 7/9/94
Great Woods, Mansfield, MA
1: "Runaway Jim"—"Foam"—"Maze"—
"Guelah"—"Scent"—"DWD"—"Horse"—
"Silent"—"Antelope"
2: 2001—"SOAM"—"Fluffhead"—"Poor
Heart"—"Tweezer"—"Lifeboy"—
"Sparkle"—BBJ—"Harry"—"Suzie"
E: "Sleeping Monkey"—"Tweezer" rep.

Sun. 7/10/94
Saratoga Performing Arts Center,
Saratoga Springs, NY
1: "Chalkdust"—"Horn"—"Peaches"—
"Rift"—"Stash"—"If I Could"—"My
Friend"—"Julius"—"Cavern"
2: "Sample"—"Bowie"—"Glide"—"Ya

Mar"—"Mike's"—"Hydrogen"—
"Weekapaug" "—"BATR"—"Coil"—
"Crimes of the Mind"*
E: "Golgi"—"Rocky Top"

Wed. 7/13/94
Big Birch Concert Pavilion,
Patterson, NY
1: "Buried Alive"—"Poor Heart"—
"Sample"—"Foam"—"Mango"—"DWD"—
"Fee"—"It's Ice"—"FEFY"—"I Didn't
Know"—"SOAM"
2: "Possum"—"Wilson" (with "Cavern"
music)—"Cavern"—"NICU"—
"Tweezer"—"Julius"—"Tweezer"—
"BBFCFM" (with "Scent" music)—
"Tweezer"—"Mound"—"Slave"—"Suzie"
E: "MSO"—"Tweezer" rep.

Thu. 7/14/94
Finger Lakes Performing Arts
Center, Canandaigua, NY
1: "Runaway Jim"—"BATR"—"PYITE"—
"Stash"—"TMWSIY"—"Avenu"—
"TMWSIY"—"Scent"—"Fluffhead"—
"Horse"—"Silent"—"Antelope"
2: 2001—"Sample"—"Maze"—"If I
Could"—"Uncle Pen"—"YEM"—
"Sparkle"—BBJ—"Harry"—"Highway to
Hell"
E: "Chalkdust"

Fri. 7/15/94
Jones Beach Theater,
Wantagh, NY
1: "Rift"—"Sample"—"Divided Sky"—
"Gumbo"—"Foam"—"Fee"—"SOAM"—
"Golgi"—"Runaway Jim"
2: "Letter to Jimmy Page"—"Bowie"—
"BATR"—"Reba"—"It's Ice"—"Yerushalim

Shel Zahav"—"Dog Faced Boy"—"Julius"—
"Setting Sail"*
E: "Sleeping Monkey"—"Rocky Top"
*first time played

Sat. 7/16/94
Sugarbush Summer Stage, Fayston, VT
1: "Golgi"—"DWD"—"N₂O"—"Stash"—
"Lizards"—"Cavern"—"Horse"—"Silent"—
"Maze"—"Sparkle"—"Sample"
2: "Antelope"—"Catapult"—"Antelope"—
"Harpua"—2001—"Harpua"—"AC/DC
Bag"—"Scent"—"Harry"—"Contact"—
"Chalkdust"
E: "Suzie"

Fri. 10/7/94
Stabler Arena, Bethlehem, PA
1: "My Friend"—"Julius"—"Glide"—"Poor
Heart"—"Divided Sky"—"Guelah"—
"Stash"—"Guyute"*—"Golgi"
2: "Maze"—"Horse"—"Silent"—"Reba"—
"Wilson"—"Scent"—"Tweezer"—
"Lifeboy"—"MSO"—"Tweezer" rep.
E: "Foreplay"*—"Long Time"*—"Cavern"
*first time played

Sat. 10/8/94
Patriot Center, Fairfax, VA
1: "Chalkdust"—"Horn"—"Sparkle"—
"DWD"—"Guyute"—"Fee"—"It's Ice"—
"Lawn Boy"—"Antelope"
2: 2001—"Sample"—"Rift"—"Mike's"—
"Simple"*—"Mike's"—"Hydrogen"—
"Weekapaug"—"Fluffhead"—"Purple
Rain"—"Harry"—"Suzie"
E: "Foreplay"—"Long Time"—"Rocky
Top"
*with a girls' soccer team

Sun. 10/9/94
A. J. Palumbo Center, Pittsburgh, PA
1: "Runaway Jim"—"Foam"—"FEFY"—
"Curtain"—"Dog Faced Boy"—"SOAM"—
"Coil"
2: "Bowie"—"BATR"—"Scent"—"YEM"—
"Amazing Grace"—"Julius"—"Contact"
E: "Sleeping Monkey"—"Poor Heart"

Mon. 10/10/94
Palace Theater, Louisville, KY
1: "Sample"—"Divided Sky"—"Horse"—
"Silent"—"Sparkle"—"Stash"—"Guyute"—
"Old Home Place"—"Ginseng Sullivan"—
"Nellie Cane"—"Chalkdust"
2: "Golgi"—"Maze"—"Esther"—
"Tweezer"—"Fee"—"Rift"—"DWD"—
"Love You"—"Slave"
E: "Foreplay"—"Long Time"—"Tweezer"
rep.

Wed. 10/12/94
Orpheum Theater, Memphis, TN
1: "My Friend"—"Reba"—"Sloth"—"Poor
Heart"—"SOAM"—"Lizards"—"Guelah"—
"Julius"—"Sweet Adeline"
2: "Peaches"—"Bowie"—"BATR"—
"Scent"—"YEM"—"Nellie Cane"—
"Foreplay"—"Long Time"—"Harry"—
"Sample"
E: "GTBT"

Thu. 10/13/94
Grove Arena, Oxford, MS
1: "Llama"—"Gumbo"—"ATR"—
"DWD"—"I Didn't Know"—"Foam"—
"FEFY"—"Sparkle"—"Stash"
2: "Old Home Place"—"Antelope"—"If I
Could"—"It's Ice"—"Amazing Grace"—
"Mike's"—"Simple"—"Mike's"—"*Yerushalim*

Shel Zabav"—"Weekapaug"—"Foreplay"—
"Long Time"—"Cavern"
E: "Fire"

Fri. 10/14/94 McAlister Auditorium, New Orleans, LA

1: "Buried Alive"—"Sample"—"Divided Sky"—"Horse"—"Silent"—"PYITE"—"Bathtub Gin"—"Sweet Adeline"—"Rift"—"Col. Forbin"—"Mockingbird"—"Julius"
2: "Curtain"—"Tweezer"—"Lifeboy"—"Guyute"—"Chalkdust"—"Nellie Cane"—"Bow Mountain Rag"*—"Foreplay"—"Long Time"—"Coil"—"Tweezer" rep.
E: "Ya Mar"∧—"Cavern"**

*first time played

∧with Michael Ray and Carl Gerhard

Sat. 10/15/94 Oak Mountain Auditorium, Pelham, AL (Dave Matthews Band opened)

1: "Wilson"—"Sparkle"—"Maze"—"Glide"—"Reba"—"DWD"—"Golgi"
2: 2001—"Runaway Jim"—"Halley's"—"Scent"—"YEM"—"Catapult"—"YEM"—"Amazing Grace"—"Foreplay"—"Long Time"—"BATR"—"Suzie"
E: "Jam"*—"The Maker"*

*with Dave Matthews Band

Sun. 10/16/95 Chattanooga Memorial Auditorium, Chattanooga, TN

1: "Rift"—"Horn"—"Foam"—"Fee"—"SOAM"—"TMWSIY"—*"Avenu"*—"TMWSIY"—"Axilla II"—"Possum"
2: "Landlady"—"Poor Heart"—"Julius"—"Fluffhead"—BBJ—"Antelope"—"Dog Faced Boy"—"Sweet Adeline"—"Sample"
E1: "Highway to Hell"
E2: "Harpua"

Tues. 10/18/94 Memorial Gym, Nashville, TN

1: "Simple"—"My Friend"—"I Didn't Know"—"Poor Heart"—"Stash"—"Tela"—"It's Ice"—"Guyute"—"Divided Sky"—"Amazing Grace"
2: "Bowie"—"Horse"—"Silent"—"Reba"—"Scent"*—"Lifeboy"*—"Old Home Place"*—"Bow Mountain Rag"*—"Nellie Cane"*—"Llama"*
E: "MSO"*

*with Bela Fleck

Thu. 10/20/94 Mahaffey Theater, St. Petersburg, FL

1: "Runaway Jim"—"Golden Lady"*—"Guelah"—"SOAM"—"Kung"—"SOAM"—"Esther"—"Julius"—"Guyute"—"Golgi"
2: "Lengthwise"—"Maze"—"McGrupp"—"Rift"—"Harry"—"Nellie Cane"—"Foreplay"—"Long Time"—"Chalkdust"
E: "Sample"

*first time played

Fri. 10/21/94 Sunrise Musical Theater, Sunrise, FL

1: "Fee"—"DWD"—"Foam"—"Mango"—"Old Home Place"—"Stash"—"Lizards"—"Dog Faced Boy"—"Antelope"
2: 2001—"Mike's"—"Simple"—"Mike's"—"Hydrogen"—"Weekapaug"—"Sleeping Monkey"—"Curtain"—"FEFY"—"Scent"—"Slave"
E: "Sweet Adeline"—"Foreplay"—"Long Time"—"Cavern"

Sat. 10/22/94 The Edge Concert Field, Orlando, FL

1: "Suzie"—"Divided Sky"—"Gumbo"—
"Axilla II"—"Rift"—"SOAM"—
"Fluffhead"—"Julius"
2: "Peaches"—"Bowie"—"Horse"—
"Silent"—"Dinner and a Movie"—
"Tweezer"—"Wilson"—"Reba"—"Amazing Grace"—"AC/DC Bag"—"Highway to Hell"
E: "Uncle Pen"—"Tweezer" rep.

Sun. 10/23/94 University of Florida, Gainesville, FL

1: "Chalkdust"—"My Friend"—
"Sparkle"—"Simple"—"Poor Heart"—
"Stash"—"Catapult"—"Stash"—"Tela"—
"Maze"—"Sample"
2: "Runaway Jim"—"BATR"—"Halley's"—
"YEM"—"DWD"—"Purple Rain"—
"Harry"—"Fee"—"GTBT"
E: "Coil"

Tues. 10/25/94 Atlanta Civic Theater, Atlanta, GA

1: "Fee"—"Llama"—"Horn"—"Julius"—
"Horse"—"Silent"—"SOAM"—"Lizards"—
"Sample"
2: "Mike's"—"Simple"—"Mango"—
"Weekapaug" "—"Yerushalim Shel Zahav"—
"Glide"—"Axilla II"—"Jesus Left Chicago"—BBJ—"If I Only Had a Brain"—"Possum"
E: "Foreplay"—"Long Time"—"Golgi"

Wed. 10/26/94 Appalachian State University Varsity Gym, Boone, NC

1: "Simple"—"It's Ice"—"NICU"—
"Antelope"—"Guyute"—"Dog Faced

Boy"—"Scent"—"Oh Kee Pa"—"Suzie"—
"Runaway Jim"
2: "Rift"—"BATR"—"Reba"—"Axilla II"—
"YEM"—"Catapult"—"Cracklin Rosie"—
"Bowie"
E: "Nellie Cane"—"Foreplay"—"Long Time"—"Amazing Grace"

Thu. 10/27/94 University Hall, University of Virginia, Charlottesville, VA

1: "Wilson"—"Sparkle"—"Maze"—"Col. Forbin"—"Mockingbird"—"Divided Sky"—"Horse"—"Silent"—"Poor Heart"—
"Cavern"
2: "Julius"—"Ya Mar"—"Tweezer"—
"Contact"—"BBFCFM"—"DWD"—"Sweet Adeline"
E: "Slave"—"Icculus"—"Tweezer" rep.

Fri. 10/28/94 Gaillard Auditorium, Charleston, SC

1: "I Didn't Know"—"Llama"—
"Guelah"—"Scent"—"Stash"—"Glide"—
"Axilla II"—"ATR"—"Sample"—"Carolina"
2: 2001—"Bowie"—"Manteca"—"Bowie"—
"Lizards"—"Rift"—"Lifeboy"—
"Chalkdust"—"Old Home Place"—"Nellie Cane"—"Foreplay"—"Long Time"
E: "Fee"—"Highway to Hell"

Sat. 10/29/94 Spartanburg Memorial Auditorium, Spartanburg, SC

1: "My Friend"—"Sparkle"—"Simple"—
"Runaway Jim"—"Foam"—"Lawn Boy"—
"SOAM"—"Buffalo Bill"—"Makisupa"—
"Rift"
2: "DWD"—"TMWSIY"—"Avenu"—
"TMWSIY"—"Sparks"—"Uncle Pen"—

"YEM"—"Bike"—"Antelope"—"Sleeping
Monkey"—"Antelope"
E: "Harry"

Mon. 10/31/94
Glens Falls Civic Center, Glens Falls, NY

1: "Frankenstein"—"Sparkle"—"Simple"—
"Divided Sky"—"Harpua"—"Julius"—
"Horse"—"Silent"—"Reba"—"Golgi"
2: "Back in The USSR"—"Dear
Prudence"—"Glass Onion"—"Ob-La-Di
Ob-La-Da"—"Wild Honey Pie"—
"Bungalow Bill"—"Guitar"—"Happiness Is
a Warm Gun"—"Martha My Dear"—" I'm
So Tired"—"Blackbird"—"Piggies"—
"Rocky Raccoon"—"Don't Pass Me By"—
"Why Don't We Do It in the Road"—"I
Will"—"Julia"—"Birthday Theme"—"Yer
Blues"—"Mother Nature's Son"—
"Everybody's Got Something To Hide
Except For Me and My Monkey"—"Sexy
Sadie"—"Helter Skelter"—"Long Long
Long"—"Revolution #1"—"Honey Pie"—
"Savoy Truffle"—"Cry Baby Cry"—
"Revolution #9" {Ringo's "Good Night"
played over speakers)
3: "Bowie"—"BATR"—"Slave"—"Rift"—
"Sleeping Monkey"—"Poor Heart"—
"Antelope"
E: "Amazing Grace"—" Costume
Contest"—"Coil"

Wed. 11/2/94
Bangor Auditorium, Bangor, ME

1: "Suzie"—"Foam"—"If I Could"—
"Maze"—"Guyute"—"Stash"—"Scent"—
"Guitar"
2: "Halley's"—"Tweezer"—"Mango"—
"Axilla II"—"Possum"—"Lizards"—
"Sample"

E: "Old Home Place"—"Foreplay"—"Long
Time"—"Tweezer" rep.

Thu. 11/3/94
Mullins Center, Amherst, MA

1: "Fee"—"Divided Sky"—"Wilson"—
"Peaches"—"Glide"—"SOAM"—"Dog
Faced Boy"—"Sparkle"—"DWD"
2: 2001—"Simple"—"Poor Heart"—
"Julius"—"YEM"—"BBFCFM"—"Harry"—
"Cavern"
E: "MSO"—"Nellie Cane"—"Amazing
Grace"—"Highway to Hell"

Fri. 11/4/94
Onandaga County War Memorial, Syracuse, NY

1: "Sample"—"It's Ice"—"BATR"—
"Bowie"—"Col. Forbin"—"Mockingbird"—
"Scent"—"Suzie"—"Chalkdust"
2: "Curtain"—"Mike's"—"Simple"—
"Mike's"—"Tela"—"Weekapaug"—"Ya
Mar"—"Golgi"—"Slave"
E: "Loving Cup"—"Rocky Top"

Sat. 11/12/94
The Mac Center, Kent, OH

1: "Runaway Jim"—"Foam"—"If I
Could"—"Guyute"—"Maze"—"Stash"—
"Esther"—"Chalkdust"
2: "Julius"—"Fluffhead"—"DWD"—"Have
Mercy"—"DWD"—"Lifeboy"—"Rift"—
"Old Home Place"—"Nellie Cane"—
"Foreplay"—"Long Time"—"Harry"—
"Golgi"
E: "Sample"

Sun. 11/13/94
Warner Theater, Erie, PA

1: "Wilson"—"Sparkle"—"Simple"—
"Reba"—"Axilla II"—"It's Ice"—"Horse"—
"Silent"—"Antelope"

2: "Suzie"—"Divided Sky"—"Lizards"—
"Tweezer"—"Mango"—"BBFCFM"—
"Amazing Grace"—"Coil"
E: "Funky Bitch"—"Tweezer" rep.

Mon. 11/14/94
Devos Hall, Grand Rapids, MI
1: "My Friend"—"Scent"—"Guelah"—
"SOAM"—"BATR"—"Landlady"—
"Maze"—"Lawn Boy"—"Cavern"
2: "Peaches"—"Bowie"—*Yerushalim Shel
Zahav*—"Slave"—"Poor Heart"—"Julius"—
"Old Home Place"—"Nellie Cane"—
"Sweet Adeline"—"YEM"
E: "Golgi"

Wed. 11/16/94
Hill Auditorium, University of
Michigan, Ann Arbor, MI
1: "Sample"—"Foam"—"FEFY"—"Reba"—
"Axilla II"—"Lizards"—"Stash"—"Pig in a
Pen"*—"Tennessee Waltz"*—"Bluegrass
Breakdown"—"Swing Low, Sweet
Chariot"*
2: "Mike's"—"Simple"—"I'm Blue, I'm
Lonesome"*—"My Long Journey
Home"*—"Chalkdust"—"Fee"—"Antelope"
E: "Amazing Grace"—"Suzie"
*with Reverend Jeff Mosier

Thu. 11/17/94
Hara Arena, Dayton, OH
1: "Helter Skelter"—"Scent"—"Maze"—
"BATR"—"Wilson"—"Divided Sky"—
"Dog Faced Boy"—"Col. Forbin"—
"Mockingbird"—"DWD"
2: *2001*—"Bowie"—"Sleeping Monkey"—
"Sparkle"—"YEM"—"Love You"—
"Slave"—"Golgi"
E: "I'm Blue, I'm Lonesome"*—"Nellie

Cane"*—"My Long Journey Home"*—
"Fixin' To Die"*
*with Reverend Jeff Mosier

Fri. 11/18/94
Wharton Center, East Lansing, MI
1: "Rift"—"AC/DC Bag"—"Julius"—
"Horse"—"Silent"—"It's Ice"—"Tela"—
"SOAM"—"Butter Them Biscuits"*∧—"My
Long Journey Home"∧
2: "Llama"—"Bathtub Gin"—"Lifeboy"—
"Poor Heart"—"Tweezer"—"Contact"—
"Possum"
E: "Sweet Baby's Arms"*∧—"Runaway
Jim"∧
*first time played
∧with Reverend Jeff Mosier

Sat. 11/19/94
Indiana University Auditorium,
Bloomington, IN
1: "Golgi"—"DWD"—"Guyute"—"Axilla
II"—"Paul and Silas"—"TMWSIY"—
"Avenu"—"Antelope"—"I'm Blue, I'm
Lonesome"*—"Butter Them Biscuits"*—
"My Long Journey Home"*
2: "Suzie"—"Sparkle"—"YEM"—"Cracklin'
Rosie"—"Harry"—"Amazing Grace"—
"GTBT"
E: "Coil"
*with Reverend Jeff Mosier

Sat. 11/19/94
Indiana University Auditorium
Parking Lot, Bloomington, IN
"Cripple Creek"—"Tennesse Waltz"—
"Old Home Place"—"Dooley"—
"Mountain Dew"—"Pig in a Pen"—"Sweet
Baby's Arms"—"My Long Journey
Home"—"Butter Them Biscuits"—"I'm
Blue, I'm Lonesome"—"Midnight

Mornlight"—"Will the Circle Be
Unbroken"

Sun. 11/20/94
Dane County Exposition Center, Madison, WI

1: "Chalkdust"—"Fee"—Scent"—"Stash"—
"If I Could"*—"Butter Them Biscuits"*—
"My Long Journey Home"*—
"Dooley"*∧—"Divided Sky"—"Sample"
2: 2001—"Bowie"—"Glide"—"Axilla II"—
"Reba"—"Simple"—"Rift"—"Terrapin"—
"Julius"—"Cavern"
E1: "Icculus"
E2: "Cavern"
*with Rev. Jeff Mosier
∧first time played

Tues. 11/22/94
Jesse Auditorium, Columbia, MO

1: "Buried Alive"—"Poor Heart"—
"Horn"—"Foam"—"Guyute"—"I Didn't
Know"—"BATR"—"DWD"—"Sweet
Adeline"
2: "Funky Bitch" "—"Yerushalim Shel
Zahav"—"Cry Baby Cry"—"Curtain"—
"Blackbird"—"Runaway Jim"—
"BBFCFM"—"I'm Blue, I'm Lonesome"—
"Butter Them Biscuits"—"My Long
Journey Home"—"Harry"—"Highway to
Hell"
E: "Lizards"

Wed. 11/23/94
Fox Theater, St. Louis, MO

1: "Wilson"—"Sparkle"—"Simple"—"It's
Ice"—"If I Could"—"Oh Kee Pa"—
"Suzie"—"Divided Sky"—"Amazing
Grace"
2: "Maze"—"Fee"—"Scent"—"Tweezer"—
"Lifeboy"—"YEM"—"Tweezer" rep.
E: "Sample"

Fri. 11/25/94
University of Illinois at Chicago Pavilion, Chicago, IL

1: "Llama"—"Guelah"—"Reba"—
"BATR"—"SOAM"—"Esther"—"Julius"—
"Golgi"
2: 2001—"Mike's"—"Simple"—"-
Harpua"—"Weekapaug"—"Mango"—
"Purple Rain"—"Antelope"
E: "GTBT"

Sat. 11/26/94
Orpheum Theater, Minneapolis, MN

1: "My Friend"—"Possum"—"Guyute"—"If
I Could"—"Foam"—"Horse"—"Silent"—
"Poor Heart"—"Cavern"
2: "Halley's"—"Bowie"—"Sweet
Adeline"—"Lizards"—"Sample"—"Slave"
E: "Rocky Top"

Mon. 11/28/94
Shroyer Gym, Bozeman, MT

1: "Chalkdust"—2001—"Scent"—
"Stash"—"Guyute"—"Sparkle"—
"Simple"*—"Divided Sky"—"Sweet
Adeline"
2: "Suzie"—"NICU"—"Tweezer"—
"Sleeping Monkey"—"Julius"
E: "Fee"—"Tweezer" rep.
*with Cameron McKenney

Wed. 11/30/94
Evergreen College Campus Center, Olympia, WA

1: "Frankenstein"—"Poor Heart"—"My
Friend"—"Reba"—"Col. Forbin"—
"Mockingbird"—"DWD"—"BATR"—"I'm
Blue, I'm Lonesome"—"Long Journey
Home"
2: "Halley's"—"Antelope"—"MSO"—
"Antelope"—"Fixin' to Die"—"Ya Mar"—

"Mike's"—"Catapult"—"McGrupp"—
"Cavern"
E: "Horse"—"Silent"—"Amazing Grace"

Thu 12/1/94
Salem Armory, Salem, OR
1: "Sample"—"Uncle Pen"—"FEFY"—
"Maze"—"Guyute"—"I Didn't Know"—
"SOAM"—"Sweet Adeline"
2: "Peaches"—"Mound"—"Tweezer"—
"BBFCFM"—"Makisupa"—"NICU"—"Jesus
Left Chicago"—"Harry"—"Golgi"
E: "Sleeping Monkey"—"Tweezer" rep.

Fri. 12/2/94
Recreation Center, University of
California at Davis, Davis, CA
1: "Poor Heart"—*2001*—"Sparkle"—
"Simple"—"It's Ice"—"Lizards"—"Stash"—
"Coil"
2: "Chalkdust"—"Bowie"*—"Buried
Alive"*—"Julius"*—"Landlady"*—
"Gumbo"*—"Caravan"*—"Suzie"*
E: "Cavern"*

*with the Giant Country Horns

Sat. 12/3/94
Event Center, San Jose State
University, San Jose, CA
1: "Wilson"—"Divided Sky"—"Guelah"—
"Scent"—"Antelope"—"Guyute"—"Sample
2: "Frankenstein"*—"Suzie"*—"Buried
Alive"*—"Gumbo"*—"Slave"*—"Touch
Me"*—"Alumni Blues" jam*—"Julius"*—
"Cavern"*
E: "Golgi"

*with the Giant Country Horns

Sun 12/4/94
Acker Gym, Chicago State
University, Chico, CA
1: "Runaway Jim"—"Foam"—"If I
Could"—"Rift"—"Tweezer"—"Fee"—
"Mound"—"Sweet Adeline"—"Possum"
2: "Maze"—"BATR"—"Reba"—"Axilla
II"—"YEM"—"Purple Rain"—"GTBT"
E: "Sleeping Monkey"—"Rocky Top"

Tues. 12/6/94
Event Center, University of
California at Santa Barbara, Santa
Barbara, CA
1: "Llama"—"Mound"—"DWD"—
"Fluffhead"—"Jesus Left Chicago"—
"Sparkle"—"Stash"—"Golgi"
2: "Curtain"—"Sample"—*2001*—"Poor
Heart"—"Mike's"—"Simple"—"Mango"—
"Weekapaug"—"Bike"—"I'm Blue, I'm
Lonesome"—"Foreplay"—"Long Time"—
"Antelope"
E: "Back in the USSR"

Wed. 12/7/94
Spreckels Theater, San Diego, CA
1: "Peaches"—"Runaway Jim"—"Sloth"—
"Ya Mar"—"SOAM"—"Guyute"—
"Lifeboy"—"Chalkdust"
2: "Rift"—"Frankenstein"—"Divided
Sky"—"Fee"—"Julius"—"I'm Blue, I'm
Lonesome"—"My Long Journey Home"—
"Amazing Grace"—"YEM"
E: "Cavern"

Thu. 12/8/94
Spreckels Theater, San Diego, CA
1: "Makisupa"—"Maze"—"AC/DC Bag"—
"Scent"—"PYITE"—"Simple"—
"Catapult"—"Simple"—"Lizards"—"Guitar"
2: "Possum"—"My Mind's"—"Axilla II"—

"Reba"—"Nellie Cane"—"Sweet
Adeline"—"Bowie"—"Golgi"
E: "Horse"—"Silent"—"Rocky Top"

Fri. 12/9/94
Mesa Amphitheater, Mesa, AZ
1: "Llama"—"Foam"—"Guyute"—
"Sparkle"—"I Didn't Know"—"It's Ice"—"If
I Could"—"Antelope"
2: "Wilson"—"Poor Heart"—"Tweezer"—
"McGrupp"—"Julius"—BBJ—"Cracklin
Rosie"—"YEM"—"Suzie"
E: "I'm Blue, I'm Lonesome"—
"Foreplay"—"Long Time"—"Tweezer" rep.

Sat. 12/10/94
Civic Auditorium,
Santa Monica, CA
1: "Fee"—"Rift"—"Stash"—"Lizards"—
"Sample"—"Divided Sky"—"Lawn Boy"—
"Chalkdust"
2: "Simple"—"Maze"—"Guyute"—2001—
"Mike's"—"Weekapaug"—"Hydrogen"—
"Why Don't We Do It in the Road"—
"Poor Heart"—"Slave"—"Cavern"
E: "Chalkdust" rep.—"GTBT"

Wed. 12/28/94
Philadelphia Civic Center,
Philadelphia, PA
1: "Mound"—"Simple"—"Julius"—
"Bathtub Gin"—"BATR"—"Axilla II"—
"Reba"—"Dog Faced Boy"—"It's Ice"—
"Antelope"
2: "Suzie"—"NICU"—"Mike's"—
"Mango"—"Weekapaug"—"Contact"—
"Llama"—"Love You"—"Coil"
E: "Bold as Love"

Thu. 12/29/94
Providence Civic Center,
Providence, RI
1: "Runaway Jim"—"Foam"—"If I
Could"—"SOAM"—"Horse"—"Silent"—
"Uncle Pen"—"I Didn't Know"—"Possum"
2: "Guyute"—"Bowie"—"Halley's"—
"Lizards"—"Cracklin' Rosie"—"GTBT"
E: "My Long Journey Home"—"Sleeping
Monkey"

Fri. 12/30/94
Madison Square Garden, New
York, NY
1: "Wilson"—"Rift"—"AC/DC Bag"—
"Sparkle"—"Simple"—"Stash"—"Fee"—
"Scent"—"Cavern"
2: "Sample"—"Poor Heart"—"Tweezer"—
"I'm Blue, I'm Lonesome"—"YEM"—
"Purple Rain"—"Harry"—"Tweezer" rep.
E: "Frankenstein"

Sat. 12/31/94
Boston Garden, Boston, MA
1: "Golgi"—"NICU"—"Antelope"*—
"Glide"—"Mound"—"Peaches"—"Divided
Sky"—"Funky Bitch"
2: "Old Home Place"—"BATR"—
"Mike's"—"Buffalo Bill"—"Mike's"—
"Yerushalim Shel Zahav"—"Weekapaug"—
"Amazing Grace"
3: "MSO"—2001—{New Year's festivities}
"Auld Lang Syne"—"Chalkdust"—
"Horse"—"Silent"—"Suzie"—"Slave"
E: "Simple"

*with Tom Marshall

Tues. 5/16/95
Lowell Memorial Auditorium, Lowell, MA (Voters for Choice Benefit with EBN and Jennifer Trynin Band)

1: "Don't You Wanna Go"*—"Ha Ha Ha"*—"Spock's Brain"*—"Strange Design"*—"Reba"—"Theme"*—"Lonesome Cowboy Bill"*—"Free"*—"Glide II"—"YEM"—"Sweet Adeline"—"Sample"

E: "I'll Come Running"*—"Gloria"*

*first time played

Wed. 6/7/95
Boise State University Pavilion, Boise, ID

1: "Possum"—"Weigh"—"Taste"*—"Strange Design"—"Stash"—"If I Could"—"Scent"—"Wedge"—"Funky Bitch"—"Slave"
2: "Ha Ha Ha"—"Maze"—"Spock's Brain"—"Theme"—"Lonesome Cowboy Bill"—"Acoustic Army"—"Sample"—"Harry"—"Suzie"

E: "Guitar"

*first time played

Thu. 6/8/95
Delta Center, Salt Lake City, UT

1: "Don't You Wanna Go"—"Ha Ha Ha"—"Runaway Jim"—"Guelah"—"Mound"—"FEFY"—"Reba"—"Prince Caspian"*—"Chalkdust"
2: "Simple"—"Rift"—"Free"—"BATR"—"Tweezer"—"Lifeboy"—"Poor Heart"—"Julius"

E: "GTBT"

*first time played

Fri. 6/9/95
Red Rocks Amphitheater, Morrison, CO

1: "My Friend"—"Divided Sky"—"Strange Design"—"Oh Kee Pa"—"AC/DC Bag"—"Theme"—"Taste"—"Sparkle"—"Antelope"
2: "SOAM"—"Wedge"—"Scent"—"Cavern"—"Bowie"—"Acoustic Army"—"Sweet Adeline"—"Slave"

E: "Coil"

Sat. 6/10/95
Red Rocks Amphitheater, Morrison, CO

1: "Makisupa"—"Llama"—"Prince Caspian"—"It's Ice"—"Free"—"Rift"—"YEM"—"Lonesome Cowboy Bill"—"Suzie"
2: "Maze"—"Fee"—"Uncle Pen"—"Mike's"—"Hydrogen"—"Weekapaug"—"Amazing Grace"—"Sample"

E: "Day in the Life"*

*first time played

Tues. 6/13/95
Riverport Amphitheater, St. Louis, MO

1: "Runaway Jim"—"Foam"—"BATR"—"Stash"—"Strange Design"—"Taste"—"Reba"—"Terrapin"—"Sparkle"—"Chalkdust"
2: "Bowie"—"Lizards"—"Axilla II"—"Theme"—"Acoustic Army"—"Harry"—"Golgi"

E: "Sweet Adeline"—"Julius"

Wed. 6/14/95
Mud Island Amphitheater, Memphis, TN

1: "Don't You Wanna Go"—"Gumbo"—"NICU"—"Mound"—"Cavern"—"Possum"—"ATR"—"Amazing Grace"—

"Horse"—"Silent"—"Spock's Brain"—
"SOAM"
2: 2001—"Poor Heart"—"Tweezer"—
"Acoustic Army"—"Guitar"
E: "Simple"—"Rocky Top"—"Tweezer"
rep.

Thu. 6/15/95
Lakewood Amphitheater,
Atlanta, GA
1: "My Friend"—"Sparkle"—"AC/DC
Bag"—"Old Home Place"—"Taste"—
"Wedge"—"Stash"—"I Didn't Know"—
"Fluffhead"—"Antelope"
2: "MSO"—"Ha Ha Ha"—"Bowie"—
"Strange Design"—"Theme"—"Scent"—
"Acoustic Army"—"Slave"
E: "BATR"—"Frankenstein"

Fri. 6/16/95
Walnut Creek Amphitheater,
Raleigh, NC
1: "Halley's"—"DWD"—"Esther"—"Ya
Mar"—"Cry Baby Cry"—"It's Ice"—"My
Mind's"—"Dog Faced Boy—Catapult"—
"SOAM"
2: "Runaway Jim"—"Free"—"Carolina"—
"YEM"*—"Coil"
E: "Bold as Love"
*with Boyd Tinsley

Sat. 6/17/95
Nissan Pavilion at Stone Ridge,
Gainesville, VA
1: "Divided Sky"—"Suzie"—"Taste"—
"Fee"—"Uncle Pen"—"Julius"—"Lawn
Boy"—"Curtain"—"Stash"
2: "Wilson"—"Maze"—"Mound"—
"Tweezer"—"Johnny B. Goode"*—
"Tweezer"—"McGrupp"—"Acoustic
Army"—"Sweet Adeline"—"Harry"—
"Sample"

E: "Three Little Birds"*∧
*first time played
∧with Dave Matthews and Leroi Moore

Mon. 6/19/95
Deer Creek Amphitheater,
Noblesville, IN
1: "Theme"—"Poor Heart"—"AC/DC
Bag"—"Tela"—"PYITE"—"Reba"—
"Strange Design"—"Rift"—"Cavern"—
"Antelope"
2: "Simple"—"Bowie"—"Mango"—"Loving
Cup"—"Sparkle"—"YEM"—"Acoustic
Army"—"Possum"
E: "Day in the Life"

Tues. 6/20/95
Blossom Music Center, Cuyahoga
Falls, OH
1: "Llama"—"Spock's Brain"—"Ginseng
Sullivan"—"Foam"—"Bathtub Gin"—"If I
Could"—"Taste"—"I Didn't Know"—
"SOAM"
2: "Halley's"—"Chalkdust"—"Prince
Caspian"—"Uncle Pen"—"Mike's"—
"Contact"—"Weekapaug"—"Cracklin'
Rosie"—"Highway to Hell"
E: "Slave"—"Amazing Grace"

Thu. 6/22/95
Finger Lakes Performing Arts
Center, Canandaigua, NY
1: "Sample"—"Scent"—"Ha Ha Ha"—
"Divided Sky"—"Guelah"—"It's Ice"—
"Strange Design"—"Maze"—"Cavern"—
"Sweet Adeline"
2: "Theme"—"Tweezer"—"Tweezer" rep.
E: "Acoustic Army"—"Guitar"

Fri. 6/23/95
Waterloo Village Music Center,
Stanhope, NJ
1: "Simple"—"Chalkdust"—"Prince
Caspian"—"Reba"—"Ginseng Sullivan"—
"Free"—"Taste"—"YEM"
2: "Runaway Jim"—"Lizards"—"Wedge"—
"Antelope"—"Harpua"*—"Llama"*—
"GTBT"*
E: "Day in the Life"
*with John Popper

Sat. 6/24/95
Mann Music Center,
Philadelphia, PA
1: "Fee"—"Rift"—"Spock's Brain"—
"Julius"—"Glide"—"Mound"—"Stash"—
"Horse"—"Silent"—"Coil"
2: 2001—"Halley's"—"Bowie"—
"Lifeboy"—"Suzie"—"Harry"—"Acoustic
Army"—"Sweet Adeline"—"Golgi"
E: "Bold as Love"

Sun. 6/25/95
Mann Music Center,
Philadelphia, PA
1: "Ya Mar"—"AC/DC Bag"—"Taste"—
"Theme"—"If I Could"—"Sparkle"—
"Divided Sky"—"I Didn't Know"—
"SOAM"
2: "Maze"—"Sample"—"Scent"—
"Mike's"—"Why Don't We Do It in the
Road"—"Weekapaug"—"Amazing
Grace"—"Cavern"
E: "BATR"—"Slave"

Mon. 6/26/95
Saratoga Performing Arts Center,
Saratoga Springs, NY
1: "My Friend"—"Don't You Wanna
Go"—"Bathtub Gin"—"NICU"—"Sloth"—

"My Mind's"—"It's Ice"—"Dog Faced
Boy"—"Tela"—"Possum"
2: "DWD"—"Free"—"Poor Heart"—
"YEM"—"Strange Design"—"Antelope"
E: "Sleeping Monkey"—"Rocky Top"

Wed. 6/28/95
Jones Beach Theater,
Wantagh, NY
1: "Axilla II"—"Foam"—"FEFY"—"Reba"—
"PYITE"—"Stash"—"Fluffhead"—
"Chalkdust"
2: "Sample"—"Poor Heart"—"Tweezer"—
"Gumbo"—"Sparkle"—"Suzie"—"Harry"—
"Tweezer" rep.
E: "Sweet Adeline"—"Guitar"

Thu. 6/29/95
Jones Beach Theater,
Wantagh, NY
1: "Runaway Jim"—"Taste"—"Horse"—
"Silent"—"Divided Sky"—"Cavern"—
"Rift"—"Simple"—"SOAM"—"Carolina"
2: "Free"—"Bowie"—"Strange Design"—
"YEM"—"Acoustic Army"—"Day in the
Life"
E: "Theme"

Fri. 6/30/95
Great Woods, Mansfield, MA
1: "AC/DC Bag"—"Scent"—"Horn"—
"Taste"—"Wedge"—"Lizards"—
"Mound"—"Fee"—"Antelope"
2: 2001—"Possum"—"Ha Ha Ha"—
"TMWSIY"—*Avenu*—"TMWSIY"—
Avenu—"Contact"—"Weekapaug"—
"Amazing Grace"—"Coil"
E: "Cracklin' Rosie"—"Golgi"

Sat. 7/1/95
Great Woods, Mansfield, MA

1: "Ya Mar"—"Llama"—"If I Could"—
"ATR"—"It's Ice"—"Prince Caspian"—
"SOAM"—"BATR"—"Chalkdust"
2: "Wilson"—"Maze"—"Theme"—"Uncle
Pen"—"Stash"—"Strange Design"—
"Acoustic Army"—"Harry"—"Suzie"
E: "Funky Bitch"

Sun 7/2/95
Sugarbush Summer Stage,
Fayston, VT

1: "Sample"—"Divided Sky"—"Gumbo"—
"Curtain"—"Julius"—"Camel Walk"—
"Reba"—"I Didn't Know"—"Rift"—
"Guitar"
2: "Runaway Jim"—"Makisupa"—
"Scent"—"Tweezer"—"Ha Ha Ha"—
"Sleeping Monkey"—"Acoustic Army"—
"Slave"
E: "Halley's"—"Tweezer"

Mon. 7/3/95
Sugarbush Summer Stage,
Fayston, VT

1: "My Friend"—"Poor Heart"—
"Antelope"—"Loving Cup"—"Sparkle"—
"It's Ice"—"If I Could"—"Maze"—"Strange
Design"—"Free"—"Cavern"
2: "Timber"—"Bowie"—"Johnny B.
Goode"—"Bowie"—"AC/DC Bag"—
"Lizards"—"BBFCFM"—"Day in the
Life"—"Possum"—"Coil"
E: "Simple"—"Amazing Grace"

Wed. 9/27/95
Cal Expo Amphitheater,
Sacramento, CA

1: "Wolfman's"—"Rift"—"Free"—"It's
Ice"—"I Didn't Know"—"Fog"*—"Strange
Design"—"Chalkdust"—"Coil"

2: "Cars Trucks and Buses"*—"AC/DC
Bag"—"Bowie"—"Billy Breathes"*—
"Keyboard Cavalry"*—"Harry"—"Hello
My Baby"*—"Day in the Life"
E: "Possum"
*first time played

Thu. 9/28/95
Summer Pops, San Diego, CA

1: "Cars Trucks and Buses"—"Runaway
Jim"—"Billy Breathes"—"Scent"—
"Stash"—"Fee"—"Fog"—"Acoustic
Army"—"Slave"
2: "Theme"—"Poor Heart"—"Don't You
Wanna Go"—"Tweezer"—"Keyboard
Cavalry"—"Amazing Grace"—"Sample"—
"Antelope"
E: "Fire"

Fri. 9/29/95
Greek Theater, Los Angeles, CA

1: "AC/DC Bag"—"Sparkle"—"Divided
Sky"—"Strange Design"—"Cars Trucks
and Buses"—"YEM"—"Sweet Adeline"—
"Suzie"
2: 2001—"Maze"—"Free"—"Ya Mar"—
"SOAM"—"Billy Breathes"—"Cryin' "*—
"Day in the Life"
E: "Chalkdust"
*first time played

Sat. 9/30/95
Shoreline Amphitheater, Mountain
View, CA

1: "My Friend"—"Cars Trucks and
Buses"—chess jam—"Reba"—"Uncle
Pen"—"Horn"—"Antelope"—"I'm Blue, I'm
Lonesome"—"Sample"
2: "Runaway Jim"—"Fog"—"If I Could"—
"Scent"—"Mike's"—"Keyboard Cavalry"—

"Weekapaug"—"Suspicious Minds"*—
"Cavern"
E: "Amazing Grace"—"GTBT"

Mon. 10/2/95
Seattle Arena, Seattle, WA
1: "Poor Heart"—"Wolfman's Brother"—
"Rift"—chess jam—"Stash"—"Acoustic
Army"—"Fog"—"Theme"—"Tela"—
"Bowie"
2: "Wilson"—"Cars Trucks and Buses"—
"Bathtub Gin"—"Llama"—"Simple"—
"Keyboard Cavalry"—"Slave"—"Hello My
Baby"—"Lizards"—"Antelope"
E: "Day in the Life"

Tues. 10/3/95
Seattle Arena, Seattle, WA
1: "Maze"—"Guelah"—"Foam"—"FEFY"—
"I'm Blue, I'm Lonesome"—"Free"—
"TMWSIY"—*Avenu*—"TMWSIY"—
"Sample"—"YEM"
2: "Timber"—"It's Ice"—"Sparkle"—
"Harry"—"Billy Breathes"—"Faht"—"Sweet
Adeline"—"SOAM"—"Coil"
E: "Rocky Top"

Thu. 10/5/95
Portland Memorial Coliseum, Portland, OR
1: "Chalkdust"—"Ha Ha Ha"—"Fog"—
"Horse"—"Silent"—"Cars Trucks and
Buses"—"Strange Design"—"Divided
Sky"—"Acoustic Army"—"Julius"—"Suzie"
2: 2001—"Runaway Jim"—"Col.
Forbin"—"Mockingbird"—"Scent"—
"Cavern"—"Bowie"—"Lifeboy"—"Amazing
Grace"
E: "Guitar"

Fri. 10/6/95
Orpheum Theater, Vancouver, BC, Canada
1: "Ya Mar"—"Stash"—"Billy Breathes"—
"Reba"—"I'm Blue, I'm Lonesome"—
"Rift"—"Free"—"Lizards"—"Sample"
2: "Poor Heart"—"Maze"—"Theme"—
"NICU"—"Tweezer"—"Keyboard
Cavalry"—"Suspicious Minds"—"Slave"
E: "Hello My Baby"—"Day in the Life"

Sat. 10/7/95
Opera House, Spokane, WA
1: "Julius"—"Gumbo"—"Fog"—"Mound"—
"Possum"—"Mango"—"Acoustic Army"—
"Wilson"—"Antelope"
2: "Makisupa"—"Cars Trucks and
Buses"—"SOAM"—"Strange Design"—"It's
Ice"—"Contact"—"Frankenstein"—
"Harry"—"Sweet Adeline"
E: "Fire"

Sun. 10/8/95
Adams Fieldhouse, Missoula, MT
1: "AC/DC Bag"—"Demand"—
"Sparkle"—"Wolfman's"—"Reba"—"I'm
Blue, I'm Lonesome"—"Prince Caspian"—
"Uncle Pen"—"Free"
2: "Keyboard Cavalry"—"Cars Trucks
and Buses"—"Timber"—"Ya Mar"—
"Sample"—"YEM"—"Suspicious Minds"—
"Dog Faced Boy"—"Bowie"—"Keyboard
Cavalry Reprise"
E: "BATR"—"Rocky Top"

Wed. 10/11/95
Compton Terrace, Phoenix, AZ
1: "Stash"—"Old Home Place"—
"Cavern"—"Divided Sky"—"If I Could"—
"Fog"—"Acoustic Army"—"Julius"—
"Sample"
2: "Possum"—"Bathtub Gin"—"Mound"—

"Mike's"—"McGrupp"—"Weekapaug"—
"Llama"—"Suzie"—"Crossroads"—"Hello
My Baby"—"Day in the Life"
E: "Chalkdust"

Fri. 10/13/95
Will Rogers Auditorium, Fort Worth, TX

1: "Ya Mar"—2001—"Maze"—"Billy
Breathes"—"I'm Blue, I'm Lonesome"—
"Prince Caspian"—"SOAM"—
"Fluffhead"—"Life on Mars"*
2: "Tube"—"Uncle Pen"—"Theme"—
"Wilson"—"Antelope"—"Keyboard
Cavalry"—"Lizards"—"Guitar"—"Sweet
Adeline"—"Coil"
E: "Bold as Love"

*first time played

Sat. 10/14/95
Austin Music Hall, Austin, TX

1: "AC/DC Bag"—"Cars Trucks and
Buses"—"Kung"—"Free"—"Stash"—
"Catapult"—"Sparkle"—"Acoustic
Army"—"It's Ice"—"Tela"—"Runaway Jim"
2: "Reba"—"Rift"—"YEM"*—"Hello My
Baby"—"Scent"—"Cavern"
E: "Day in the Life"

*with John Medeski, Billy Martin, and Chris Wood

Sun. 10/15/95
Austin Music Hall, Austin, TX

1: "Buried Alive"—"Poor Heart"—
"Slave"—"I Didn't Know"—"Demand"—
"Llama"—"Foam"—"Strange Design"—"I'm
Blue, I'm Lonesome"—"Bowie"
2: "Julius"—"Simple"—"Tweezer"—
"Lizards"—"Sample"—"Suspicious
Minds"—"Harry"—"Tweezer" rep.
E: "Funky Bitch"

Tues. 10/17/95
State Palace Theater, New Orleans, LA

1: "Sample"—"Stash"—"Uncle Pen"—
"AC/DC Bag"—"Maze"—"Glide"—
"Sparkle"—"Free"—"Strange Design"—
"Amazing Grace"
2: "Mound"—"Prince Caspian"—"Fog"—
"Suzie"—"Keyboard Cavalry"—"Jam"*
E: "My Long Journey Home"—"I'm Blue,
I'm Lonesome"

*with John Medeski, Billy Martin, and Chris Wood

Thu. 10/19/95
Municipal Theater, Kansas City, MO

1: "Cars Trucks and Buses"—"Runaway
Jim"—"Horn"—"PYITE"—"Esther"—
"Chalkdust"—"Theme"—"Acoustic
Army"—"SOAM"—"Billy Breathes"—
"Cavern"
2: "Frankenstein"—"Poor Heart"—
"Mike's"—"Hydrogen"—"Weekapaug"—
"Lawn Boy"—"BBFCFM"—"Kung"—
"Suspicious Minds"—"Possum"
E: "Day in the Life"

Fri. 10/20/95
Five Seasons Arena, Cedar Rapids, IA

1: "My Friend"—"Ya Mar"—"Ha Ha
Ha"—"Divided Sky"—"Fee"—"Rift"—
"Free"—"Hello My Baby"—"Amazing
Grace"—"Amazing Grace" rep.*
2: "Timber"—"Scent"—"Simple"—
"Maze"—"Gumbo"—"Guitar"—"My Long
Journey Home"—"I'm Blue, I'm
Lonesome"—"BATR"—"Antelope"
E: "Sleeping Monkey"—"Rocky Top"

*with electric instruments

Sat. 10/21/95
Pershing Auditorium, Lincoln, NE

1: "Tweezer" rep.—"Chalkdust"—
"Guelah"—"Reba"—"Wilson"—"Cars
Trucks and Buses"—"Kung"—"Lizards"—
"Strange Design"—"Acoustic Army"—
"GTBT"—"Tweezer" rep.
2: 2001—"Bowie"—"Lifeboy"—
"Sparkle"—"YEM"—"Purple Rain"—
"Harry"—"Suzie"
E: "Highway to Hell"

Sun. 10/22/95
Assembly Hall, Champaign, IL

1: "AC/DC Bag"—"My Mind's"—
"Sloth"—"Runaway Jim"—"Weigh"—
"NICU"—"FEFY"—"It's Ice"—"Poor
Heart"—"Sample"—"I'm Blue, I'm
Lonesome"—"Stash"
2: "Golgi"—"Possum"—"Catapult"—
"Curtain"—"Tweezer"—"Makisupa"—
"BBFCFM"—"Life on Mars"—"Uncle
Pen"—"Slave"—"Cavern"
E: "Sweet Adeline"—"Coil"

Tues. 10/24/95 Dane County
Coliseum, Madison, WI

1: "My Friend"—"Paul and Silas"—
"Fog"—"Fee"—"Llama"—"Horse"—
"Silent"—"Demand"—"Maze"—
"Wolfman's"—"Acoustic Army"—"Prince
Caspian"—"SOAM"
2: "Julius"—"Theme"—"BATR"—"YEM"—
"Sleeping Monkey"—"Antelope"—
"Contact"—"Cavern"
E: "Day in the Life"

Wed. 10/25/95
St. Paul Civic Center, St. Paul, MN

1: "Ya Mar"—"Sample"—"Divided Sky"—
"Wedge"—"Scent"—"Free"—"Strange

Design"—"My Long Journey Home"—
"I'm Blue, I'm Lonesome"—"Chalkdust"
2: "Reba"—"Life on Mars"—"Cars Trucks
and Buses"—"Mike's"—"Sparkle"—
"Weekapaug"—"Suzie"—"Crossroads"
E: "Fire"

Fri. 10/27/95
Wing Stadium, Kalamazoo, MI

1: "Runaway Jim"—"Fluffhead"—"Fog"—
"Horn"—"I Didn't Know"—"Rift"—
"Stash"—"Fee"—"Suspicious Minds"
2: 2001—"Bowie"—"Dog Faced Boy"—
"Poor Heart"—"Simple"—"McGrupp"—
"Keyboard Cavalry"—"BATR"—"Possum"
E: "Life on Mars"

Sat. 10/28/95
The Palace, Auburn Hills, MI

1: "AC/DC Bag"—"Mound"—"Timber"—
"Uncle Pen"—"Sample"—"Lizards"—"Billy
Breathes"—"Acoustic Army"—"Prince
Caspian"—"Antelope"
2: "Maze"—"Theme"—"Scent"—"YEM"—
"Strange Design"—"Frankenstein"—
"Chalkdust"
E: "Guitar"

Sun. 10/29/95
Louisville Gardens, Louisville, KY

1: "Buried Alive"—"Poor Heart"—
"Julius"—"PYITE"—"Cars Trucks and
Buses"—"Horse"—"Silent"—"SOAM"—
"NICU"—"Gumbo"—"Slave"—"Sweet
Adeline"
2: "Makisupa"—"Bowie"—"Mango"—"It's
Ice"—"Kung"—"It's Ice"—"Shaggy Dog"—
"Possum"—"Lifeboy"—"Amazing Grace"
E: "Funky Bitch"

Tues. 10/31/95
Rosemont Horizon, Chicago, IL
1: "Icculus"—"Divided Sky"—"Wilson"—
"Ya Mar"—"Sparkle"—"Free"—"Guyute"—
"Antelope"—"Harpua"
2: "I Am the Sea"—"Real Me"—
"Quadrophenia"—"Cut My Hair"—"Punk
Meets the Godfather"—"I'm One"—
"Dirty Jobs"—"Helpless Dancer"—"Is It in
My Head"—"I've Had Enough"—"5:15"—
"Sea and Sand"—"Drowned"—"Bell
Boy"—"Dr. Jimmy"—"The Rock"—"Love
Reign O'er Me"
3: "YEM"—"Jesus Left Chicago"*—"Day
in the Life"—"Suzie"**
E: "My Generation"
second set with the Giant Country Horns
*with Dave Grippo
**with Dave Grippo, Don Glasgo, Joey Somerville

Thu. 11/9/95
Fox Theater, Atlanta, GA
1: "Tweezer" rep."—"Divided Sky"—
"Prince Caspian"—"PYITE"—"Simple"—
"Reba"—"Tela"—"Sample"
2: "Theme"—"Julius"—"Lizards"—
"Bathtub Gin"—"TMWSIY"—"Avenu"—
"TMWSIY"—"Life on Mars"—"Hello My
Baby"—"Coil"
E: "Loving Cup"

Fri. 11/10/95
Fox Theater, Atlanta, GA
1: "BATR"—"Runaway Jim"—"Fog"—"Old
Home Place"—"It's Ice"—"Dog Faced
Boy"—"Maze"—"Guyute"—"Cavern"
2: "Free"—"Scent"—"YEM"—
"Crossroads"—"YEM"—"Strange
Design"—"Sparkle"—"AC/DC Bag"—
"Sweet Adeline"
E: "Harry Hood"

Sat. 11/11/95
Fox Theater, Atlanta, GA
1: "Cars Trucks and Buses"—"Mike's"—
"Day in the Life"—"Poor Heart"—
"Weekapaug"—"Horse"—"Silent"—"Ya
Mar"—"Stash"—"Amazing Grace"—
"Fee"—"Chalkdust"
2: 2001—"Bowie"—"Suzie"—"Uncle
Pen"—"Fluffhead"—"Sleeping Monkey"—
"Frankenstein"—"Suspicious Minds"—
"Antelope"
E: "Acoustic Army"—"GTBT"

Sun. 11/12/95
O'Connell Center, Gainesville, FL
1: "My Friend"—"Llama"—"BATR"—
"Guelah"—"Reba"—"I Didn't Know"—
"Fog"—"If I Could"—"SOAM"—"Hello
My Baby"
2: "Curtain"—"Tweezer"—"Keyboard
Cavalry"—"Sample"—"Slave"—"Cracklin'
Rosie"—"Possum"—"Tweezer" rep.
E: "Fire"

Tues. 11/14/95
**University of Central Florida
Arena, Orlando, FL**
1: "Chalkdust"—"Foam"—"Billy
Breathes"—"Divided Sky"—"Esther"—
"Free"—"Julius"—"I'm Blue, I'm
Lonesome"—"Cavern"
2: "Maze"—"Gumbo"—"Stash"—
"Manteca"—"Stash"—"Dog Faced Boy"—
"Stash"—"Strange Design"—"YEM"
E: "Wedge"—"Rocky Top"

Wed. 11/15/95
Sundome, Tampa, FL
1: "Poor Heart"—"AC/DC Bag"—
"FEFY"—"Rift"—"Prince Caspian"—
"Sparkle"—"SOAM"—"Sweet Adeline"—
"Coil"

2: "Wilson"—"Theme"—"Scent"—
"Mike's"—"Life on Mars"—
"Weekapaug"—"Fee"—"Guitar"
E: "Suzie"

Thu. 11/16/95
The Auditorium, West Palm Beach, FL

1: "Cars Trucks and Buses"—"Runaway Jim"—chess jam—"Horn"—"Mound"—
"Ya Mar"—"Simple"—"Timber"—
"Guyute"—"Funky Bitch"
2: "Day in the Life"—"Bowie"—
"Lifeboy"—"Uncle Pen"—"Ha Ha Ha"—
"Harry"—"If I Only Had a Brain"—
"Amazing Grace"—"Possum"*
E: "Brown Eyed Girl"∧

*with Butch Trucks

∧with Jimmy Buffett

Sat. 11/18/95
The Coliseum, North Charleston, SC

1: "Dinner and a Movie"—"BATR"—
"Reba"—"Lawn Boy"—"PYITE"—"Slave"—
"I'm Blue, I'm Lonesome"—"Sample"
2: "AC/DC Bag"—"Sparkle"—"Free"—"I'm So Tired"—"YEM"—"Contact"—
"BBFCFM"—"Acoustic Army"—
"BBFCFM"—"Cavern"
E: "Bill Bailey"*

*with Dr. Jack McConnell

Sun. 11/19/95
Charlotte Coliseum, Charlotte, NC

1: "Makisupa"—"Maze"—"Poor Heart"—
"Rift"—"Stash"—"Strange Design"—"It's Ice"—"Hello My Baby"—"Julius"—"Coil"
2: "Theme"—2001—"Curtain"—
"Tweezer"—"Billy Breathes"—"Scent"—
"Harry"—"Suzie"
E: "Life on Mars"—"Tweezer" rep.

Tues. 11/21/95
Lawrence Joel Coliseum, Winston-Salem, NC

1: "Fee"—"Chalkdust"—"Prince Caspian"—"Divided Sky"—"Long Journey Home"—"I'm Blue, I'm Lonesome"—
"Guyute"—"My Friend"—"Dog Faced Boy"—"Runaway Jim"
2: "Simple"—"Bowie"—"Take Me to the River"*—"Bowie"—"Glide"—"Ya Mar"—
"Mike's"—"Keyboard Cavalry"—
"Suspicious Minds"—"Carolina"—"Day in the Life"
E: "GTBT"

*first time played

Wed. 11/22/95
US Air Arena, Landover, MD

1: "Cars Trucks and Buses"—"Wilson"—
"Antelope"—"Fluffhead"—"Uncle Pen"—
"Cavern"—"Fog"—"Lizards"—"Sample"—
"Sweet Adeline"
2: "Rift"—"Free"—"Llama"—"BATR"—
"YEM"—"Strange Design"
E: "Poor Heart"—"Frankenstein"

Fri. 11/24/95
Pittsburgh Civic Arena, Pittsburgh, PA

1: "Oh Kee Pa"—"AC/DC Bag"—
"Curtain"—"Sparkle"—"Stash"—"Tela"—
"I'm Blue, I'm Lonesome"—"Maze"—
"Suzie"
2: "Chalkdust"—"Theme"—"Reba"—
"Catapult"—"Scent"—"Bathtub Gin"—
"Acoustic Army"—"Bike"—"Fee"—"Julius"
E: "Life on Mars"—"Rocky Top"

Sat. 11/25/95
Hampton Coliseum, Hampton, VA

1: "Poor Heart"—"Day in the Life"—
"Bowie"—"Billy Breathes"—"Fog"—

"BATR"—"Rift"—"Wolfman's"—"Runaway Jim"

2: "Timber"—"Kung"—"Mike's"—trading places jam—"Keyboard Cavalry"—"Mike's"—"Long Journey Home"—"I'm Blue, I'm Lonesome"—"Strange Design"—"Weekapaug"—"Harry"—"Hello My Baby"—"Poor Heart"

E: "Fire"

Tues. 11/28/95
Civic Coliseum, Knoxville, TN

1: "Stash"—"Dinner and a Movie"—"BATR"—"Foam"—"I Didn't Know"—"Divided Sky"—"Guyute"—"Hello My Baby"—"Sample"

2: 2001—"Maze"—"Suzie"—"Uncle Pen"—"Free"—"Wind Beneath My Wings"*—"Antelope"—"Contact"—"BBFCFM"—"Funky Bitch"

E: "Coil

*first time played (with Colonel Bruce Hampton onstage reading a newspaper)

Wed. 11/29/95
Municipal Auditorium, Nashville, TN

1: "AC/DC Bag"—"Ya Mar"—"Reba"—"If I Could"—"It's Ice"—"Theme"—"Acoustic Army"—"Fee"—"SOAM"

2: "Timber"—"Sparkle"—"Simple"—"Possum"—"YEM"—"Fog"*—"Poor Heart"*—"I'm Blue, I'm Lonesome"*—"Long Journey Home"*—"Slave"*

E: "Day in the Life"

*with Bela Fleck

Thu. 11/30/95 Ervin J. Nutter Center, Dayton, OH

1: "Sample"—"Curtain"—"Ha Ha Ha"—"Julius"—"NICU"—"Bathtub Gin"—"Rift"—"FEFY"—"Lizards"—"Fire"

2: "Cars Trucks and Buses"—"Tweezer"—"Makisupa"—"Antelope"—"Scent"—"Free"—"Strange Design"—"Amazing Grace"

E: "Harry"

Fri. 12/1/95
Hershey Park Arena, Hershey, PA

1: "Buried Alive"—"DWD"—"Theme"—"Poor Heart"—"Wolfman's"—"Chalkdust"—"Col. Forbin"—"Mockingbird"—"Stash"—"Cavern"

2: "Halley's"—"Mike's"—"Weekapaug"—"Mango"—"Wilson"—"Suspicious Minds"—"Bowie"—"Catapult"—"Bowie"

E: "Suzie"

Sat. 12/2/95
New Haven Coliseum, New Haven, CT

1: "Prince Caspian"—"Runaway Jim"—"Mound"—"Guelah"—"Reba"—"MSO"—"Free"—"Fog"—"BATR"—"Possum"

2: 2001—"Maze"—"Simple"—"Faht"—"Tweezer"—"Day in the Life"—"Golgi"—"Coil"—"Tweezer" rep.

E: "Bold as Love"

Mon. 12/4/95
Mullins Center, Amherst, MA

1: "Julius"—"Gumbo"—"Divided Sky"—"PYITE"—"Stash"—"My Mind's"—"Axilla II"—"Horse"—"Silent"—"Hello My Baby"—"Guitar"

2: "Timber"—"Sparkle"—"Ya Mar"—"Antelope"—"Billy Breathes"—"Cars Trucks and Buses"—"YEM"—"Sample"—"Frankenstein"

E: "BATR"—"Rocky Top"

Tues. 12/5/95
Mullins Center, Amherst, MA

1: "Horn"—"Chalkdust"—"Fog"—
"Lizards"—"Free"—"Esther"—"Bowie"—
"I'm Blue, I'm Lonesome"
2: "Poor Heart"—"Bathtub Gin"—
"Keyboard Cavalry"—"Scent"—
"Lifeboy"—"Harry"—"Cavern"
E: "Theme"—"Sweet Adeline"

Thu. 12/7/95
Niagara Falls Convention Center, Niagara Falls, NY

1: "Old Home Place"—"Curtain"—"AC/
DC Bag"—"Demand"—"Rift"—"Slave"—
"Guyute"—"BATR"—"Possum"—"Hello
My Baby"
2: "SOAM"—"Strange Design"—"Fog"—
"Reba"—"Julius"—"Sleeping Monkey"—
"Sparkle"—"Mike's"—"Weekapaug"—
"Amazing Grace"
E: "Uncle Pen"

Fri. 12/8/95
Cleveland State University Convocation Center, Cleveland, OH

1: "Sample"—"Poor Heart"—"Simple"—
"Runaway Jim"—"Fluffhead"—"It's Ice"—
"Acoustic Army"—"Prince Caspian"—
"GTBT"
2: 2001—"Tweezer"—"Kung"—
"Tweezer"—"Love You"—"Coil"—
"Tweezer" rep."—"Antelope"
E: "Come Together"*—"Day in the Life"
*first time played

Sat. 12/9/95
Knickerbocker Arena, Albany, NY

1: "Maze"—"Theme"—"NICU"—
"Sloth"—"Rift"—"BATR"—"Free"—"Billy
Breathes"—"Dog Faced Boy"—"Chalkdust"

2: "Timber"—"Wilson"—"Gumbo"—
"YEM"—"Lawn Boy"—"Slave"—
"Crossroads"—"Sweet Adeline"
E: "Loving Cup"

Mon. 12/11/95
Cumberland County Civic Center, Portland, ME

1: "My Friend"—"Ha Ha Ha"—"Stash"—
"Prince Caspian"—"Reba"—"Dog Log"—
"Llama"—"Dog Log"—"Tube"—
"McGrupp"—"Julius"—"Cavern"
2: "Curtain"—"Bowie"—"Mango"—
"Fog"—"Scent"—"Harry"—"Suspicious
Minds"—"Funky Bitch"*
E: "Guitar"*
*with Warren Haynes

Tues. 12/12/95
Providence Civic Center, Providence, RI

1: "Ya Mar"—"Sample"—"Divided Sky"—
"Lifeboy"—"PYITE"—"Horse"—"Silent"—
"Antelope"—"I'm Blue, I'm Lonesome"—
"Coil"
2: "Free"—"Sparkle"—"DWD"—
"Lizards"—"Simple"—"Runaway Jim"
E: "Fire"

Thu. 12/14/95
Broome County Arena, Binghamton, NY

1: "Suzie"—"Llama"—"Horn"—"Foam"—
"Makisupa"—"SOAM"—"Tela"—"Fog"—
"MSO"—"Frankenstein"
2: "Curtain"—"Tweezer"—"Timber"—
"Tweezer"—"Keyboard Cavalry"—
"Halley's"—"NICU"—"Slave"
E: "Bold as Love"

Fri. 12/15/95
Corestates Spectrum,
Philadelphia, PA
1: "Chalkdust"—"Harry"—"Wilson"—
"Maze"—"Ha Ha Ha"—"Suspicious
Minds"—"Cars Trucks and Buses"—
"BATR"—"Free"—"Possum"
2: "Tweezer" rep.—"Runaway Jim"—"It's
Ice"—"Bathtub Gin"—trading places
jam—2001—"Bowie"—"Sweet Adeline"
E: "GTBT"—"Tweezer" rep.

Sat. 12/16/95
Olympic Center, Lake Placid, NY
1: "Buried Alive"—"AC/DC Bag"—
"Fog"—"Ya Mar"—"Sloth"—"Divided
Sky"—"Dog Faced Boy"—"Julius"—"Suzie"
2: "Sample"—"Reba"—"Scent"—
"Cavern"—"Mike's"—"Simple"—
"Weekapaug"—"Coil"
E: "Fire"

Sun. 12/17/95
Olympic Center, Lake Placid, NY
1: "My Friend"—"Poor Heart"—"Day in
the Life"—"Antelope"—"Mango"—
"Tube"—"Stash"—"Lizards"—"Chalkdust"
2: "BATR"—"Maze"—"Free"—2001—
"Harry"—"Sparkle"—"Tweezer"—
"Tweezer" rep.
E: "Hello My Baby"—"Runaway Jim"

Thu. 12/28/95
Worcester Centrum,
Worcester, MA
1: "SOAM"—"Gumbo"—"Curtain"—
"Julius"—"Guyute"—"Horn"—"Rift"—
"FEFY"—"Possum"
2: "Timber"—"Theme"—"Wilson"—
"Buried Alive"—"Tweezer"—"I Didn't
Know"—"Uncle Pen"—"Slave"
E: "Fee"—"Tweezer" rep.

Fri. 12/29/95
Worcester Centrum,
Worcester, MA
1: "My Friend"—"Poor Heart"—
"DWD"—"Fog"—"NICU"—"Stash"—
"Fluffhead"—"Llama"—"Sweet Adeline"
2: "Makisupa"—"Cars Trucks and
Buses"—"Bathtub Gin"—"Real Me"—
"Bathtub Gin"—"McGrupp"—
"BBFCFM"—"Bass Jam"*—"La Grange"—
"BATR"—"Fire"
E: "Golgi"
*with Jim Stinnette

Sat. 12/30/95
Madison Square Garden, New
York, NY
1: "Prince Caspian"—2001—"Suzie"—
"Bowie"—"Simple"—"It's Ice"—"Kung"—
"It's Ice"—"TMWSIY"—"Avenu"—
"TMWSIY"—"Divided Sky"—"Sample"
2: "Ya Mar"—"Free"—"Harry"—"AC/DC
Bag"—"Lifeboy"—"Scent"—"Cavern"—
"Antelope"
E: "Day in the Life"

Sun. 12/31/95
Madison Square Garden, New
York, NY
1: "PYITE"—"Sloth"—"Reba"—"Coil"—
"Maze"—"Col. Forbin"—"Shine"—
"Mockingbird"—"Sparkle"—"Chalkdust"
2: "Drowned"—"Lizards"—"Axilla II"—
"Runaway Jim"—"Strange Design"—
"Hello My Baby"—"Mike's Song"
3: "Auld Lang Syne"—"Weekapaug"—
"Sea and Sand"—"YEM"—"Sanity"—
"Frankenstein"
E: "Johnny B. Goode"

Fri. 4/26/96
New Orleans Jazz and Heritage
Festival, New Orleans, LA
"Ya Mar"—"AC/DC Bag"—"Sparkle"—
"Stash"—"Cars Trucks and Buses"*—
"YEM"—"Wolfman's"—"Scent"—2001—
"Harry"—"Simple"—"Day in the Life"—
"Bowie"
E: "Hello My Baby"—"Cavern"
*with Michael Ray

thu. 6/6/96
Joyous Lake, Woodstock, NY
(The Third Ball)
1: "SOAM"—"Poor Heart"—"Runaway
Jim"—"Funky Bitch"—"Theme"—
"BBFCFM"—"Scent"—"Highway to Hell"
2: "AC/DC Bag"—"YEM"—"Chalkdust"—
"Sparkle"—"Stash"—"Waste"*—"Character
Zero"—"Bowie"—"Fee"—"Sample"
E: "Ya Mar"—"Fire"
*first time played

index